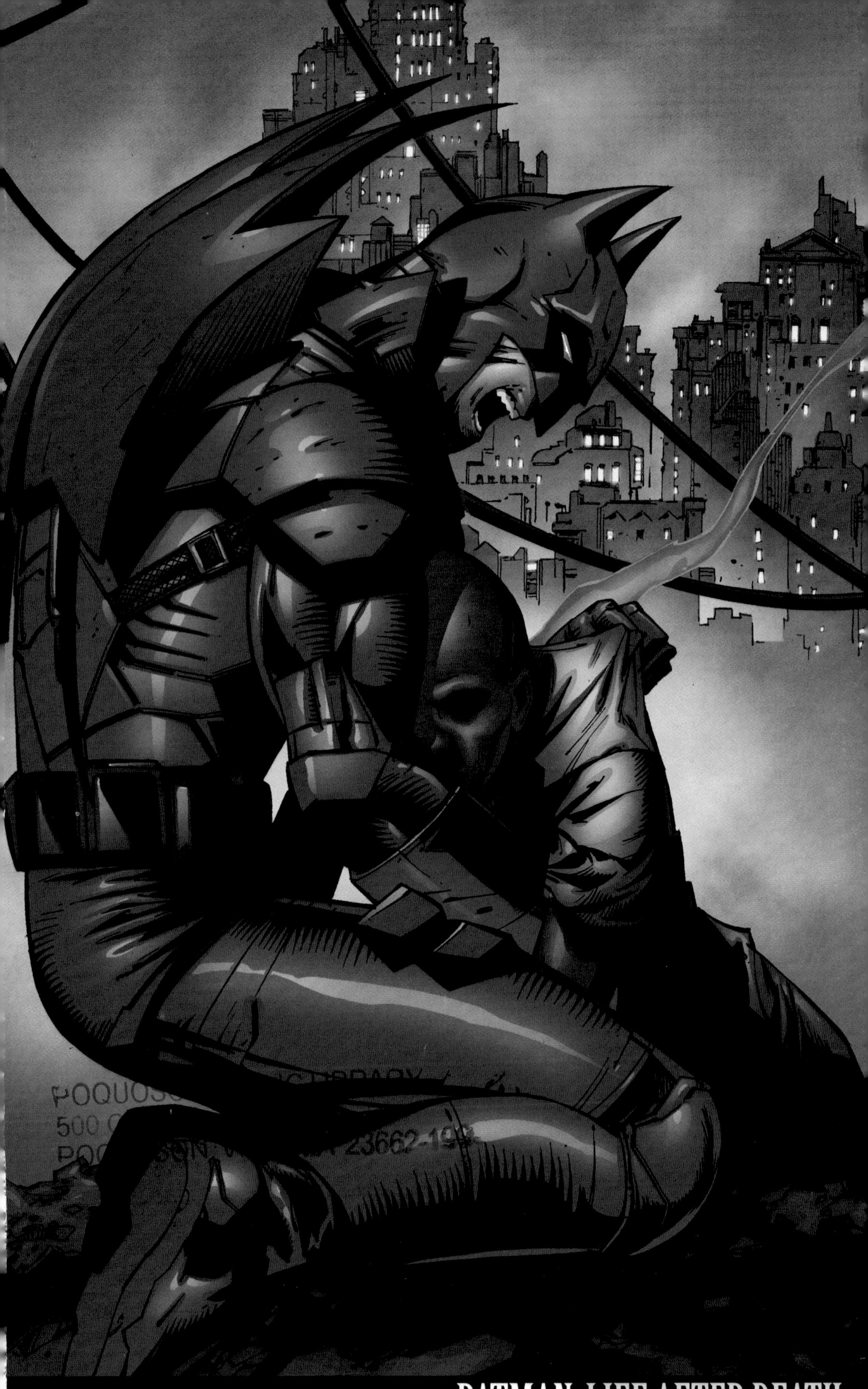

BATMAN: LIFE AFTER DEATH

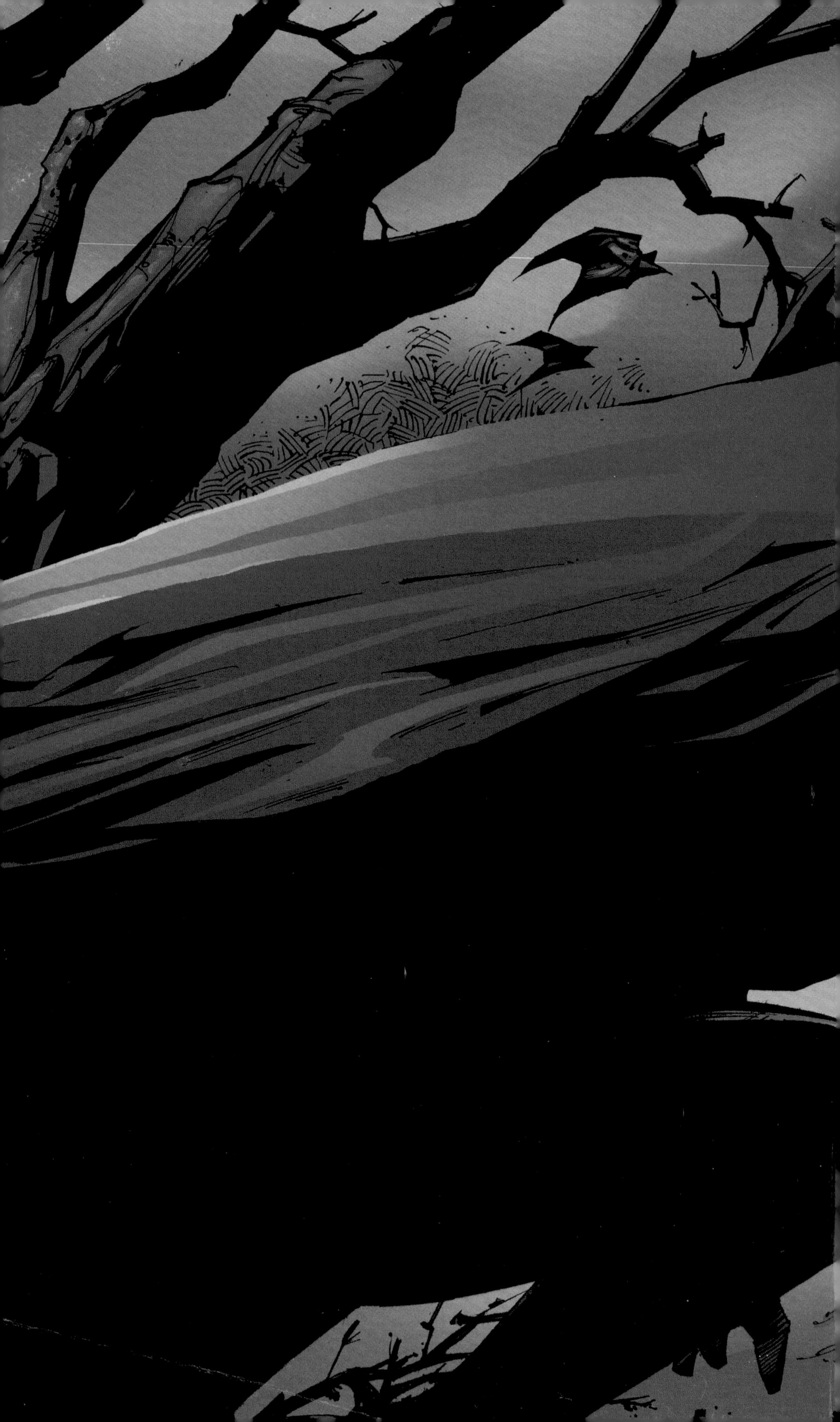

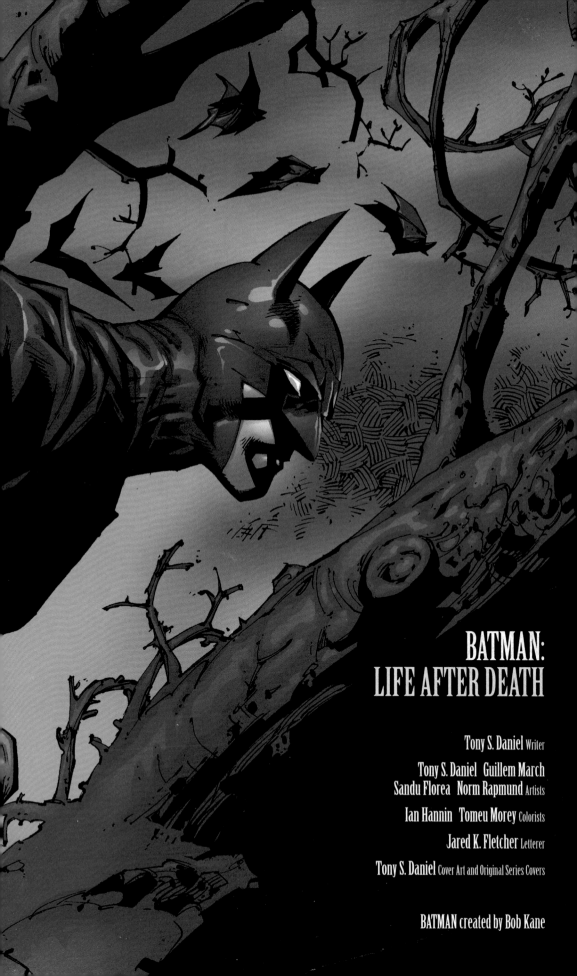

BATMAN: LIFE AFTER DEATH

Tony S. Daniel Writer

Tony S. Daniel   Guillem March
Sandu Florea   Norm Rapmund Artists

Ian Hannin   Tomeu Morey Colorists

Jared K. Fletcher Letterer

Tony S. Daniel Cover Art and Original Series Covers

BATMAN created by Bob Kane

Mike Marts Editor – Original Series
Janelle Siegel Assistant Editor – Original Series
Bob Harras Group Editor – Collected Editions
Scott Nybakken Editor
Robbin Brosterman Design Director – Books

DC COMICS
Diane Nelson President
Dan DiDio and Jim Lee Co-Publishers
Geoff Johns Chief Creative Officer
Patrick Caldon EVP – Finance and Administration
John Rood EVP – Sales, Marketing and Business Development
Amy Genkins SVP – Business and Legal Affairs
Steve Rotterdam SVP – Sales and Marketing
John Cunningham VP – Marketing
Terri Cunningham VP – Managing Editor
Alison Gill VP – Manufacturing
David Hyde VP – Publicity
Sue Pohja VP – Book Trade Sales
Alysse Soll VP – Advertising and Custom Publishing
Bob Wayne VP – Sales
Mark Chiarello Art Director

BATMAN: LIFE AFTER DEATH

Published by DC Comics. Cover and compilation Copyright
© 2010 DC Comics. All Rights Reserved. Originally published
in single magazine form in BATMAN 692-699. Copyright ©
2009, 2010 DC Comics. All Rights Reserved. All characters,
their distinctive likenesses and related elements featured in
this publication are trademarks of DC Comics. The stories,
characters and incidents featured in this publication are
entirely fictional. DC Comics does not read or accept
unsolicited submissions of ideas, stories or artwork.

DC Comics, 1700 Broadway, New York, NY 10019
A Warner Bros. Entertainment Company
Printed by Quad/Graphics, Versailles, KY, USA
9/15/10. First Printing.
HC ISBN: 78-1-4012-2834-7 SC ISBN: 978-1-4012-2975-7

SUSTAINABLE
FORESTRY
INITIATIVE

Certified Fiber Sourcing
www.sfiprogram.org

Fiber used in this product line meets the
sourcing requirements of the SFI program.
www.sfiprogram.org PWC-SFICOC-260

Table of Contents

LIFE AFTER DEATH

Pencils by **Tony S. Daniel** Colors by **Ian Hannin**

Riddle Me This

Pencils and inks by **Guillem March** Colors by **Tomeu Morey**

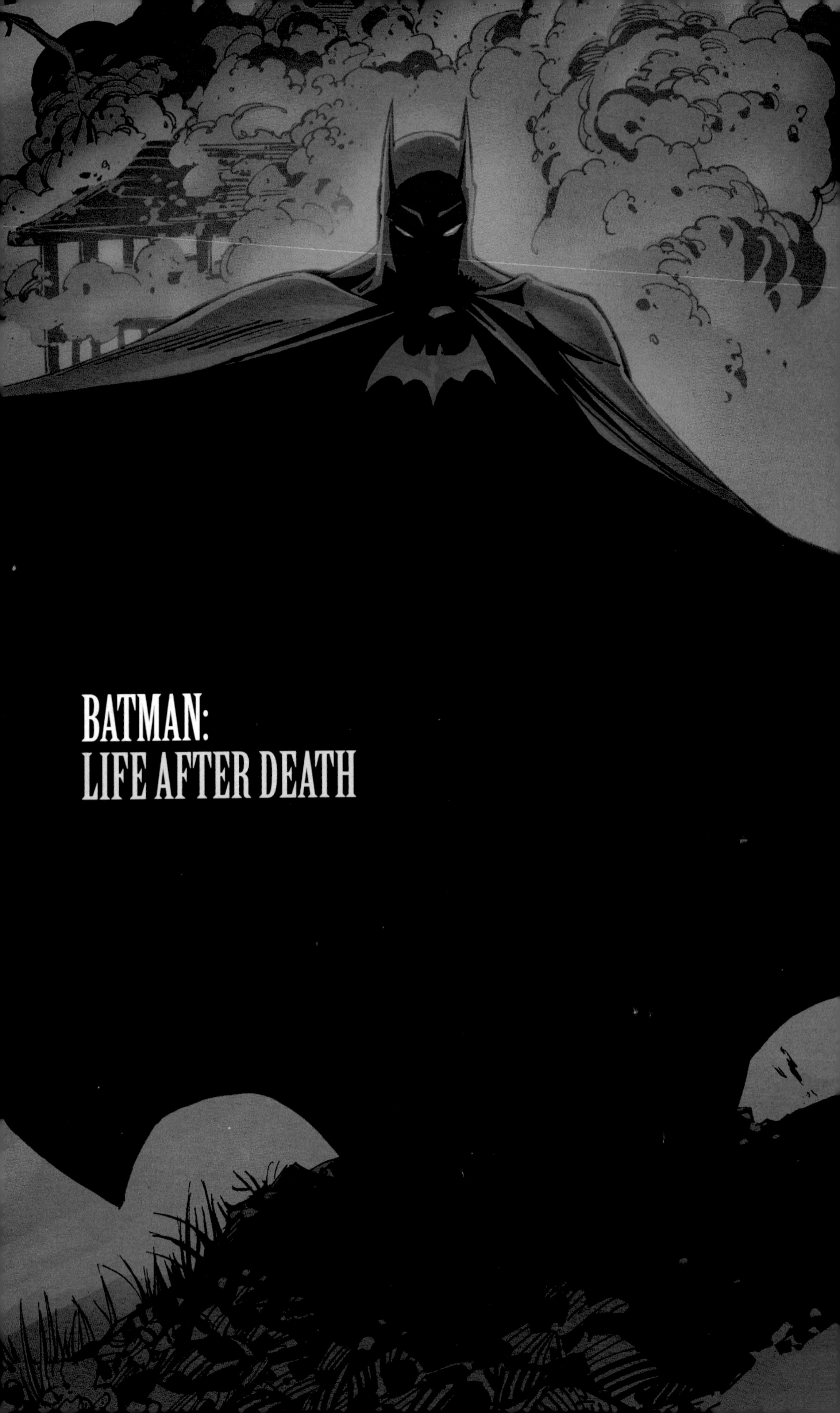
BATMAN:
LIFE AFTER DEATH

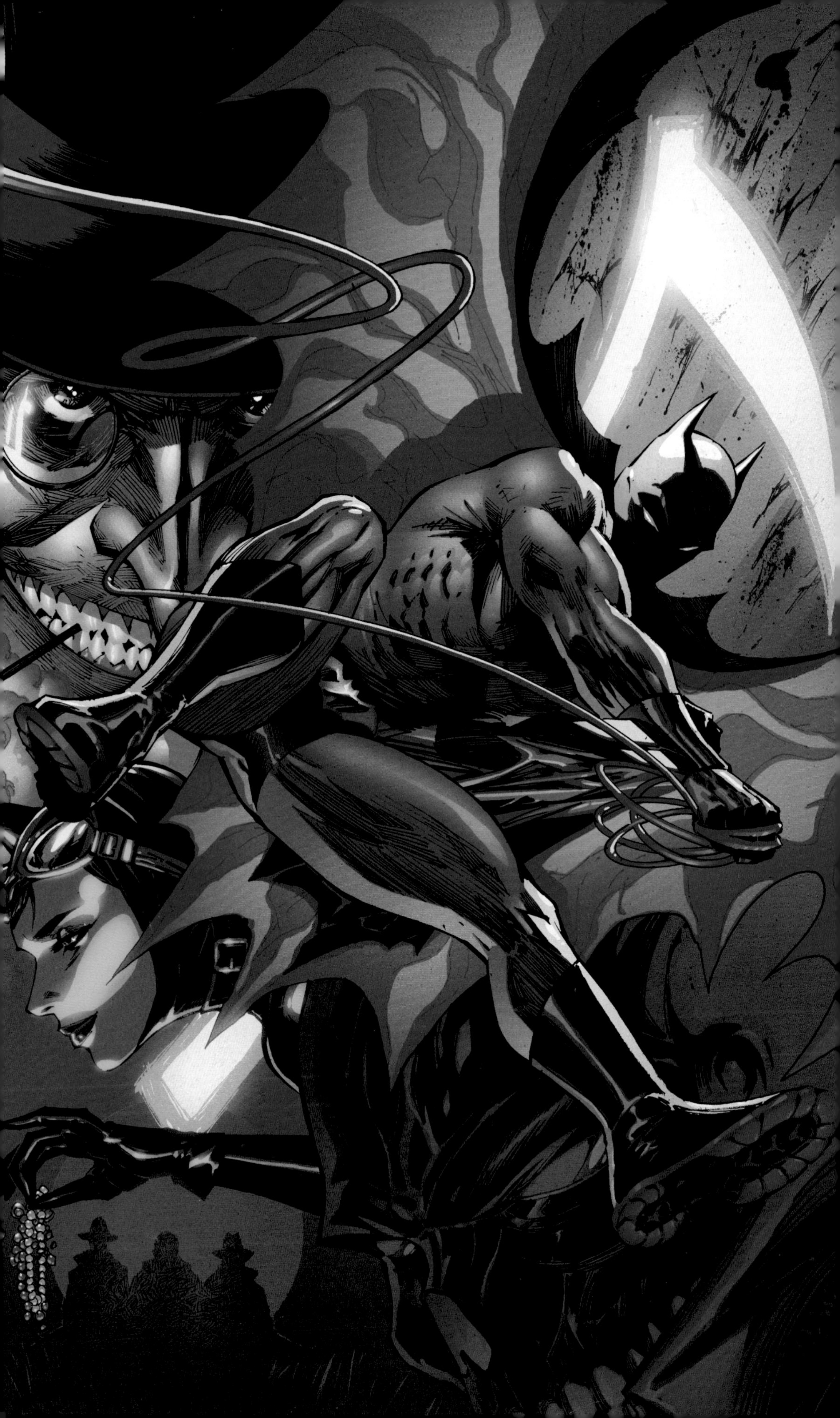

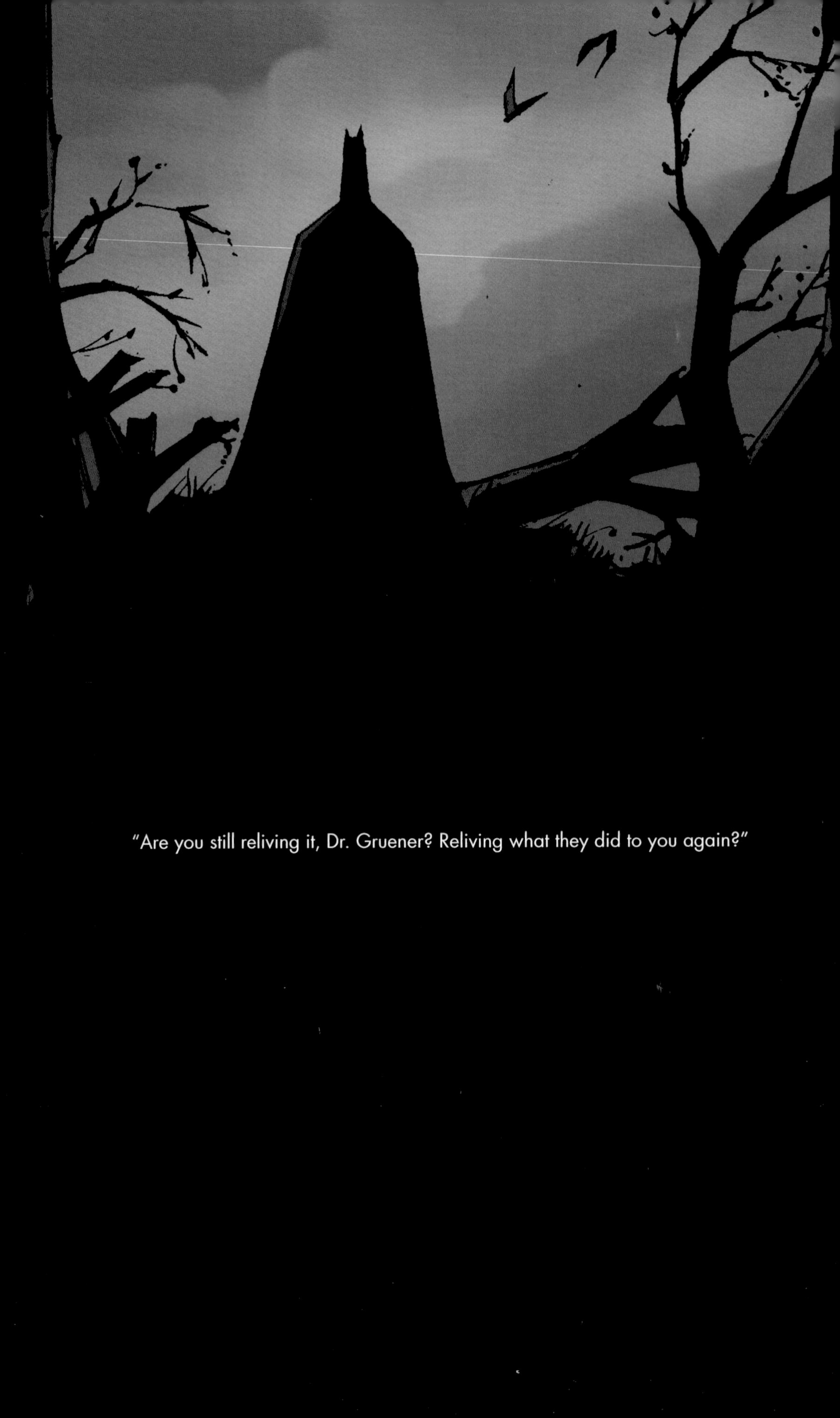
"Are you still reliving it, Dr. Gruener? Reliving what they did to you again?"

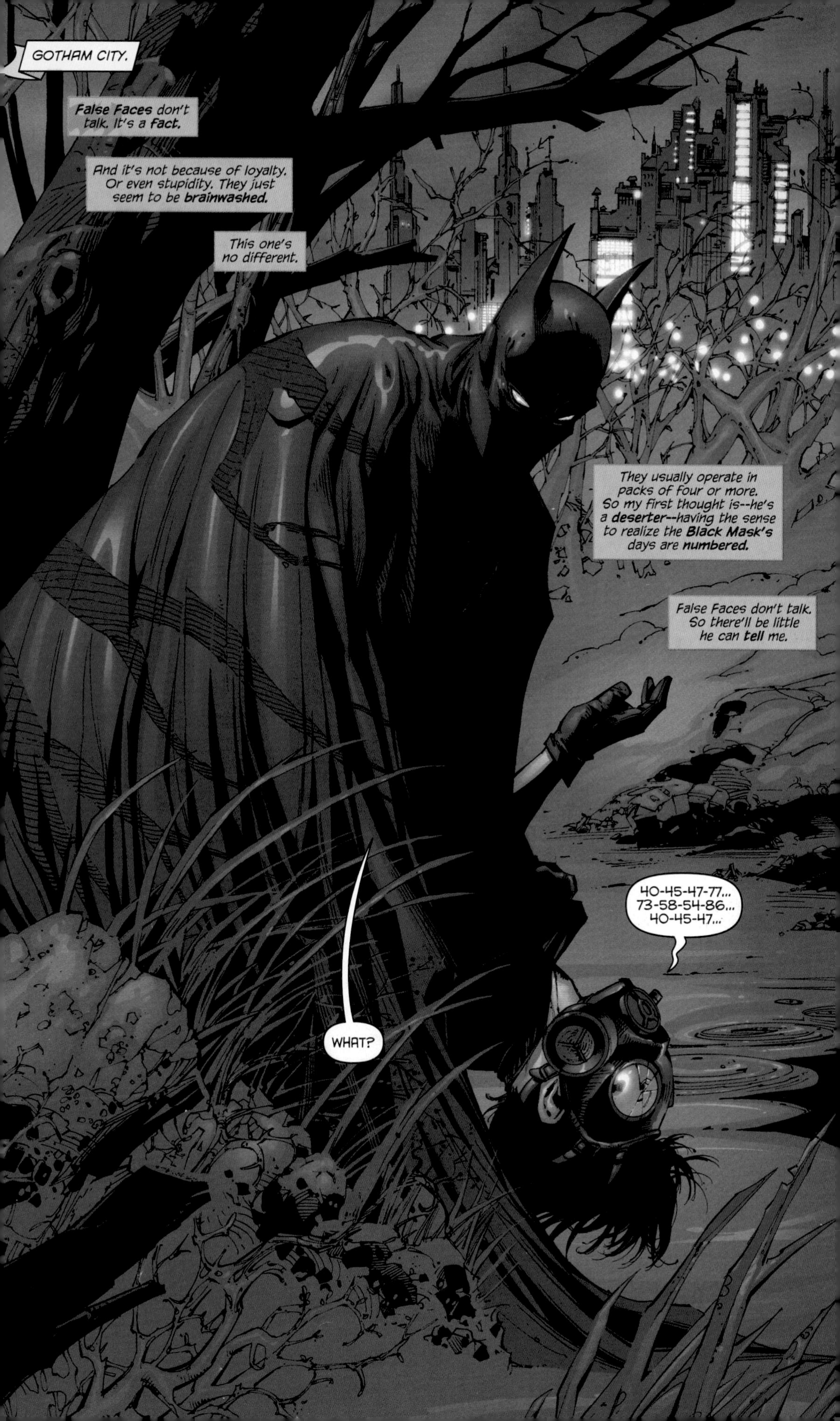

GOTHAM CITY.
False Faces don't talk. It's a fact.
And it's not because of loyalty. Or even stupidity. They just seem to be brainwashed.
This one's no different.
They usually operate in packs of four or more. So my first thought is--he's a deserter--having the sense to realize the Black Mask's days are numbered.
False Faces don't talk. So there'll be little he can tell me.
40-45-47-77... 73-58-54-86... 40-45-47...
WHAT?

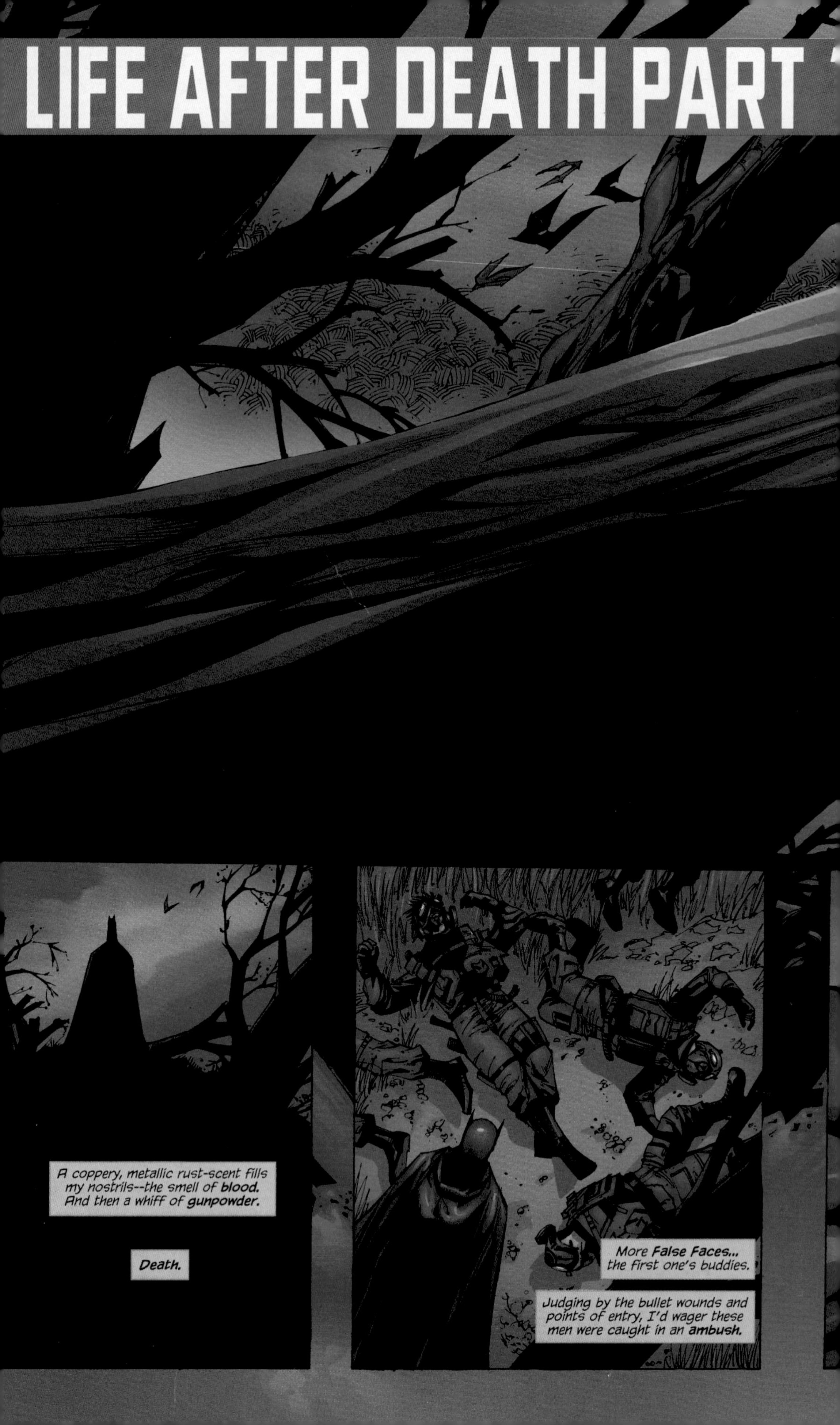
LIFE AFTER DEATH PART
A coppery, metallic rust-scent fills my nostrils--the smell of blood. And then a whiff of gunpowder.
Death.
More False Faces... the first one's buddies.
Judging by the bullet wounds and points of entry, I'd wager these men were caught in an ambush.

THE AWAKENING

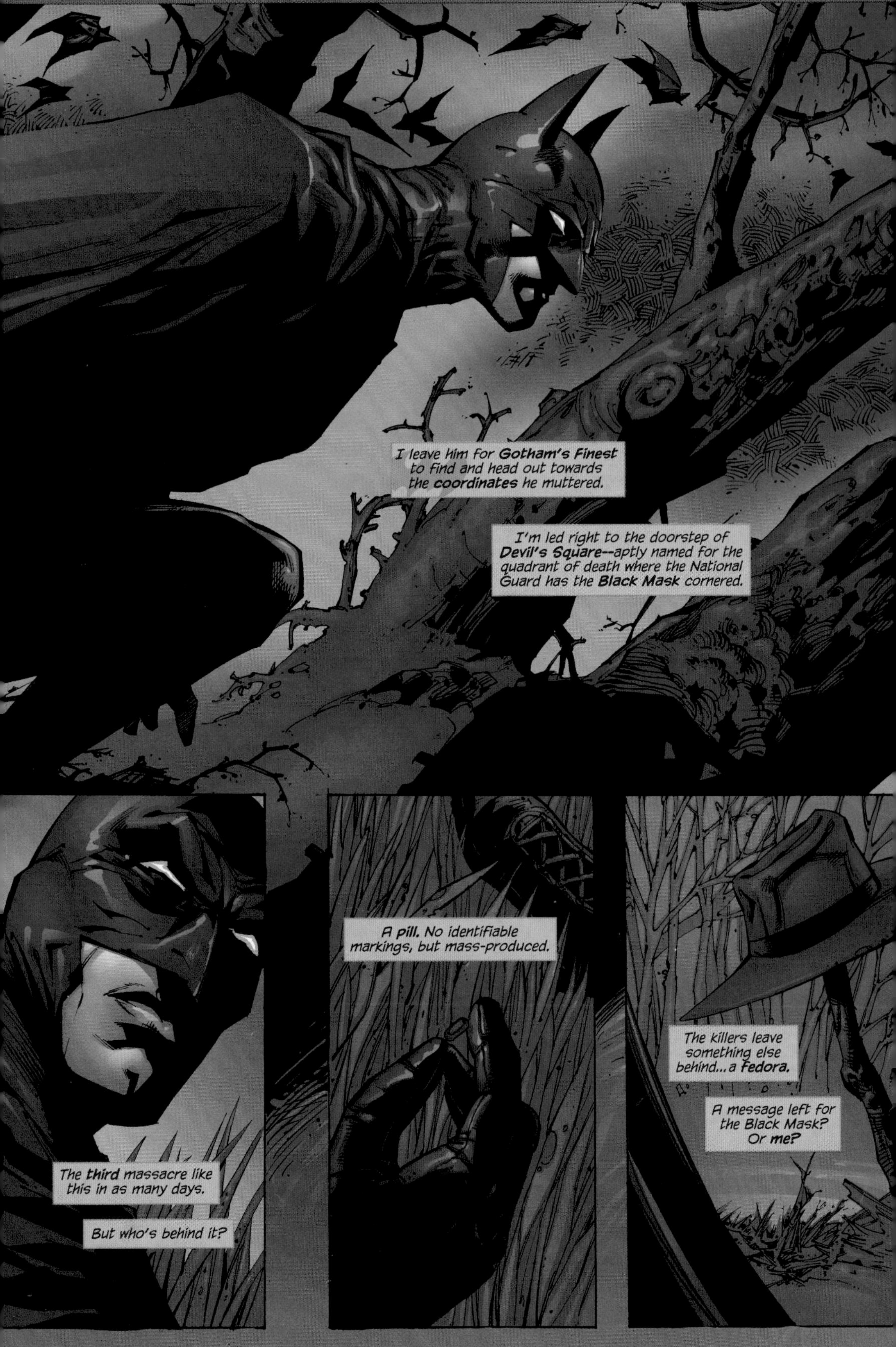
I leave him for Gotham's Finest to find and head out towards the coordinates he muttered.
I'm led right to the doorstep of Devil's Square--aptly named for the quadrant of death where the National Guard has the Black Mask cornered.
The third massacre like this in as many days.
But who's behind it?
A pill. No identifiable markings, but mass-produced.
The killers leave something else behind... a Fedora.
A message left for the Black Mask? Or me?

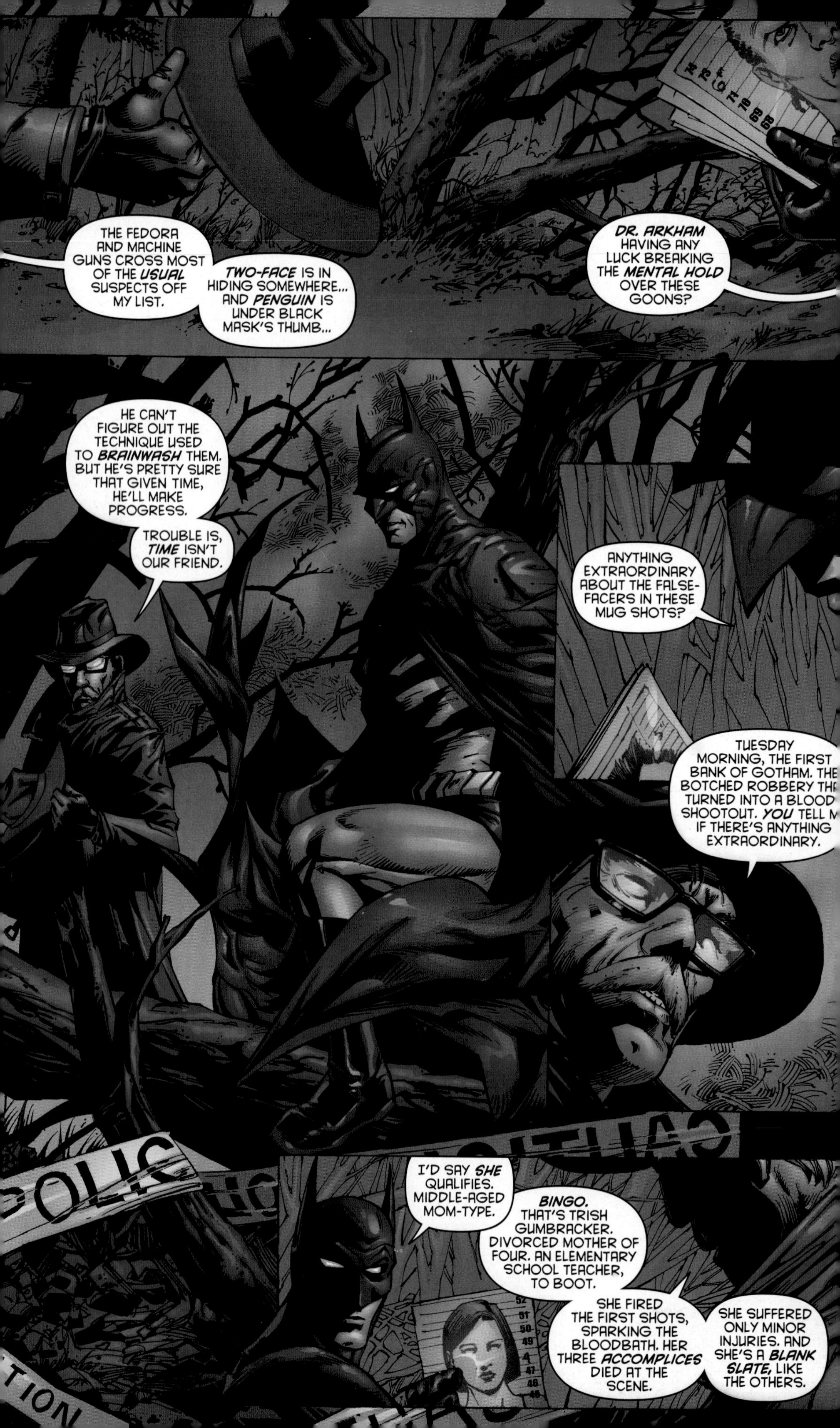
THE FEDORA AND MACHINE GUNS CROSS MOST OF THE *USUAL* SUSPECTS OFF MY LIST.
TWO-FACE IS IN HIDING SOMEWHERE... AND *PENGUIN* IS UNDER BLACK MASK'S THUMB...
DR. ARKHAM HAVING ANY LUCK BREAKING THE *MENTAL HOLD* OVER THESE GOONS?
HE CAN'T FIGURE OUT THE TECHNIQUE USED TO *BRAINWASH* THEM. BUT HE'S PRETTY SURE THAT GIVEN TIME, HE'LL MAKE PROGRESS.
TROUBLE IS, *TIME* ISN'T OUR FRIEND.
ANYTHING EXTRAORDINARY ABOUT THE FALSE-FACERS IN THESE MUG SHOTS?
TUESDAY MORNING, THE FIRST BANK OF GOTHAM. THE BOTCHED ROBBERY THA TURNED INTO A BLOOD SHOOTOUT. *YOU* TELL M IF THERE'S ANYTHING EXTRAORDINARY.
I'D SAY *SHE* QUALIFIES. MIDDLE-AGED MOM-TYPE.
BINGO. THAT'S TRISH GUMBRACKER. DIVORCED MOTHER OF FOUR. AN ELEMENTARY SCHOOL TEACHER, TO BOOT.
SHE FIRED THE FIRST SHOTS, SPARKING THE BLOODBATH. HER THREE *ACCOMPLICES* DIED AT THE SCENE.
SHE SUFFERED ONLY MINOR INJURIES. AND SHE'S A *BLANK SLATE,* LIKE THE OTHERS.

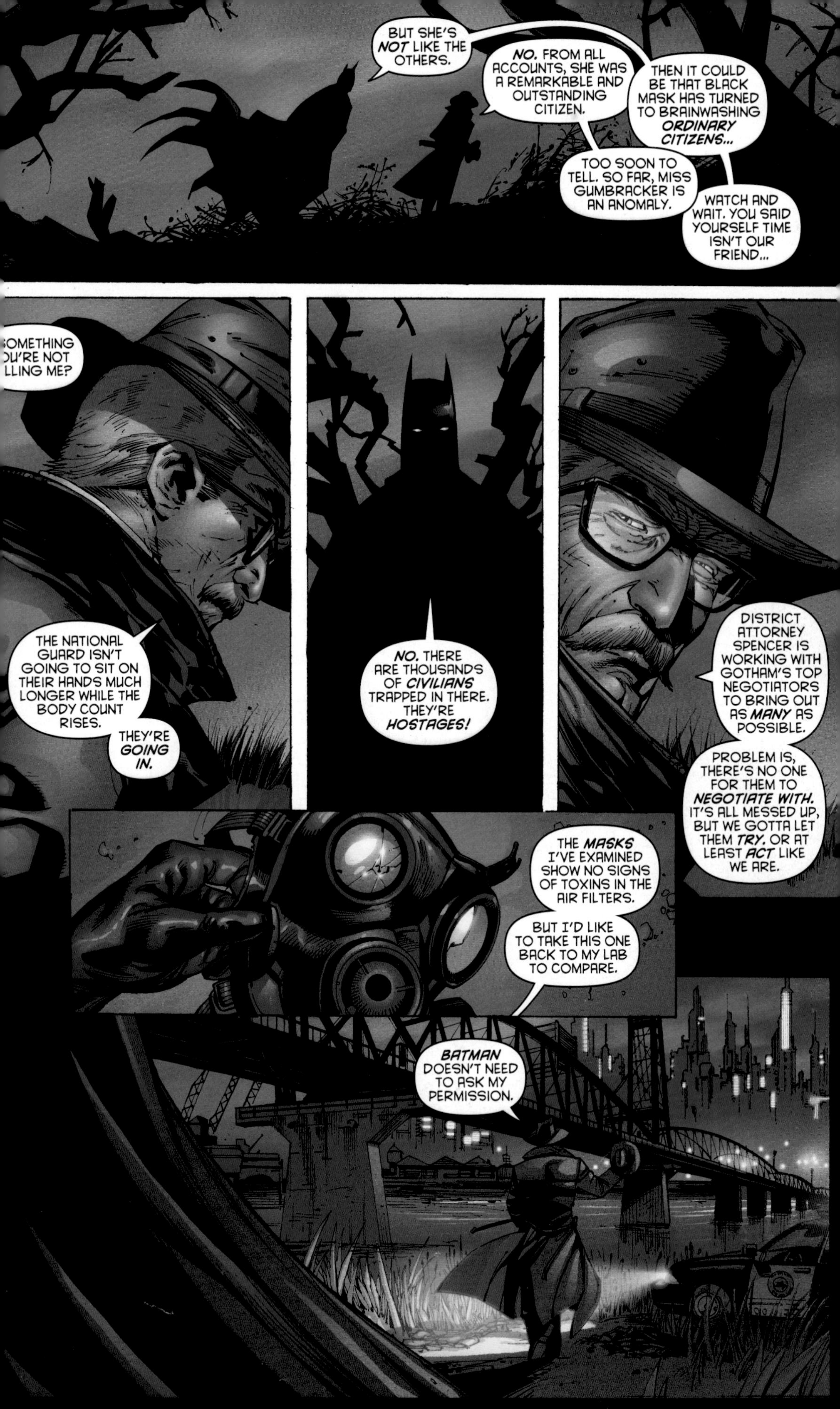

BUT SHE'S NOT LIKE THE OTHERS.
NO. FROM ALL ACCOUNTS, SHE WAS A REMARKABLE AND OUTSTANDING CITIZEN.
THEN IT COULD BE THAT BLACK MASK HAS TURNED TO BRAINWASHING ORDINARY CITIZENS...
TOO SOON TO TELL. SO FAR, MISS GUMBRACKER IS AN ANOMALY.
WATCH AND WAIT. YOU SAID YOURSELF TIME ISN'T OUR FRIEND...
OMETHING OU'RE NOT LLING ME?
THE NATIONAL GUARD ISN'T GOING TO SIT ON THEIR HANDS MUCH LONGER WHILE THE BODY COUNT RISES.
THEY'RE GOING IN.
NO. THERE ARE THOUSANDS OF CIVILIANS TRAPPED IN THERE. THEY'RE HOSTAGES!
DISTRICT ATTORNEY SPENCER IS WORKING WITH GOTHAM'S TOP NEGOTIATORS TO BRING OUT AS MANY AS POSSIBLE.
PROBLEM IS, THERE'S NO ONE FOR THEM TO NEGOTIATE WITH. IT'S ALL MESSED UP, BUT WE GOTTA LET THEM TRY. OR AT LEAST ACT LIKE WE ARE.
THE MASKS I'VE EXAMINED SHOW NO SIGNS OF TOXINS IN THE AIR FILTERS.
BUT I'D LIKE TO TAKE THIS ONE BACK TO MY LAB TO COMPARE.
BATMAN DOESN'T NEED TO ASK MY PERMISSION.

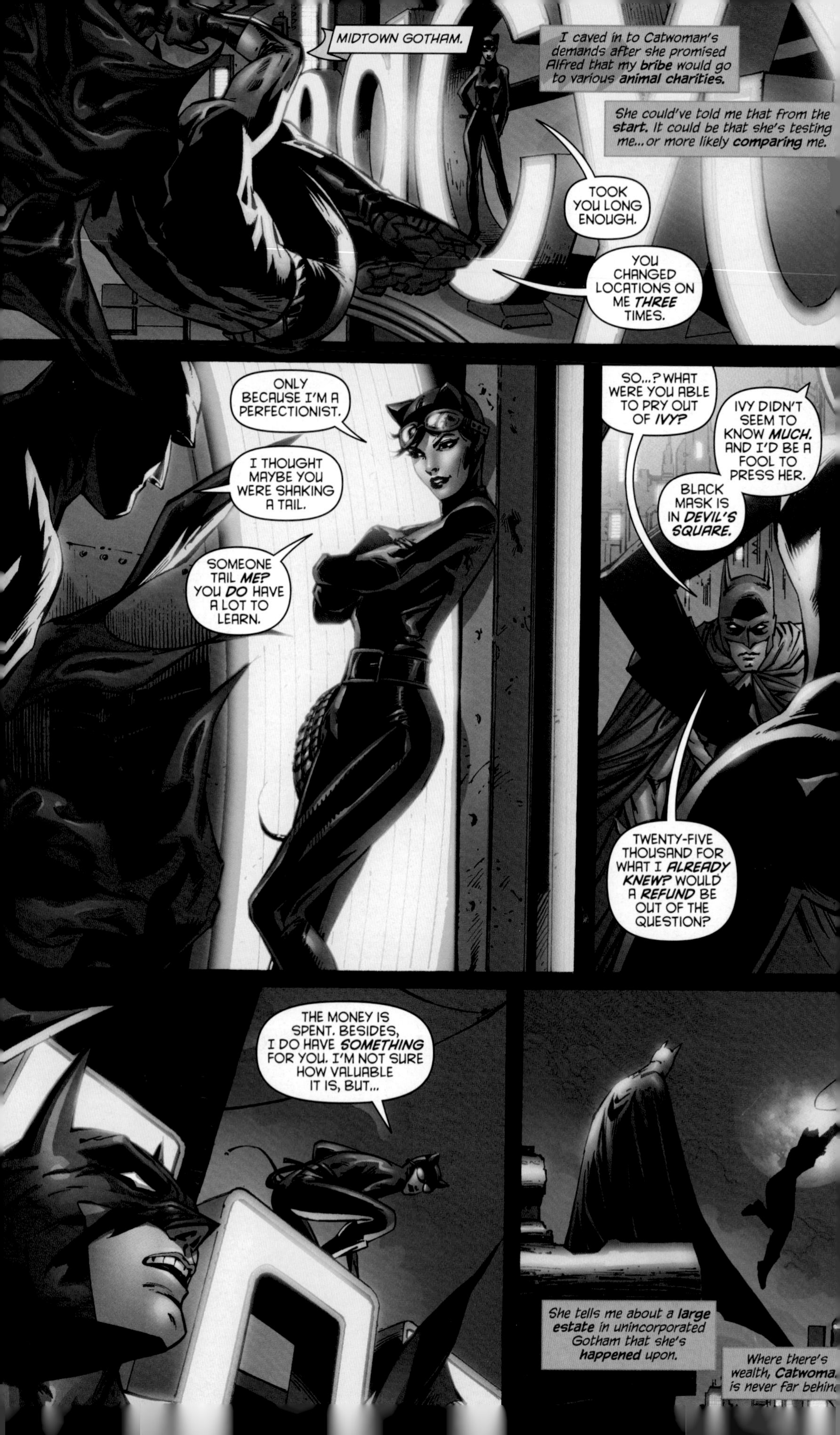
MIDTOWN GOTHAM.
I caved in to Catwoman's demands after she promised Alfred that my bribe would go to various animal charities.
She could've told me that from the start. It could be that she's testing me...or more likely comparing me.
TOOK YOU LONG ENOUGH.
YOU CHANGED LOCATIONS ON ME THREE TIMES.
ONLY BECAUSE I'M A PERFECTIONIST.
I THOUGHT MAYBE YOU WERE SHAKING A TAIL.
SOMEONE TAIL ME? YOU DO HAVE A LOT TO LEARN.
SO...? WHAT WERE YOU ABLE TO PRY OUT OF IVY?
IVY DIDN'T SEEM TO KNOW MUCH. AND I'D BE A FOOL TO PRESS HER.
BLACK MASK IS IN DEVIL'S SQUARE.
TWENTY-FIVE THOUSAND FOR WHAT I ALREADY KNEW? WOULD A REFUND BE OUT OF THE QUESTION?
THE MONEY IS SPENT. BESIDES, I DO HAVE SOMETHING FOR YOU. I'M NOT SURE HOW VALUABLE IT IS, BUT...
She tells me about a large estate in unincorporated Gotham that she's happened upon.
Where there's wealth, Catwoman is never far behind

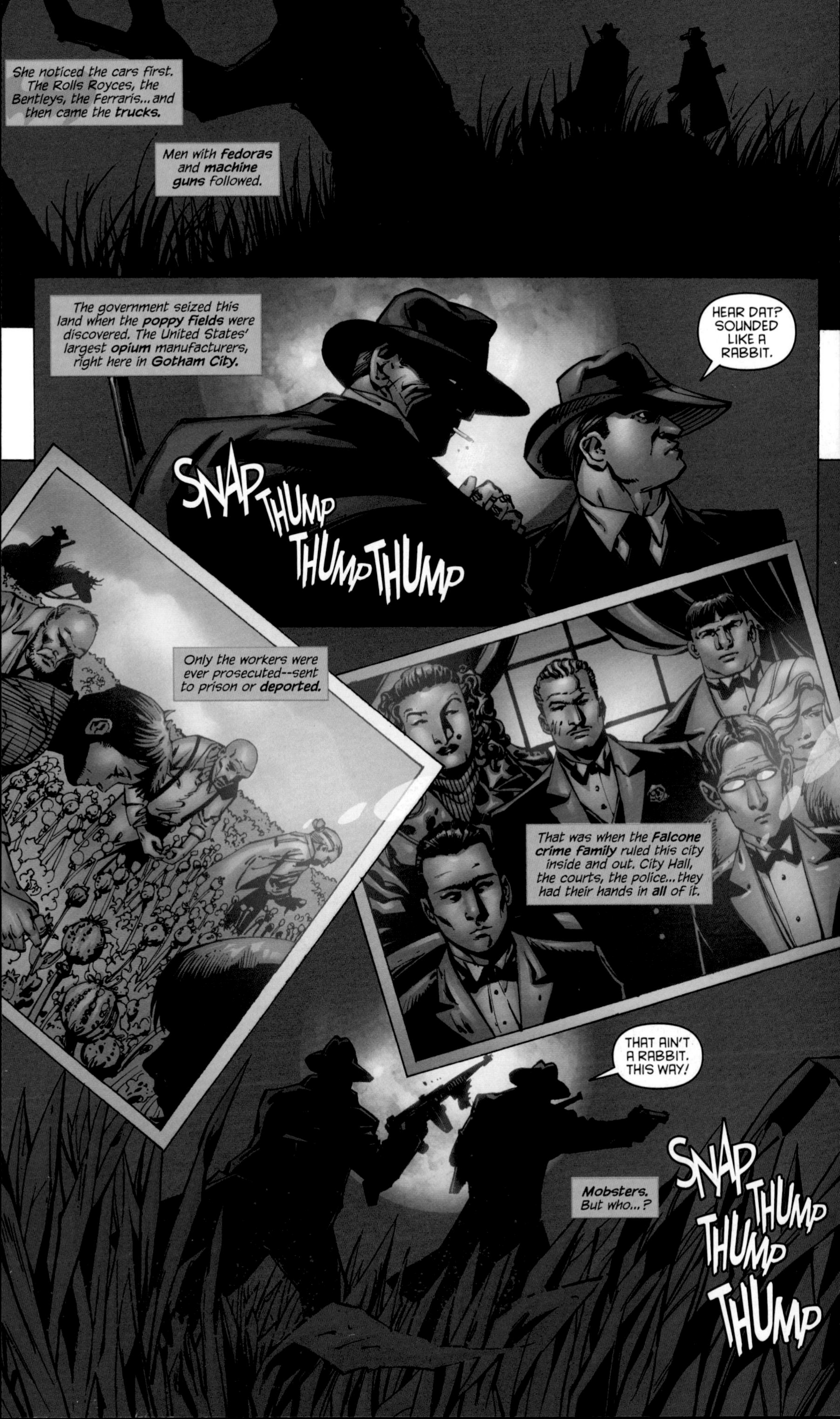
She noticed the cars first. The Rolls Royces, the Bentleys, the Ferraris...and then came the **trucks.**
Men with **fedoras** and **machine guns** followed.
The government seized this land when the **poppy fields** were discovered. The United States' largest **opium** manufacturers, right here in **Gotham City.**
HEAR DAT? SOUNDED LIKE A RABBIT.
SNAP THUMP THUMP THUMP
Only the workers were ever prosecuted--sent to prison or **deported.**
That was when the **Falcone crime family** ruled this city inside and out. City Hall, the courts, the police...they had their hands in **all** of it.
THAT AIN'T A RABBIT. THIS WAY!
Mobsters. But who...?
SNAP THUMP THUMP THUMP

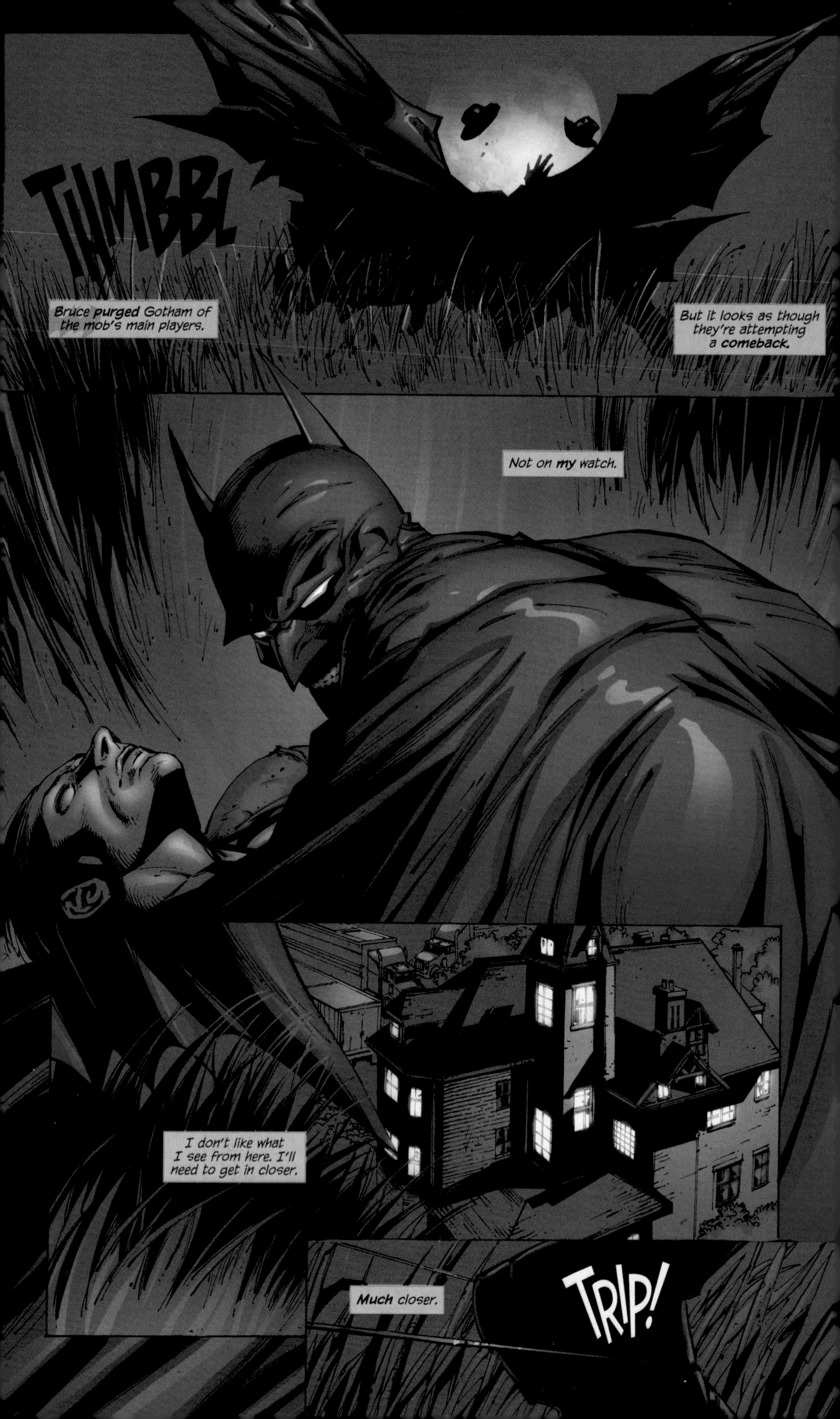
THMBBL
Bruce purged Gotham of the mob's main players.
But it looks as though they're attempting a comeback.
Not on my watch.
I don't like what I see from here. I'll need to get in closer.
Much closer.
TRIP!

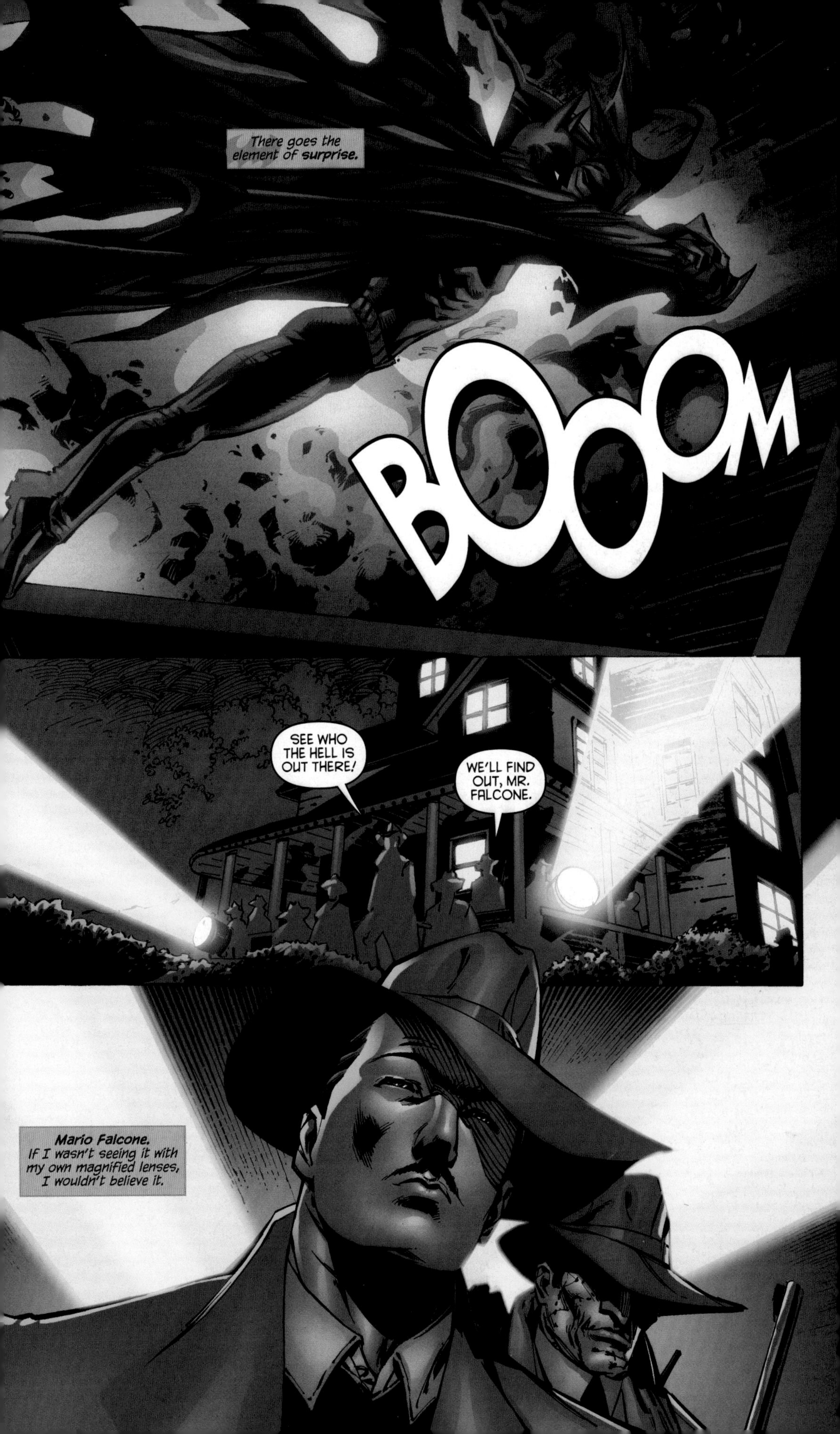
There goes the element of surprise.
BOOOM
SEE WHO THE HELL IS OUT THERE!
WE'LL FIND OUT, MR. FALCONE.
Mario Falcone. If I wasn't seeing it with my own magnified lenses, I wouldn't believe it.

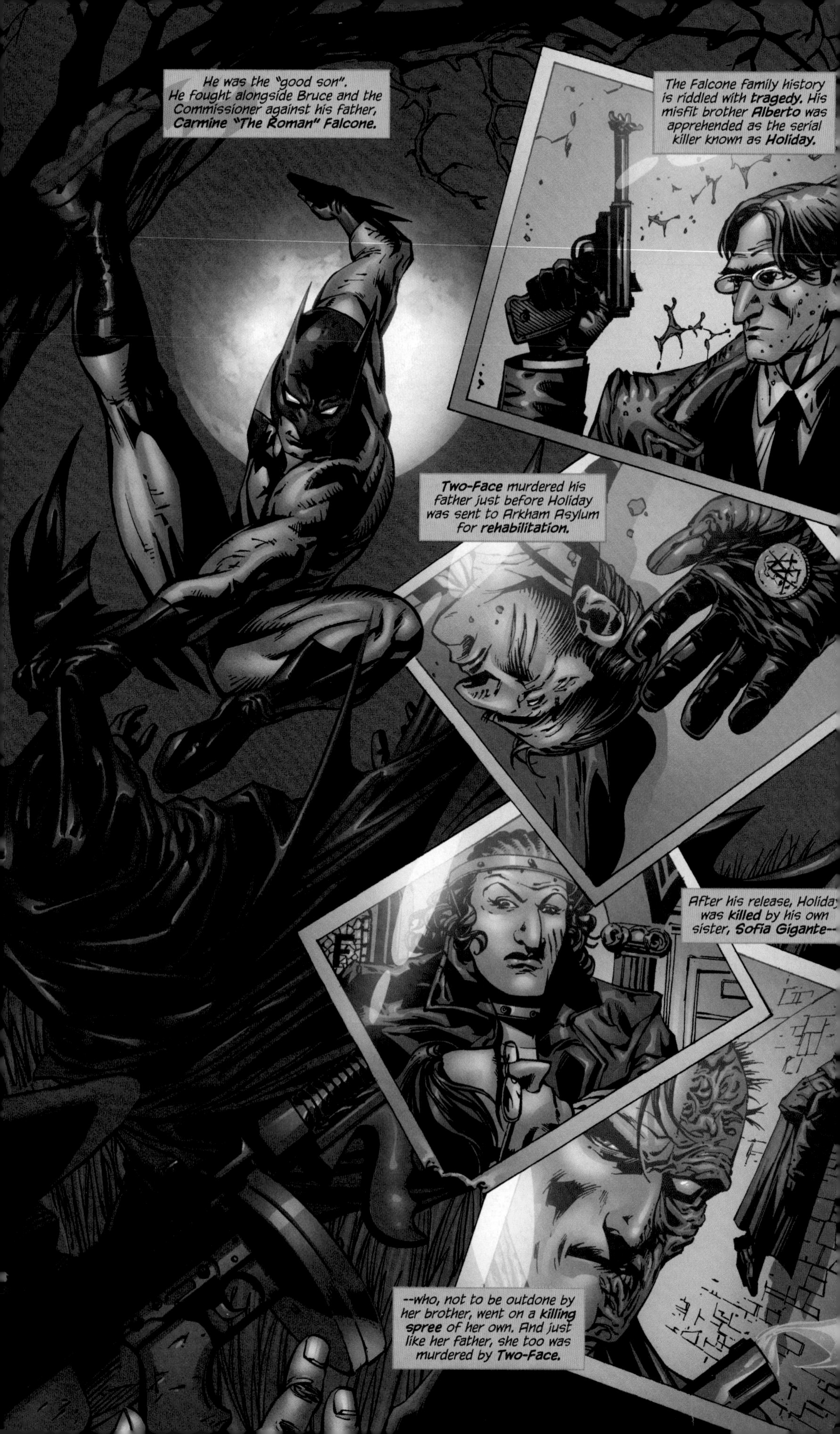
He was the "good son". He fought alongside Bruce and the Commissioner against his father, **Carmine "The Roman" Falcone.**
The Falcone family history is riddled with **tragedy.** His misfit brother **Alberto** was apprehended as the serial killer known as **Holiday.**
Two-Face murdered his father just before Holiday was sent to Arkham Asylum for **rehabilitation.**
After his release, Holiday was **killed** by his own sister, **Sofia Gigante--**
--who, not to be outdone by her brother, went on a **killing spree** of her own. And just like her father, she too was murdered by **Two-Face.**

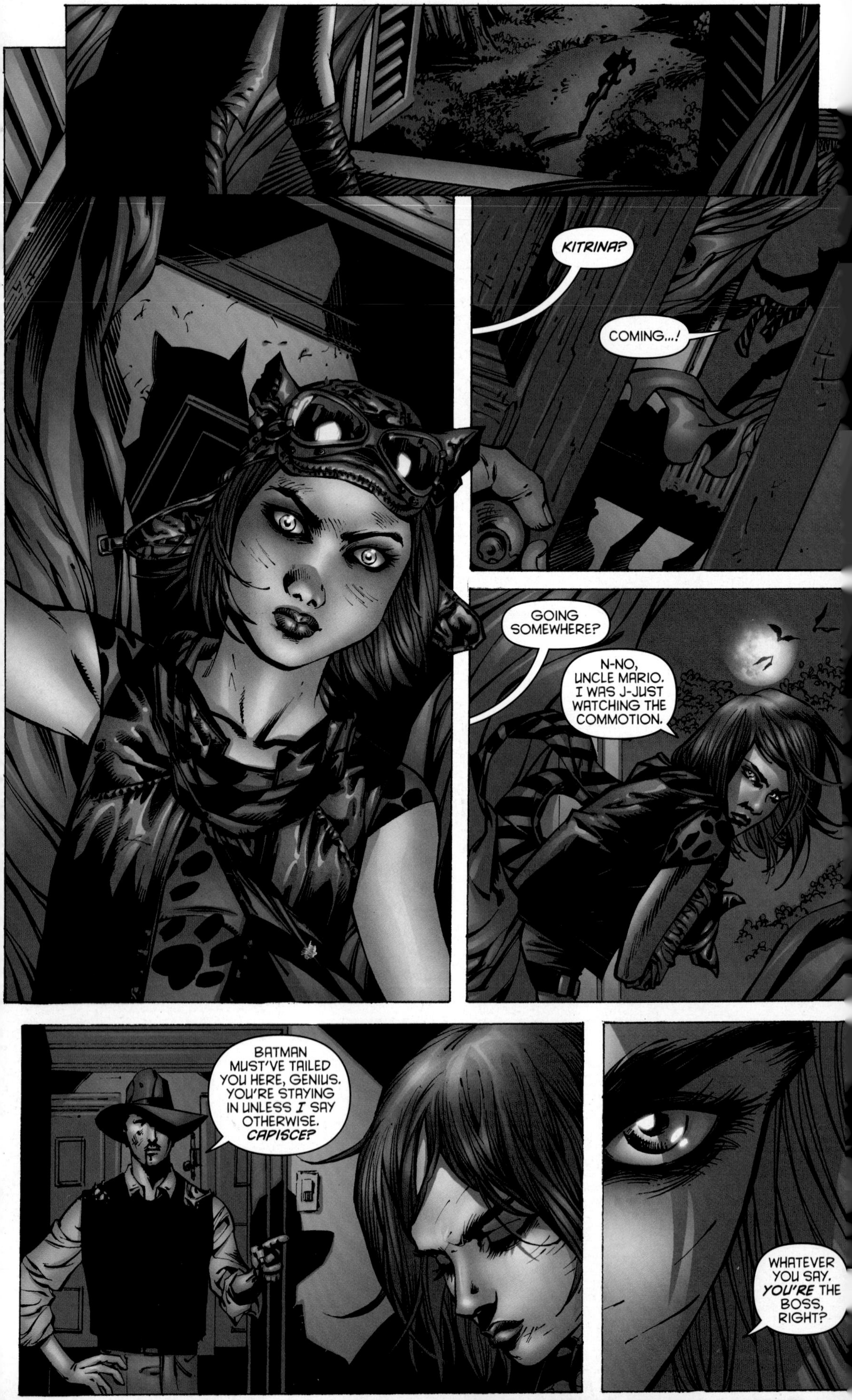
KITRINA?
COMING...!
GOING SOMEWHERE?
N-NO, UNCLE MARIO. I WAS J-JUST WATCHING THE COMMOTION.
BATMAN MUST'VE TAILED YOU HERE, GENIUS. YOU'RE STAYING IN UNLESS *I* SAY OTHERWISE. *CAPISCE?*
WHATEVER YOU SAY. *YOU'RE* THE BOSS, RIGHT?

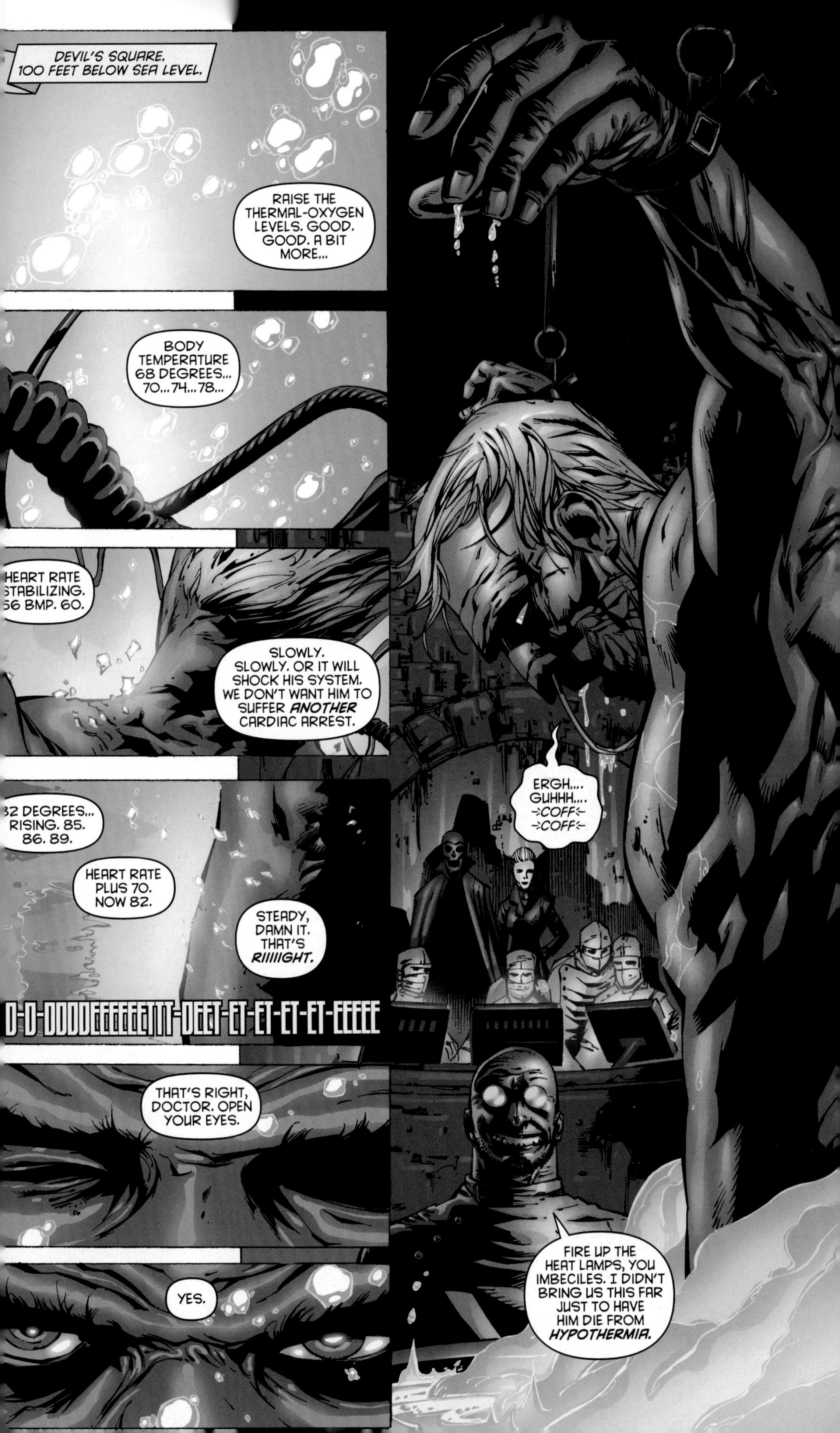
DEVIL'S SQUARE. 100 FEET BELOW SEA LEVEL.
RAISE THE THERMAL-OXYGEN LEVELS. GOOD. GOOD. A BIT MORE...
BODY TEMPERATURE 68 DEGREES... 70... 74... 78...
HEART RATE STABILIZING. 56 BMP. 60.
SLOWLY. SLOWLY. OR IT WILL SHOCK HIS SYSTEM. WE DON'T WANT HIM TO SUFFER *ANOTHER* CARDIAC ARREST.
82 DEGREES... RISING. 85. 86. 89.
HEART RATE PLUS 70. NOW 82.
STEADY, DAMN IT. THAT'S *RIIIIGHT.*
D-D-DDDDEEEEEEETTT-DEET-ET-ET-ET-ET-EEEEE
THAT'S RIGHT, DOCTOR. OPEN YOUR EYES.
YES.
ERGH.... GUHHH.... *COFF* *COFF*
FIRE UP THE HEAT LAMPS, YOU IMBECILES. I DIDN'T BRING US THIS FAR JUST TO HAVE HIM DIE FROM *HYPOTHERMIA.*

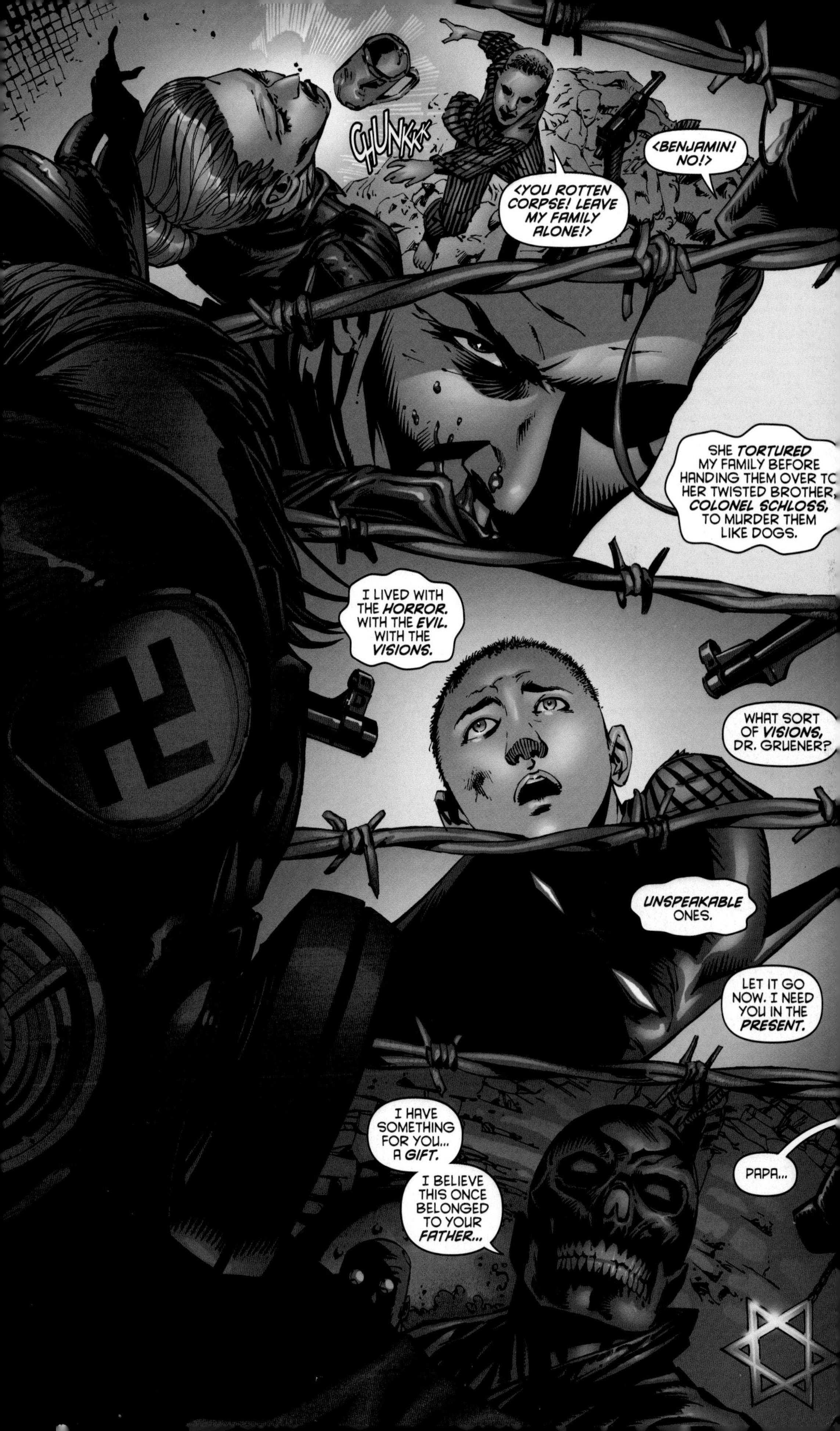
CHUNKKK
<BENJAMIN! NO!>
<YOU ROTTEN CORPSE! LEAVE MY FAMILY ALONE!>
SHE TORTURED MY FAMILY BEFORE HANDING THEM OVER TO HER TWISTED BROTHER, COLONEL SCHLOSS, TO MURDER THEM LIKE DOGS.
I LIVED WITH THE HORROR. WITH THE EVIL. WITH THE VISIONS.
WHAT SORT OF VISIONS, DR. GRUENER?
UNSPEAKABLE ONES.
LET IT GO NOW. I NEED YOU IN THE PRESENT.
I HAVE SOMETHING FOR YOU... A GIFT.
I BELIEVE THIS ONCE BELONGED TO YOUR FATHER...
PAPA...

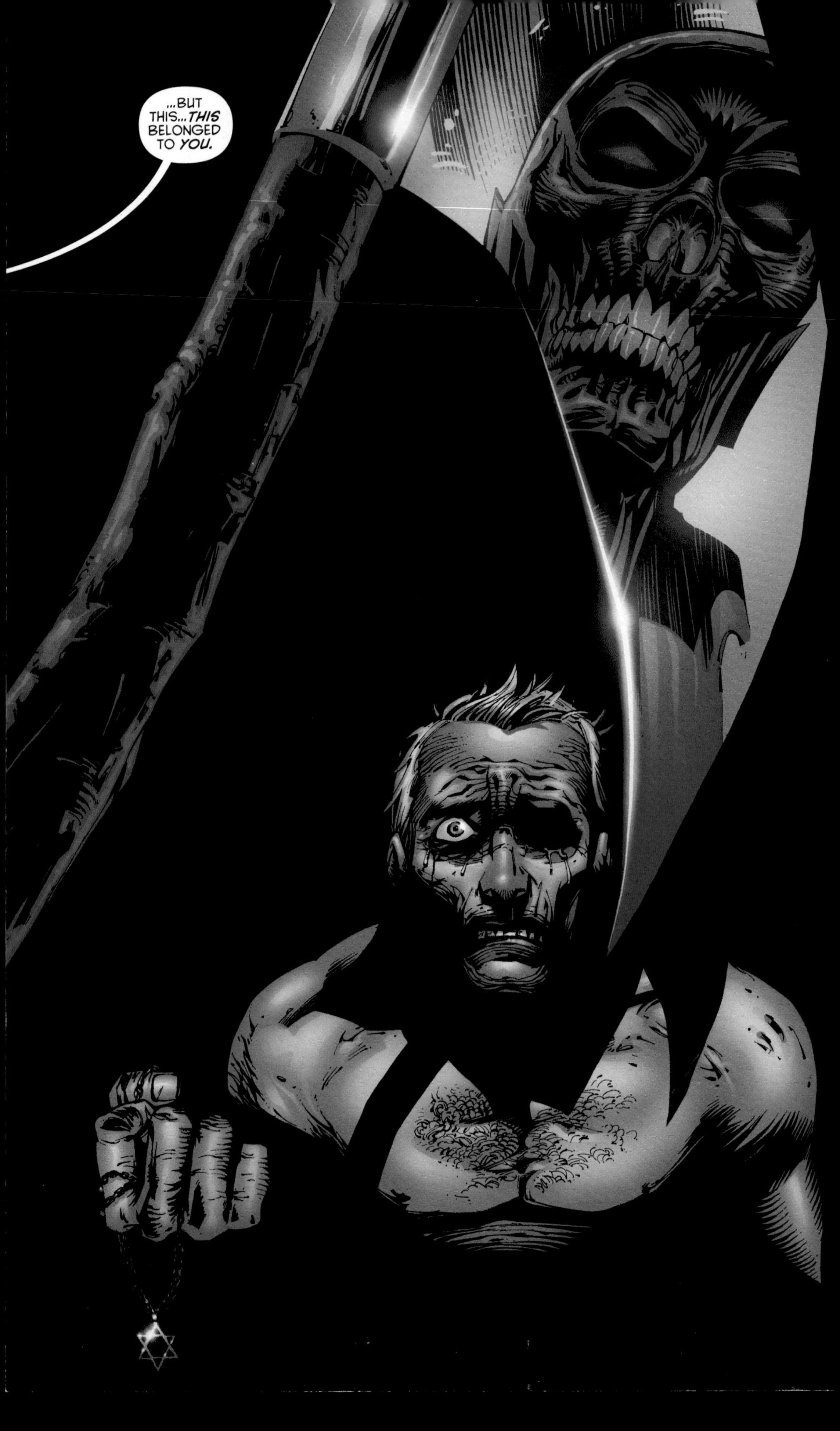
...BUT THIS...*THIS* BELONGED TO *YOU.*

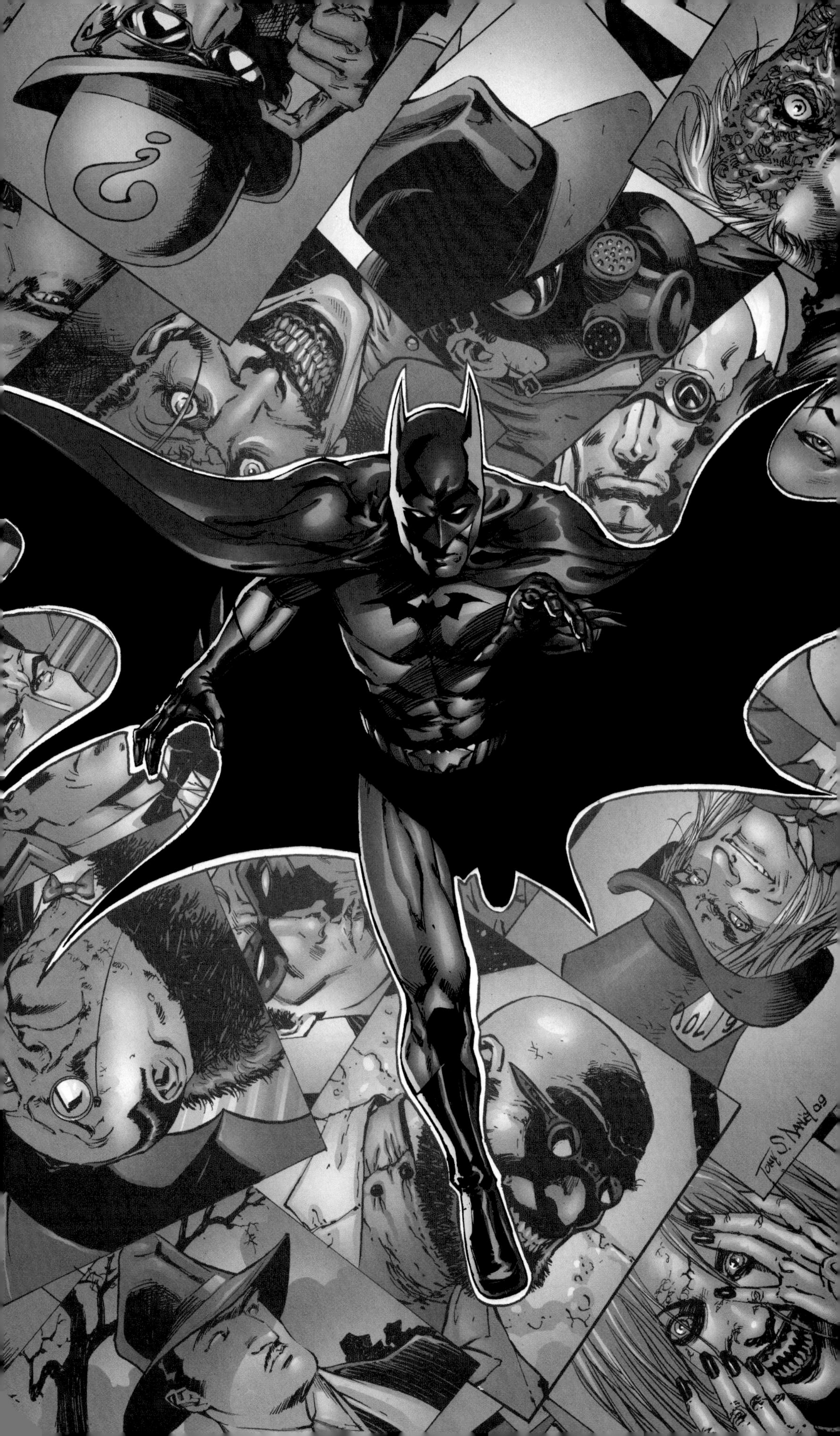

"I have an hour and a half of darkness left. That's all I need to get started."

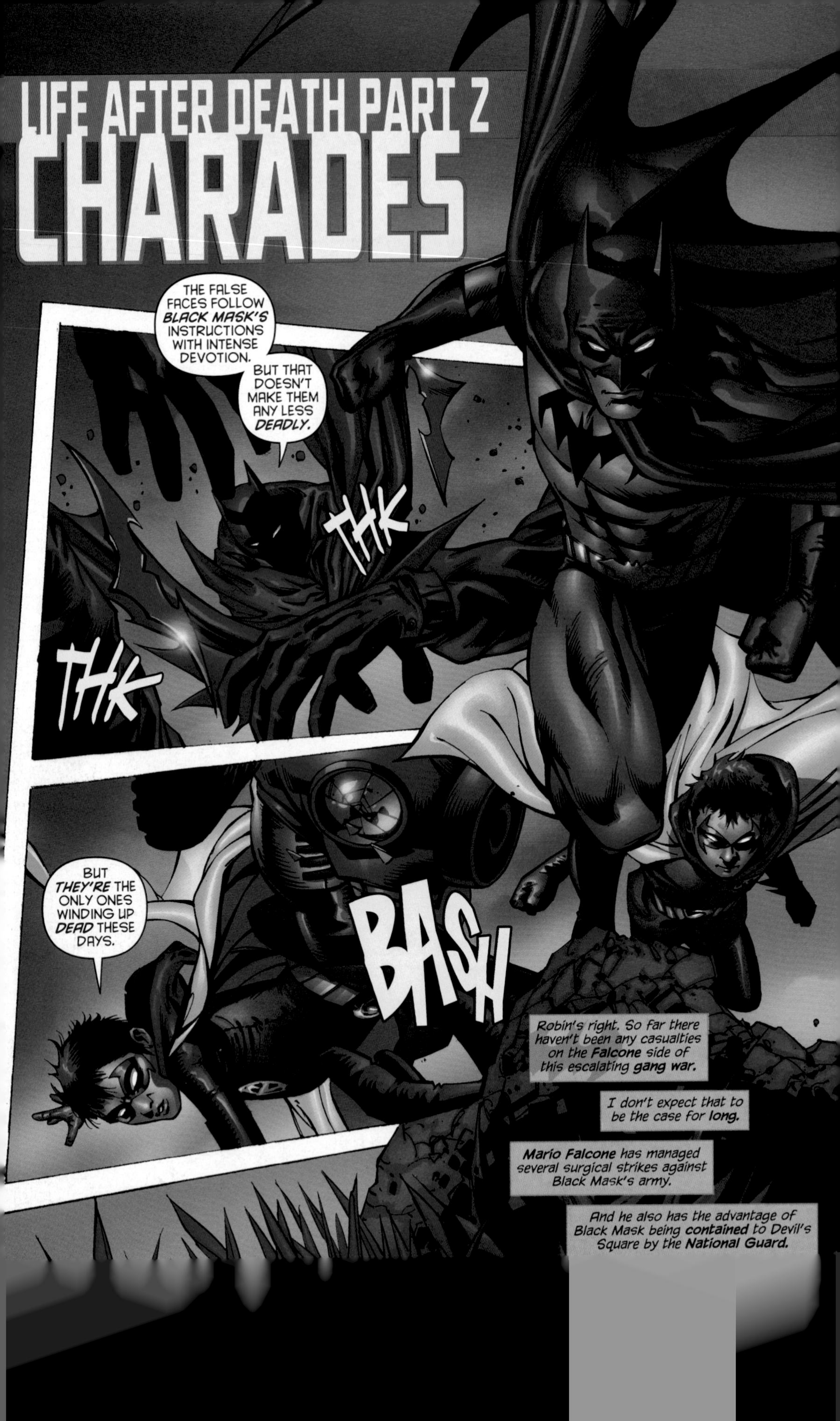

LIFE AFTER DEATH PART 2
CHARADES
THE FALSE FACES FOLLOW BLACK MASK'S INSTRUCTIONS WITH INTENSE DEVOTION.
BUT THAT DOESN'T MAKE THEM ANY LESS DEADLY.
THK
THK
BUT THEY'RE THE ONLY ONES WINDING UP DEAD THESE DAYS.
BASH
Robin's right. So far there haven't been any casualties on the Falcone side of this escalating gang war.
I don't expect that to be the case for long.
Mario Falcone has managed several surgical strikes against Black Mask's army.
And he also has the advantage of Black Mask being contained to Devil's Square by the National Guard.

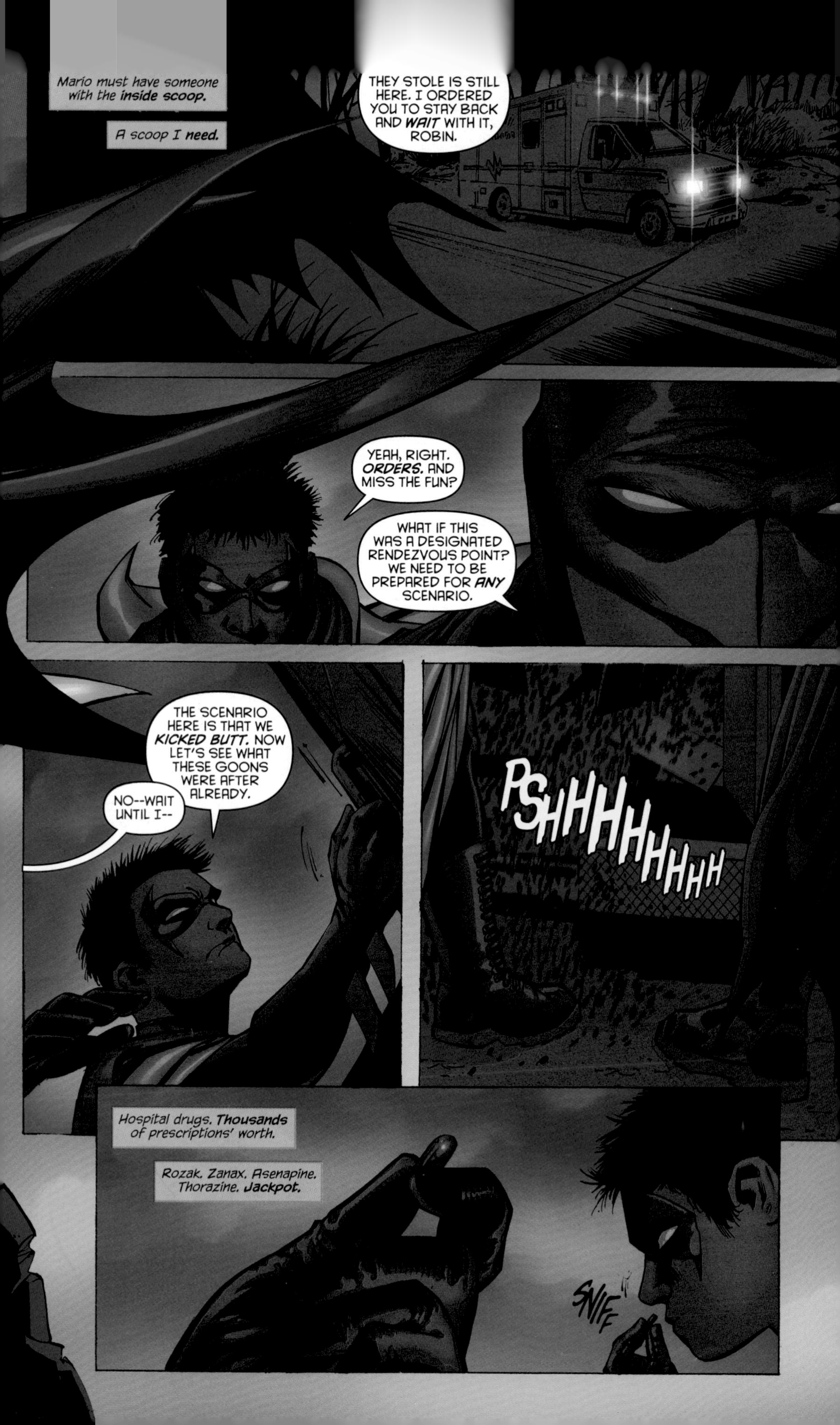
Mario must have someone with the inside scoop.
A scoop I need.
THEY STOLE IS STILL HERE. I ORDERED YOU TO STAY BACK AND WAIT WITH IT, ROBIN.
YEAH, RIGHT. ORDERS. AND MISS THE FUN?
WHAT IF THIS WAS A DESIGNATED RENDEZVOUS POINT? WE NEED TO BE PREPARED FOR ANY SCENARIO.
THE SCENARIO HERE IS THAT WE KICKED BUTT. NOW LET'S SEE WHAT THESE GOONS WERE AFTER ALREADY.
NO--WAIT UNTIL I--
PSHHHHHHHHH
Hospital drugs. Thousands of prescriptions' worth.
Rozak. Zanax. Asenapine. Thorazine. Jackpot.
SNIFF

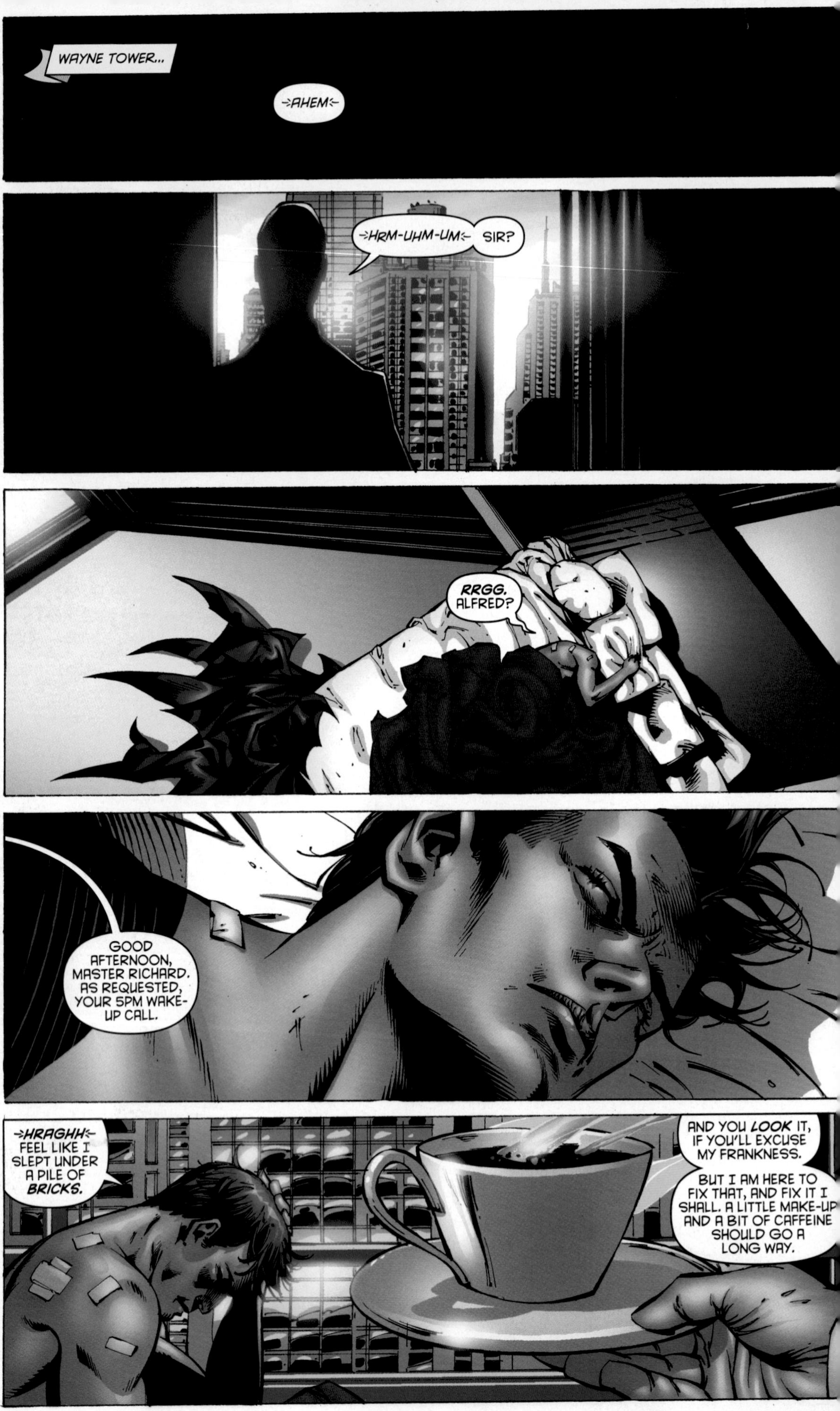
WAYNE TOWER...
AHEM
HRM-UHM-UM SIR?
RRGG. ALFRED?
GOOD AFTERNOON, MASTER RICHARD. AS REQUESTED, YOUR 5PM WAKE-UP CALL.
HRAGHH FEEL LIKE I SLEPT UNDER A PILE OF BRICKS.
AND YOU LOOK IT, IF YOU'LL EXCUSE MY FRANKNESS.
BUT I AM HERE TO FIX THAT, AND FIX IT I SHALL. A LITTLE MAKE-UP AND A BIT OF CAFFEINE SHOULD GO A LONG WAY.

I'M *WAAAY* OUT OF MY ELEMENT HERE, ALFRED. HOBNOBBING WITH GOTHAM'S SOCIALITES ISN'T MY THING.

STATUS AND OPULENCE DOESN'T GIVE ONE SHARP TEETH.

THOUGH BEING INVITED TO THE ARKHAM RESEARCH BENEFIT MORE THAN QUALIFIES YOU AS ONE OF *THEM*.

WELL, THEY'LL HAVE TO SETTLE FOR A BIT OF *ACTING* ON MY PART.

QUITE. BUT DON'T WORRY, MASTER RICHARD. YOU WON'T BE PLAYING THE PART ALONE.

FLIK

NO?

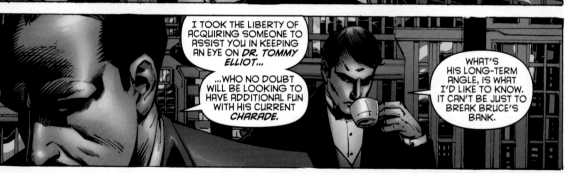

I TOOK THE LIBERTY OF ACQUIRING SOMEONE TO ASSIST YOU IN KEEPING AN EYE ON *DR. TOMMY ELLIOT*...

...WHO NO DOUBT WILL BE LOOKING TO HAVE ADDITIONAL FUN WITH HIS CURRENT *CHARADE*.

WHAT'S HIS LONG-TERM ANGLE, IS WHAT I'D LIKE TO KNOW. IT CAN'T BE JUST TO BREAK BRUCE'S BANK.

IT SEEMS "MASTER BRUCE" HAS BEEN INVITED TO JOIN THE *GOTHAM SHIELD COMMITTEE*...

...AN ELITE GROUP OF *EXPERTS* FORMED TO DISCUSS NEW IDEAS FOR THE FUTURE STABILITY OF OUR FAIR CITY.

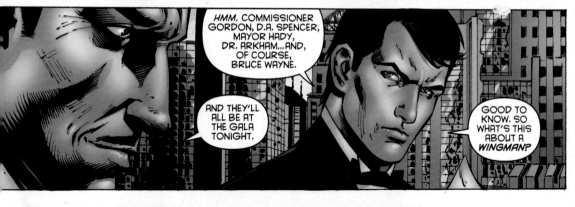

HMM. COMMISSIONER GORDON, D.A. SPENCER, MAYOR HADY, DR. ARKHAM...AND, OF COURSE, BRUCE WAYNE.

AND THEY'LL ALL BE AT THE GALA TONIGHT.

GOOD TO KNOW. SO WHAT'S THIS ABOUT A *WINGMAN*?

A sea of diamonds and furs. They could've cancelled this shindig and put the money towards Arkham's New Asylum.

It's a wonder these events aren't targeted by thieves more often.

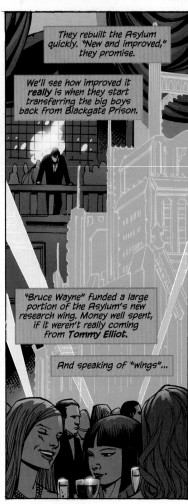

They rebuilt the Asylum quickly. "New and improved," they promise.

We'll see how improved it really is when they start transferring the big boys back from Blackgate Prison.

"Bruce Wayne" funded a large portion of the Asylum's new research wing. Money well spent, if it weren't really coming from Tommy Elliot.

And speaking of "wings"...

...here's mine, Helena Bertinelli, a.k.a. The Huntress.

PRETTY SWANKY, HUH?

THE PARTY? I SUPPOSE.

I MEANT THE *DRESS*. AND THANKS FOR GOING TO THE TROUBLE OF BUYING IT. OR IS IT *ALFRED* I SHOULD BE THANKING?

I THOUGHT WE WEREN'T GOING TO DRAW ATTENTION TO OURSELVES...

TRUST ME, WITH *THIS* CROWD--ANYTHING *OFF THE RACK* IS DRAWING ATTENTION.

SO WHERE'S OUR OLD FRIEND "BRUCE"?

OVER MY LEFT SHOULDER. TEN YARDS, TALKING TO THE *GENE-CORE* DOCTORS. THAT'S *DOCTOR SINGH* TOMMY IS TALKING TO-- THEIR FOUNDER.

I'VE READ ABOUT HIM. HE SOMEHOW GOT THE FDA TO APPROVE HIS THERAPY FOR CLINICAL TRIALS IN ARKHAM.

IT'S ALL ABOUT THE BENJAMINS.

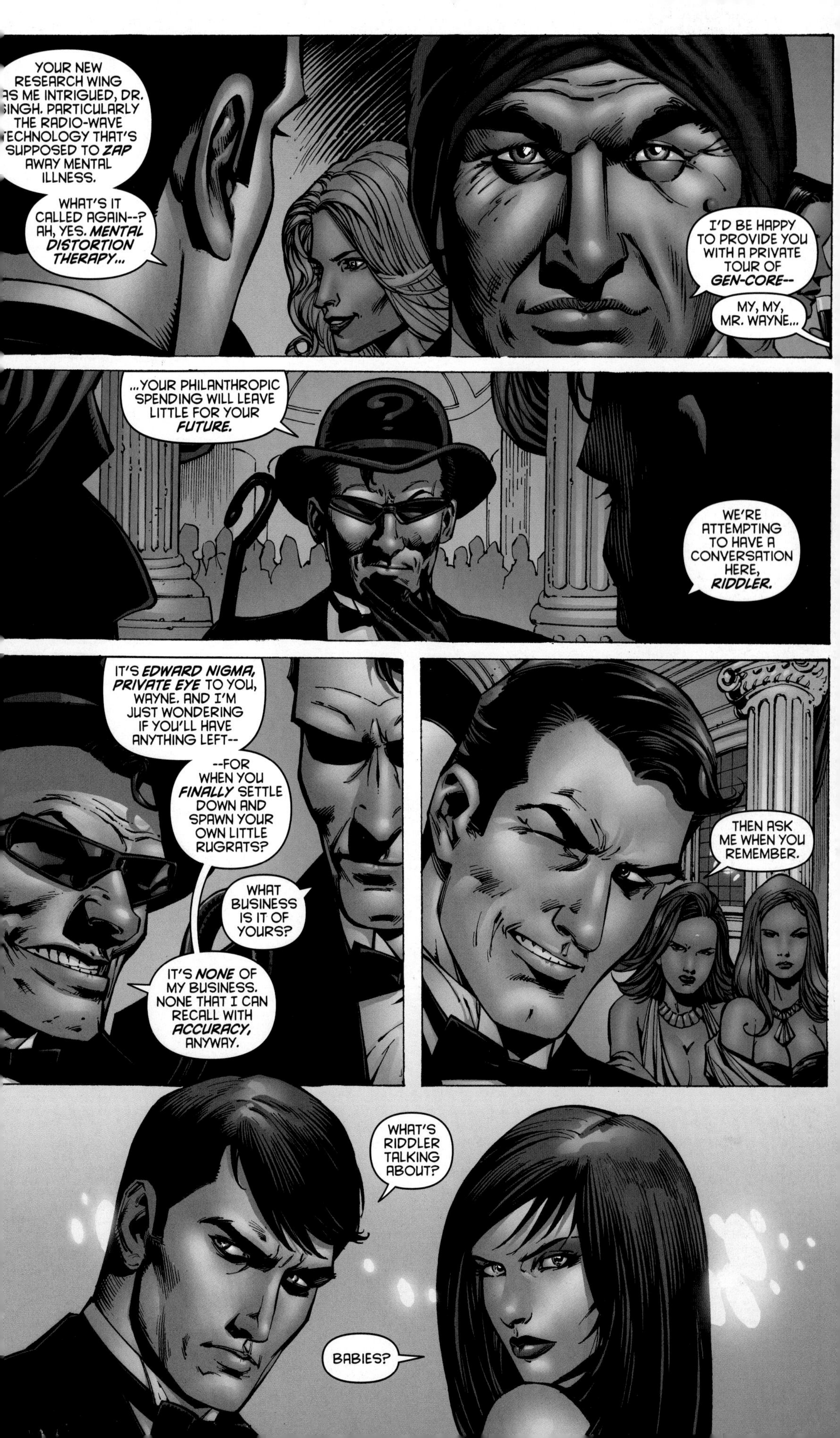
YOUR NEW RESEARCH WING HAS ME INTRIGUED, DR. SINGH. PARTICULARLY THE RADIO-WAVE TECHNOLOGY THAT'S SUPPOSED TO ZAP AWAY MENTAL ILLNESS.
WHAT'S IT CALLED AGAIN--? AH, YES. MENTAL DISTORTION THERAPY...
I'D BE HAPPY TO PROVIDE YOU WITH A PRIVATE TOUR OF GEN-CORE--
MY, MY, MR. WAYNE...
...YOUR PHILANTHROPIC SPENDING WILL LEAVE LITTLE FOR YOUR FUTURE.
WE'RE ATTEMPTING TO HAVE A CONVERSATION HERE, RIDDLER.
IT'S EDWARD NIGMA, PRIVATE EYE TO YOU, WAYNE. AND I'M JUST WONDERING IF YOU'LL HAVE ANYTHING LEFT--
--FOR WHEN YOU FINALLY SETTLE DOWN AND SPAWN YOUR OWN LITTLE RUGRATS?
WHAT BUSINESS IS IT OF YOURS?
IT'S NONE OF MY BUSINESS. NONE THAT I CAN RECALL WITH ACCURACY, ANYWAY.
THEN ASK ME WHEN YOU REMEMBER.
WHAT'S RIDDLER TALKING ABOUT?
BABIES?

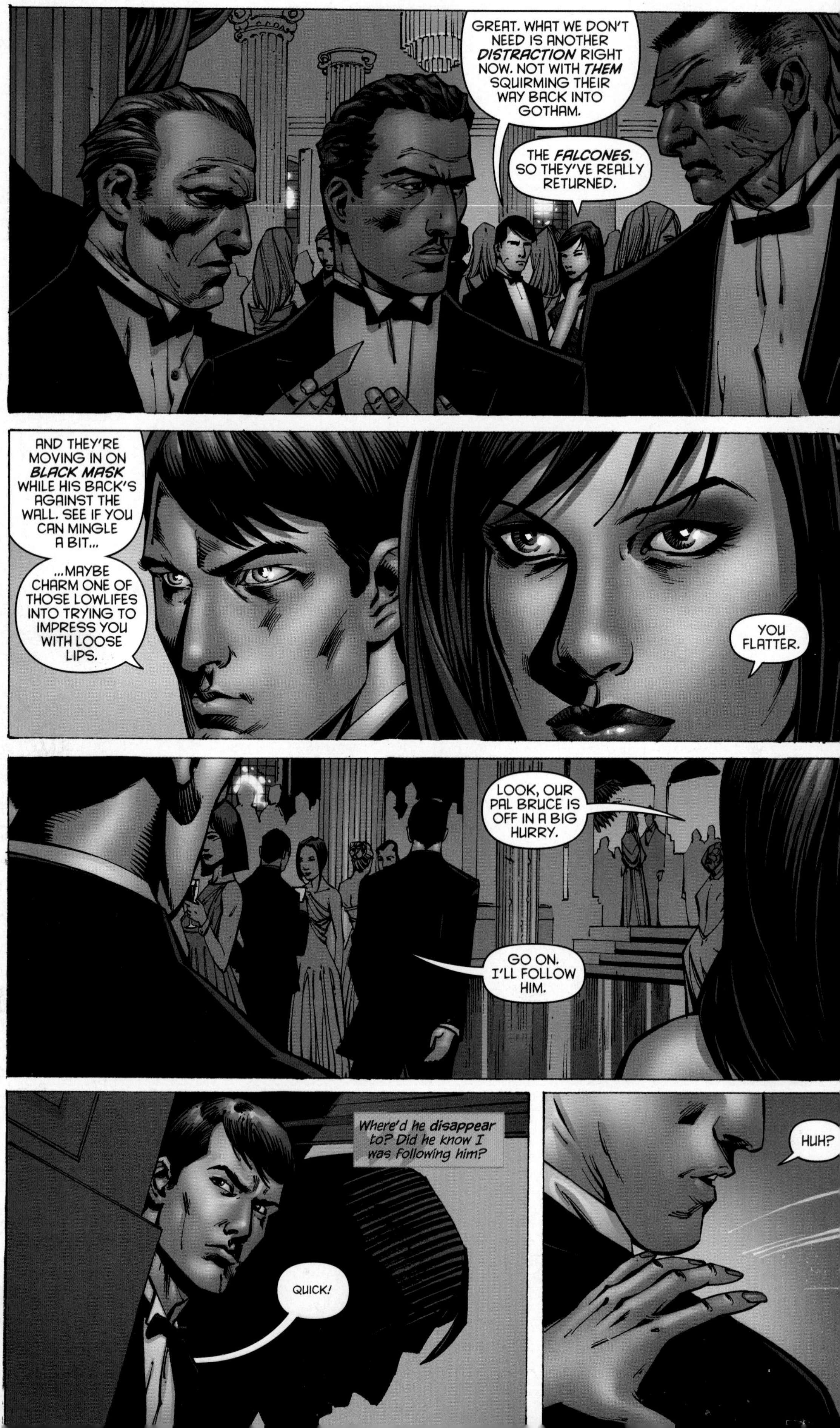
GREAT. WHAT WE DON'T NEED IS ANOTHER DISTRACTION RIGHT NOW. NOT WITH THEM SQUIRMING THEIR WAY BACK INTO GOTHAM.
THE FALCONES. SO THEY'VE REALLY RETURNED.
AND THEY'RE MOVING IN ON BLACK MASK WHILE HIS BACK'S AGAINST THE WALL. SEE IF YOU CAN MINGLE A BIT...
...MAYBE CHARM ONE OF THOSE LOWLIFES INTO TRYING TO IMPRESS YOU WITH LOOSE LIPS.
YOU FLATTER.
LOOK, OUR PAL BRUCE IS OFF IN A BIG HURRY.
GO ON. I'LL FOLLOW HIM.
Where'd he disappear to? Did he know I was following him?
QUICK!
HUH?

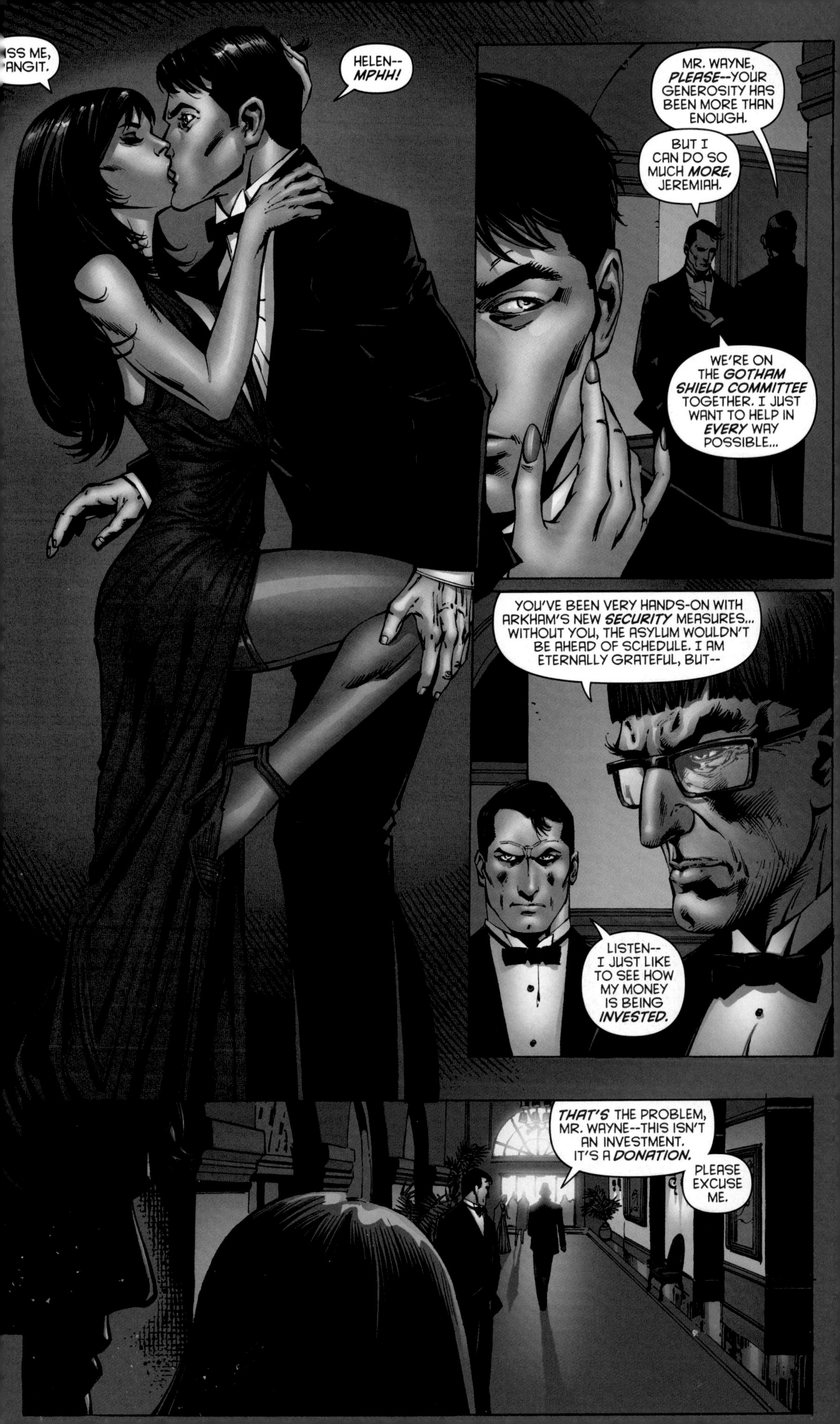
ISS ME,
ANGIT.
HELEN--
MPHH!
MR. WAYNE, PLEASE--YOUR GENEROSITY HAS BEEN MORE THAN ENOUGH.
BUT I CAN DO SO MUCH MORE, JEREMIAH.
WE'RE ON THE GOTHAM SHIELD COMMITTEE TOGETHER. I JUST WANT TO HELP IN EVERY WAY POSSIBLE...
YOU'VE BEEN VERY HANDS-ON WITH ARKHAM'S NEW SECURITY MEASURES... WITHOUT YOU, THE ASYLUM WOULDN'T BE AHEAD OF SCHEDULE. I AM ETERNALLY GRATEFUL, BUT--
LISTEN-- I JUST LIKE TO SEE HOW MY MONEY IS BEING INVESTED.
THAT'S THE PROBLEM, MR. WAYNE--THIS ISN'T AN INVESTMENT. IT'S A DONATION.
PLEASE EXCUSE ME.

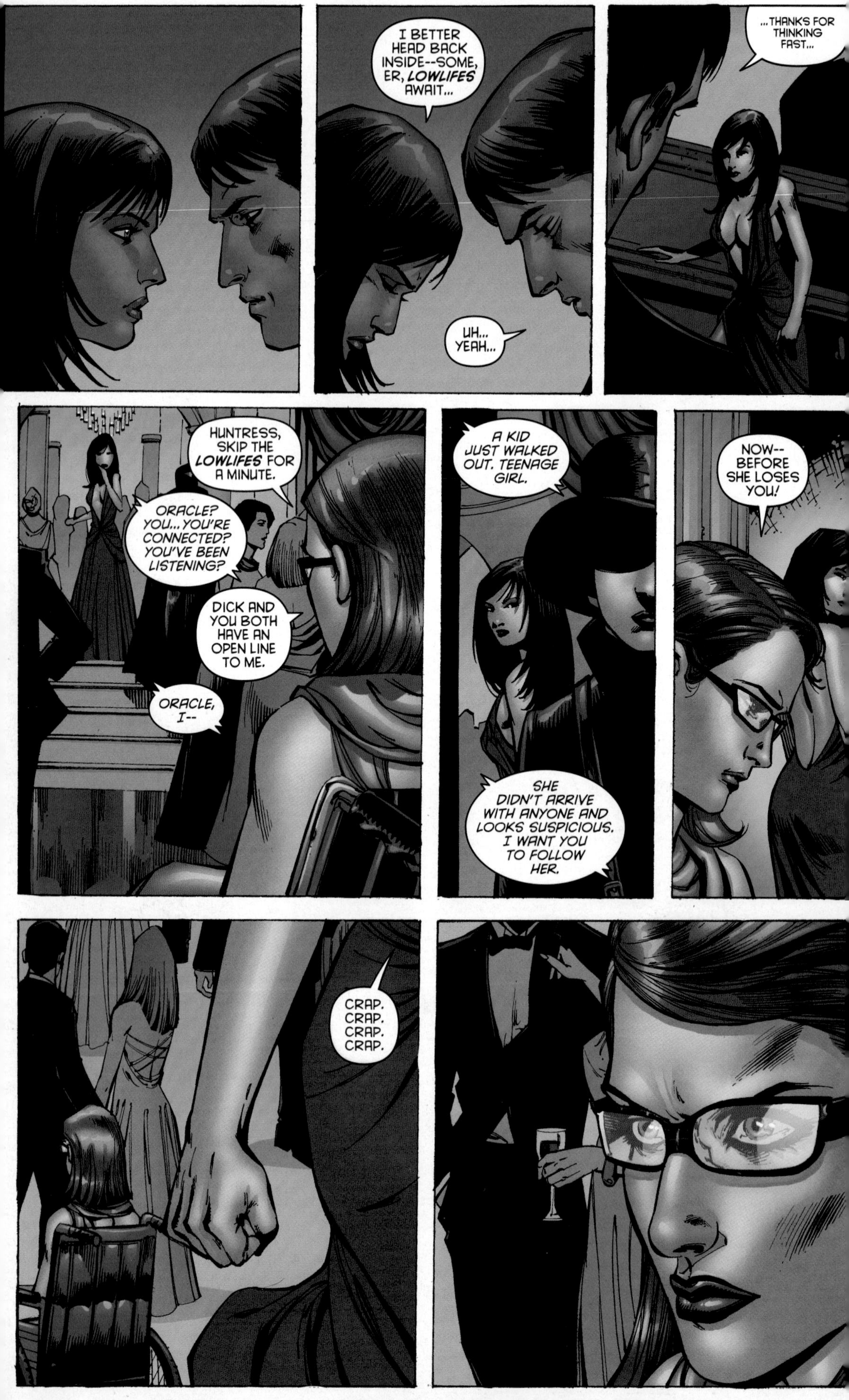
I BETTER HEAD BACK INSIDE--SOME, ER, LOWLIFES AWAIT...
UH... YEAH...
...THANKS FOR THINKING FAST...
HUNTRESS, SKIP THE LOWLIFES FOR A MINUTE.
ORACLE? YOU... YOU'RE CONNECTED? YOU'VE BEEN LISTENING?
DICK AND YOU BOTH HAVE AN OPEN LINE TO ME.
ORACLE, I--
A KID JUST WALKED OUT. TEENAGE GIRL.
SHE DIDN'T ARRIVE WITH ANYONE AND LOOKS SUSPICIOUS. I WANT YOU TO FOLLOW HER.
NOW-- BEFORE SHE LOSES YOU!
CRAP. CRAP. CRAP. CRAP.

DAG!

YOU'RE BEING FOLLOWED, KITRINA.

LIKE I DON'T KNOW. AND *DON'T* TALK TO ME. YOU'RE RUINING MY INNER CHI.

HEY--!

HIT THE ALARM! ⟩COFF⟨ ⟩COFF⟨

TSSSSSS

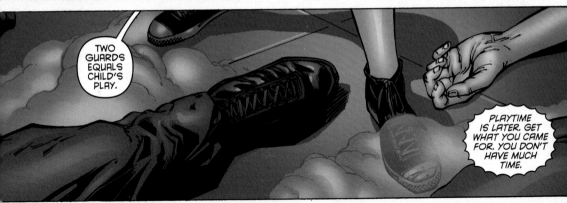

TWO GUARDS EQUALS CHILD'S PLAY.

PLAYTIME IS LATER. GET WHAT YOU CAME FOR. YOU DON'T HAVE MUCH TIME.

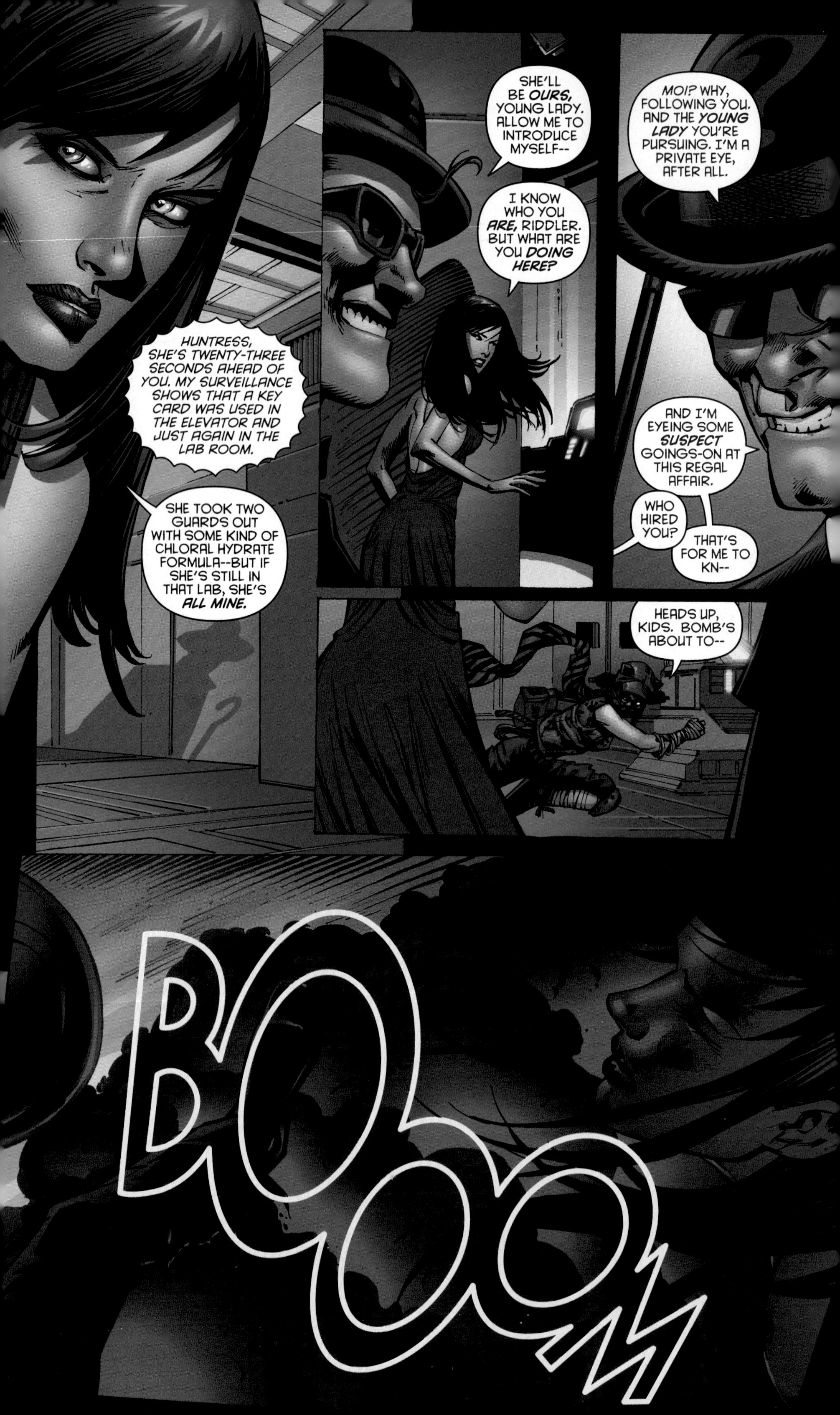
HUNTRESS, SHE'S TWENTY-THREE SECONDS AHEAD OF YOU. MY SURVEILLANCE SHOWS THAT A KEY CARD WAS USED IN THE ELEVATOR AND JUST AGAIN IN THE LAB ROOM.
SHE TOOK TWO GUARDS OUT WITH SOME KIND OF CHLORAL HYDRATE FORMULA--BUT IF SHE'S STILL IN THAT LAB, SHE'S ALL MINE.
SHE'LL BE OURS, YOUNG LADY. ALLOW ME TO INTRODUCE MYSELF--
I KNOW WHO YOU ARE, RIDDLER. BUT WHAT ARE YOU DOING HERE?
MOI? WHY, FOLLOWING YOU. AND THE YOUNG LADY YOU'RE PURSUING. I'M A PRIVATE EYE, AFTER ALL.
AND I'M EYEING SOME SUSPECT GOINGS-ON AT THIS REGAL AFFAIR.
WHO HIRED YOU?
THAT'S FOR ME TO KN--
HEADS UP, KIDS. BOMB'S ABOUT TO--
BOOOOM

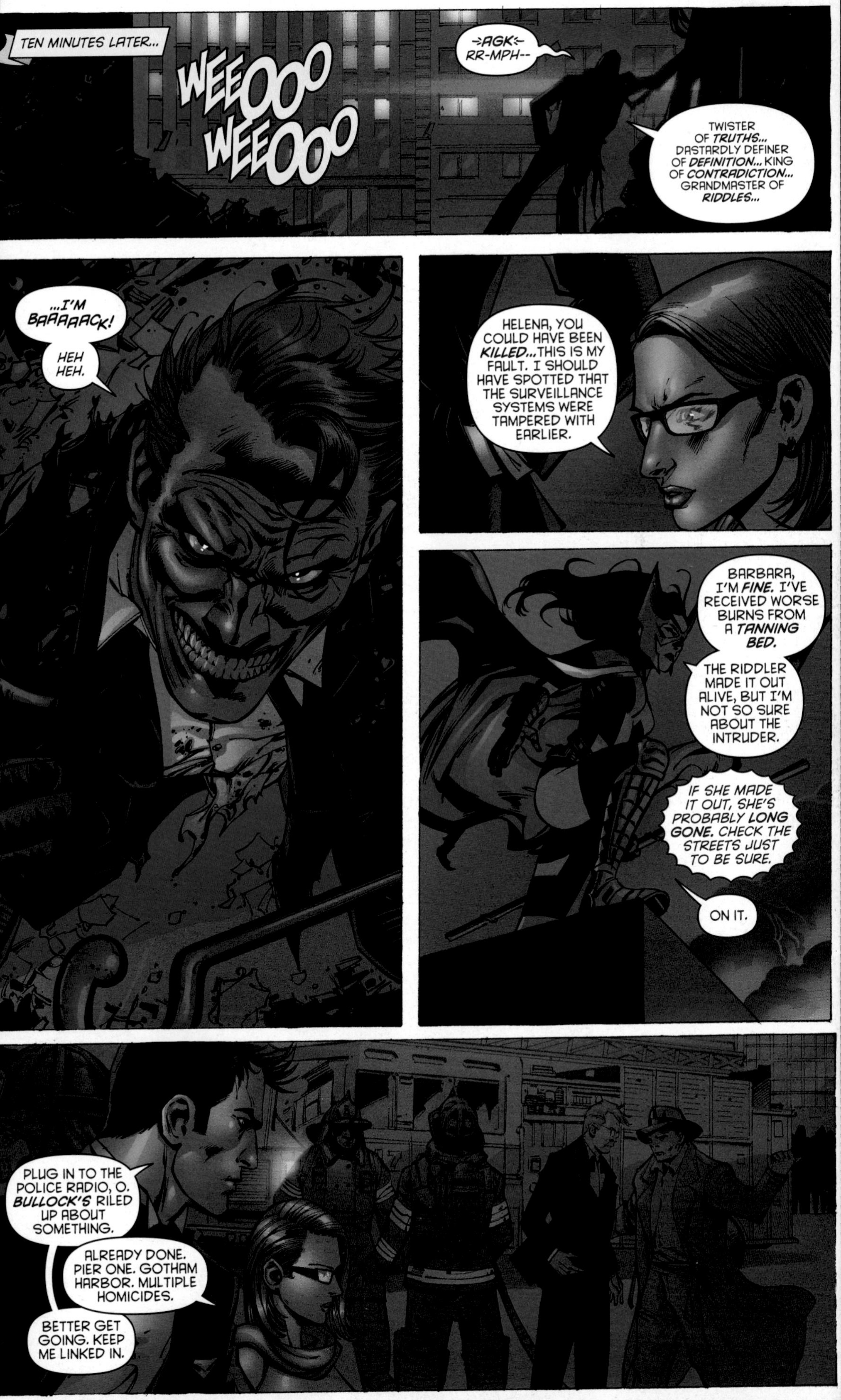
TEN MINUTES LATER...
WEEOOO WEEOOO
->AGK<- RR-MPH--
TWISTER OF TRUTHS... DASTARDLY DEFINER OF DEFINITION... KING OF CONTRADICTION... GRANDMASTER OF RIDDLES...
...I'M BAAAAACK!
HEH HEH.
HELENA, YOU COULD HAVE BEEN KILLED... THIS IS MY FAULT. I SHOULD HAVE SPOTTED THAT THE SURVEILLANCE SYSTEMS WERE TAMPERED WITH EARLIER.
BARBARA, I'M FINE. I'VE RECEIVED WORSE BURNS FROM A TANNING BED.
THE RIDDLER MADE IT OUT ALIVE, BUT I'M NOT SO SURE ABOUT THE INTRUDER.
IF SHE MADE IT OUT, SHE'S PROBABLY LONG GONE. CHECK THE STREETS JUST TO BE SURE.
ON IT.
PLUG IN TO THE POLICE RADIO, O. BULLOCK'S RILED UP ABOUT SOMETHING.
ALREADY DONE. PIER ONE. GOTHAM HARBOR. MULTIPLE HOMICIDES.
BETTER GET GOING. KEEP ME LINKED IN.

GOTHAM HARBOR...

WELL, THE OTHER SHOE HAS DROPPED.

AND EVERY *OTHER* BODY PART. MUST'VE BEEN SOME *BONFIRE*, HUH? THERE'S LIKE FIFTEEN--SIXTEEN BODIES IN THAT *HEAP*.

I COUNT *EIGHT*, SERGEANT. SO FAR. THE MEDICAL EXAMINER WILL HAVE TO PRY THEM APART. THE HEAT FROM THE FIRE FUSED SOME BONES TOGETHER.

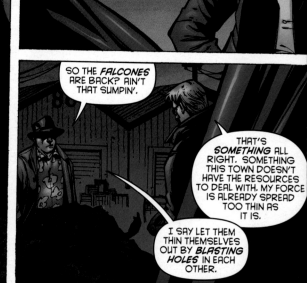

WHAT DO YOU THINK WENT DOWN HERE WITH FALCONE'S MEN, BATMAN?

SO THE *FALCONES* ARE BACK? AIN'T THAT SUMPIN'.

THAT'S *SOMETHING* ALL RIGHT. SOMETHING THIS TOWN DOESN'T HAVE THE RESOURCES TO DEAL WITH. MY FORCE IS ALREADY SPREAD TOO THIN AS IT IS.

I SAY LET THEM THIN THEMSELVES OUT BY *BLASTING HOLES* IN EACH OTHER.

FALCONE'S MEN DIDN'T STAND A CHANCE AGAINST WHOEVER *CUT* THEM UP.

WHAT ARE YOU SAYING? THESE GUYS WERE CHOPPED UP, BUT *SURELY* THAT WAS DONE *AFTER*--

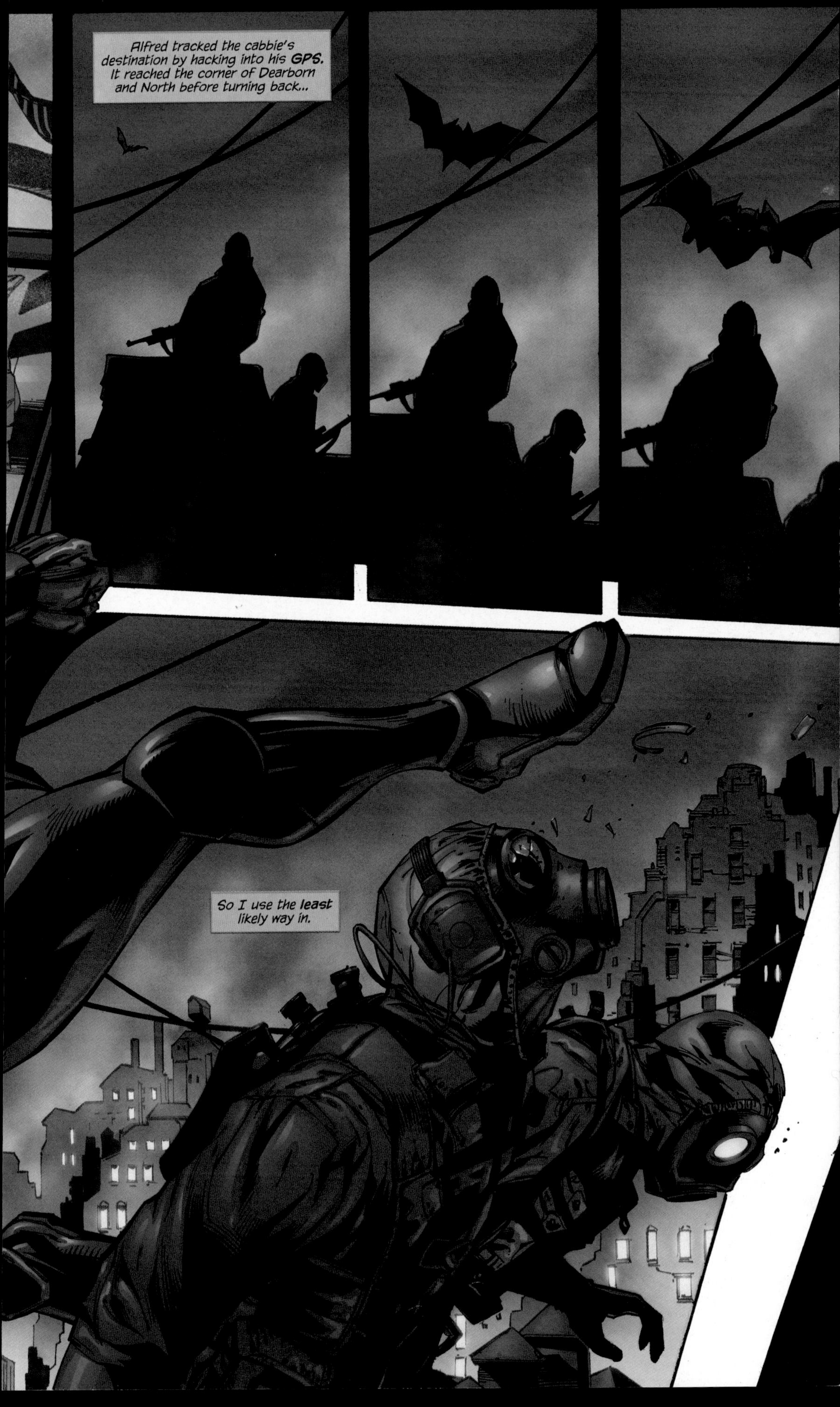
Alfred tracked the cabbie's destination by hacking into his GPS. It reached the corner of Dearborn and North before turning back...
So I use the least likely way in.

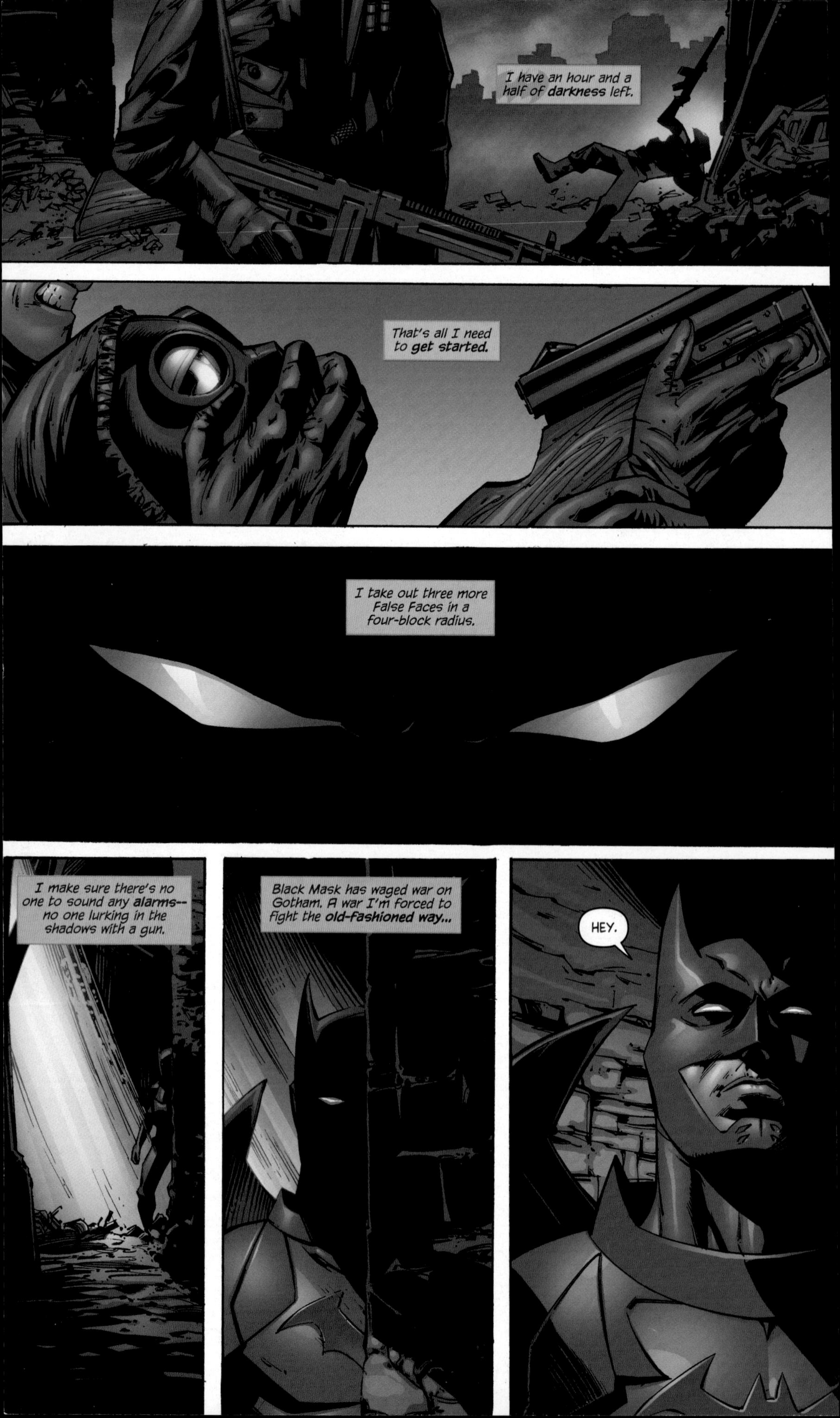
I have an hour and a half of darkness left.
That's all I need to get started.
I take out three more False Faces in a four-block radius.
I make sure there's no one to sound any alarms--no one lurking in the shadows with a gun.
Black Mask has waged war on Gotham. A war I'm forced to fight the old-fashioned way...
HEY.

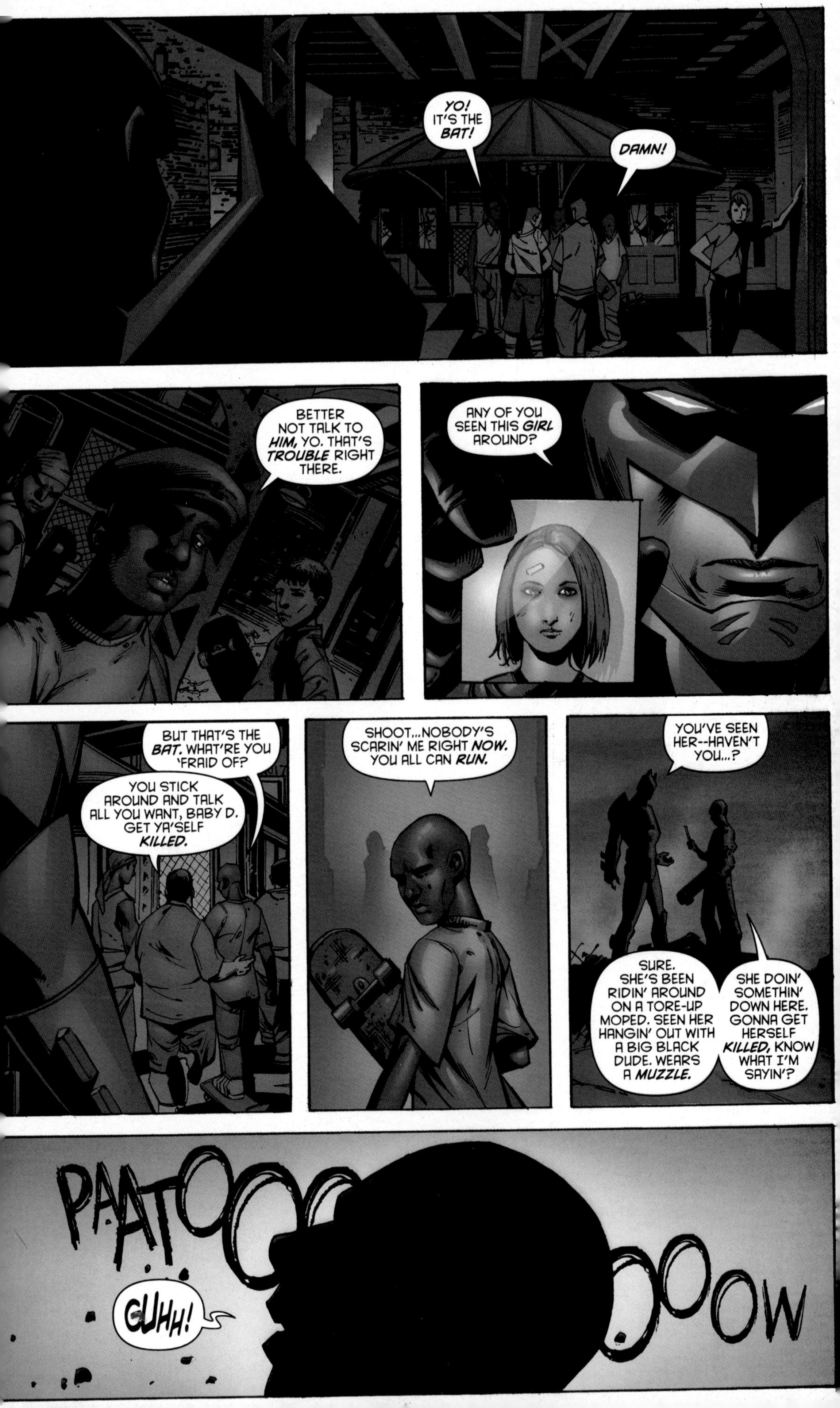

YO! IT'S THE BAT!
DAMN!
BETTER NOT TALK TO HIM, YO. THAT'S TROUBLE RIGHT THERE.
ANY OF YOU SEEN THIS GIRL AROUND?
BUT THAT'S THE BAT. WHAT'RE YOU 'FRAID OF?
YOU STICK AROUND AND TALK ALL YOU WANT, BABY D. GET YA'SELF KILLED.
SHOOT...NOBODY'S SCARIN' ME RIGHT NOW. YOU ALL CAN RUN.
YOU'VE SEEN HER--HAVEN'T YOU...?
SURE. SHE'S BEEN RIDIN' AROUND ON A TORE-UP MOPED. SEEN HER HANGIN' OUT WITH A BIG BLACK DUDE. WEARS A MUZZLE.
SHE DOIN' SOMETHIN' DOWN HERE. GONNA GET HERSELF KILLED, KNOW WHAT I'M SAYIN'?
PAATOOOOOOOW
GUHH!

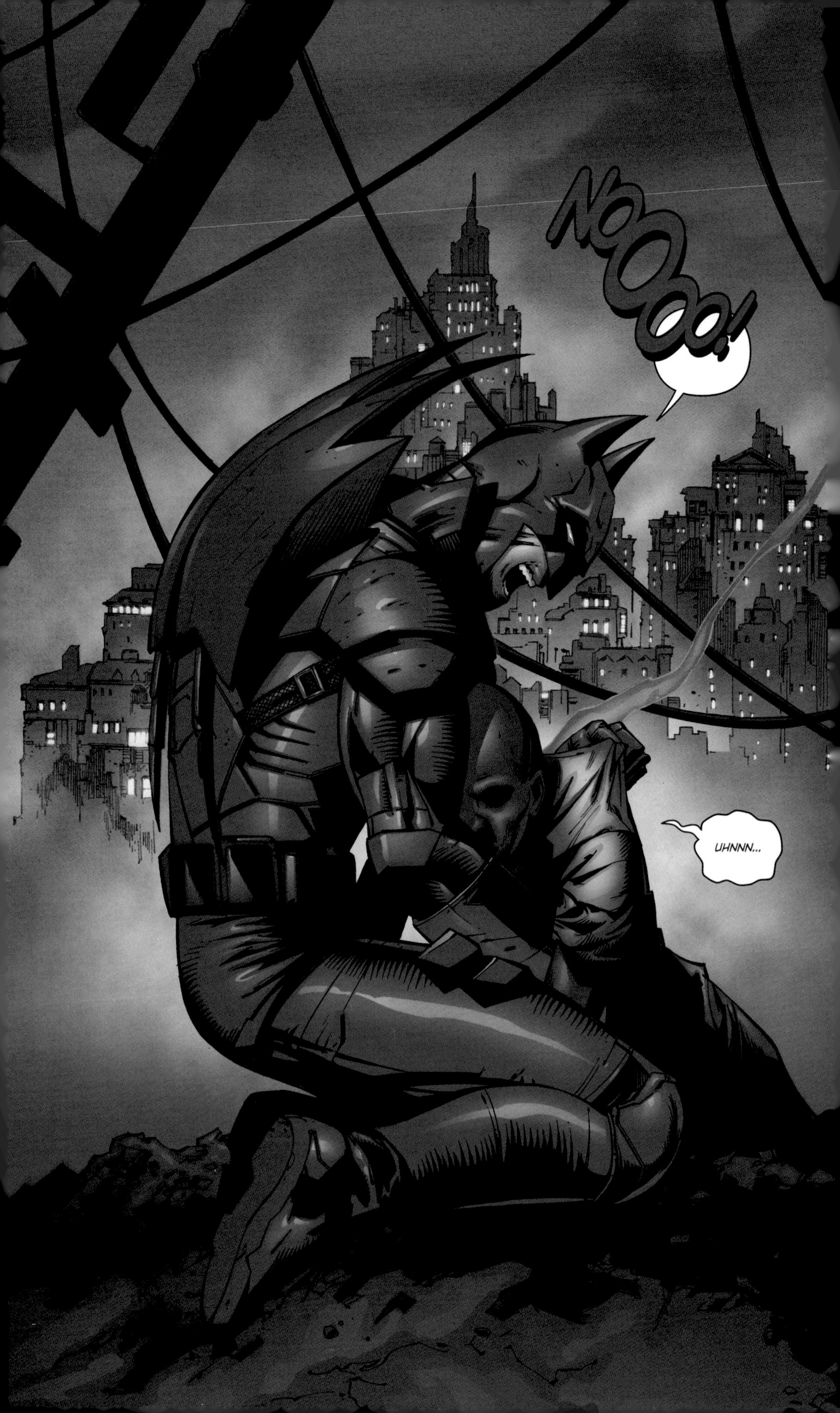
NOOOOO!
UHNNN...

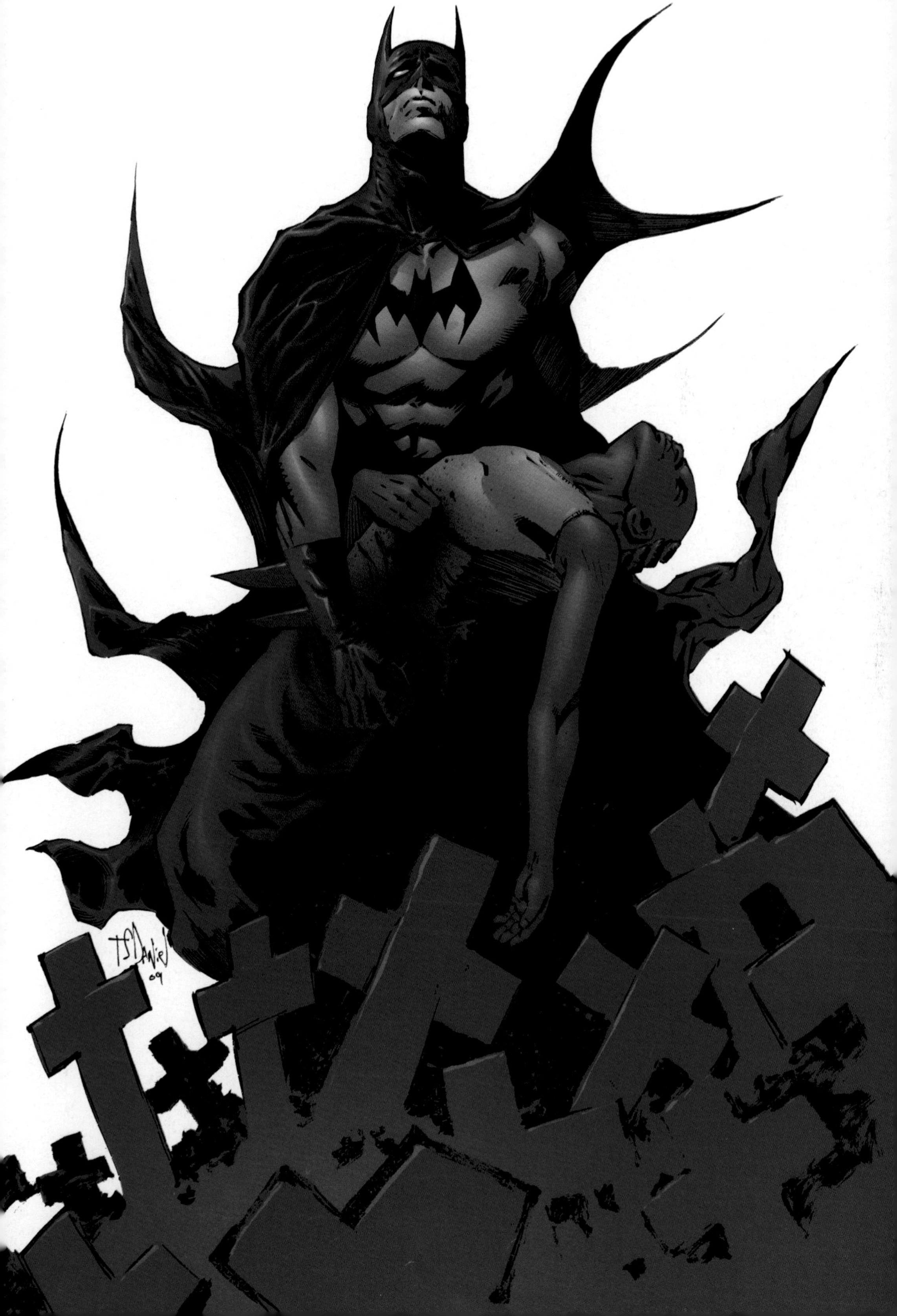

"Children of Gotham, fear no more —
for I will purge your city of the animals that seek to destroy you."

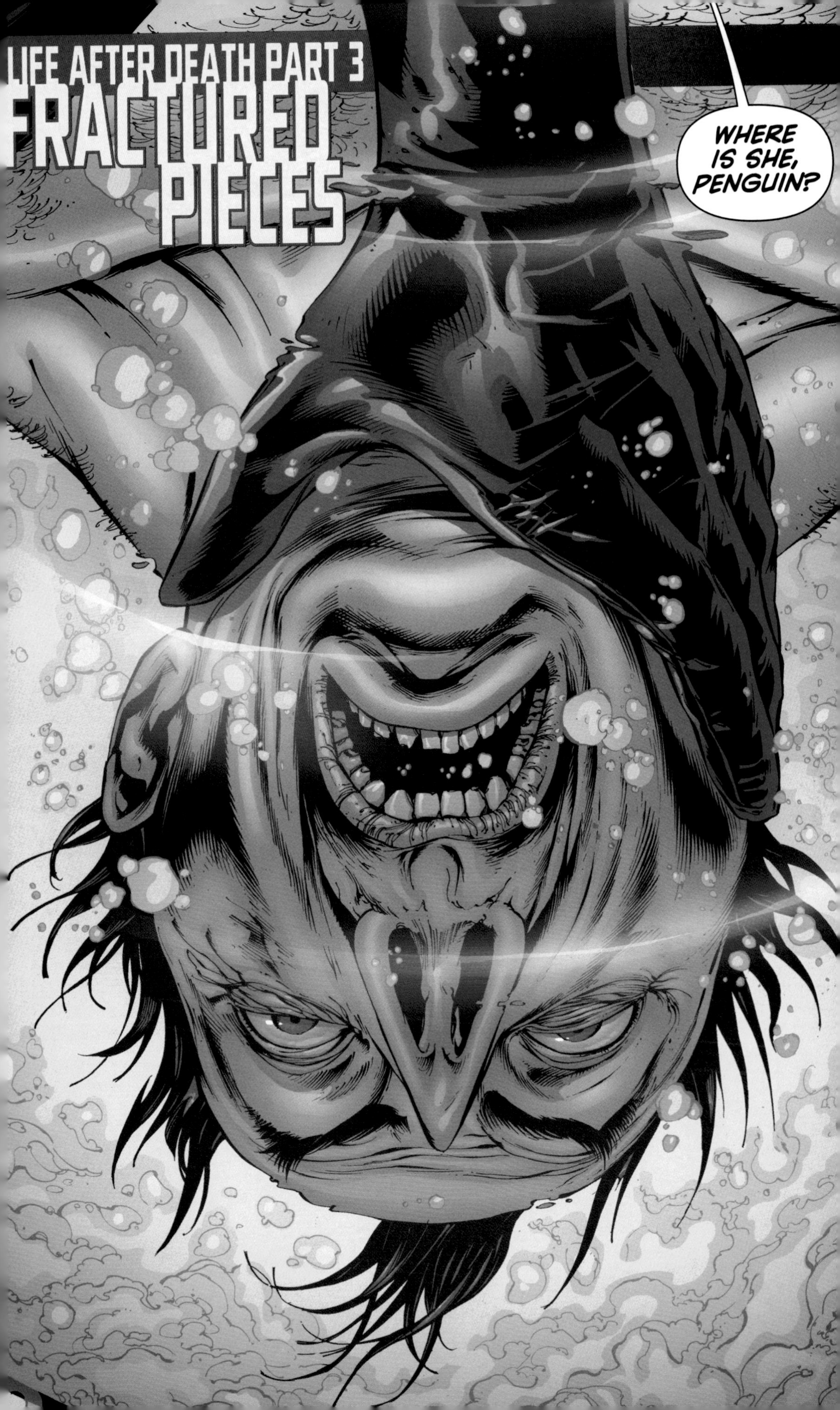
LIFE AFTER DEATH PART 3
FRACTURED PIECES
WHERE IS SHE, PENGUIN?

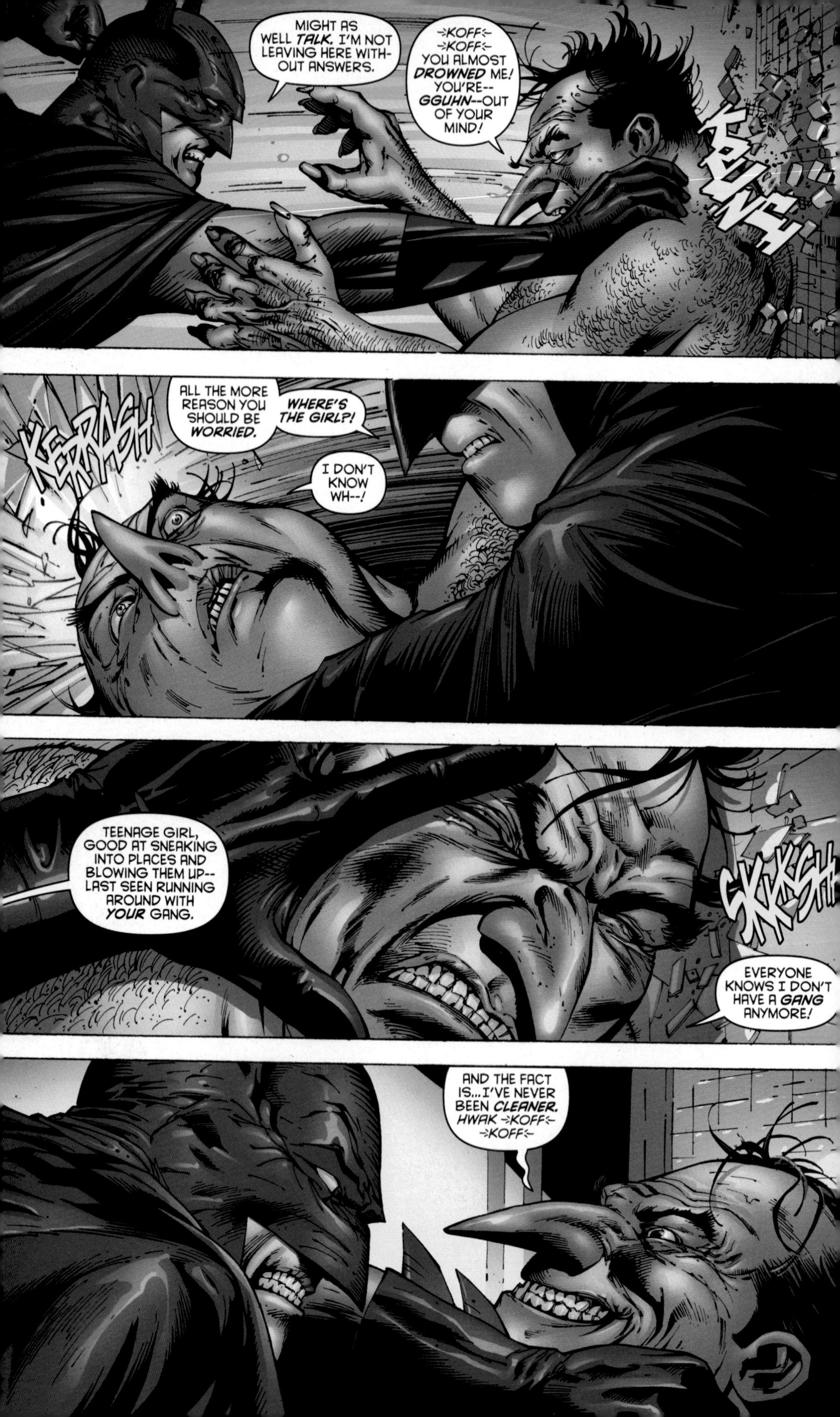
MIGHT AS WELL *TALK*. I'M NOT LEAVING HERE WITH-OUT ANSWERS.
-KOFF- -KOFF- YOU ALMOST *DROWNED* ME! YOU'RE-- *GGUHN*--OUT OF YOUR MIND!
ALL THE MORE REASON YOU SHOULD BE *WORRIED*.
WHERE'S THE GIRL?!
I DON'T KNOW WH--!
TEENAGE GIRL, GOOD AT SNEAKING INTO PLACES AND BLOWING THEM UP-- LAST SEEN RUNNING AROUND WITH *YOUR* GANG.
EVERYONE KNOWS I DON'T HAVE A *GANG* ANYMORE!
AND THE FACT IS...I'VE NEVER BEEN *CLEANER*. HWAK -KOFF- -KOFF-

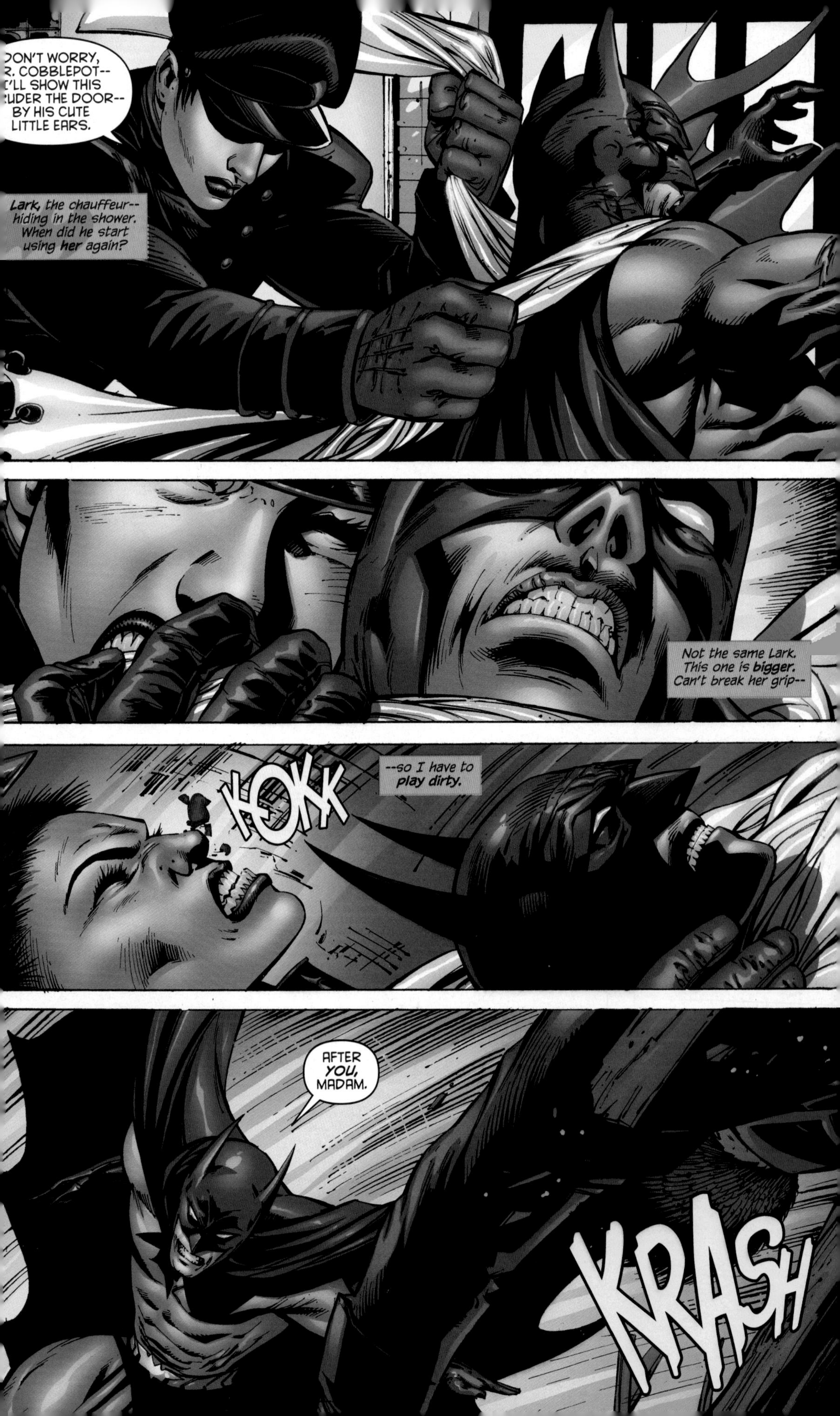
DON'T WORRY, R. COBBLEPOT-- 'LL SHOW THIS UDER THE DOOR-- BY HIS CUTE LITTLE EARS.
Lark, the chauffeur-- hiding in the shower. When did he start using her again?
Not the same Lark. This one is bigger. Can't break her grip--
KOKK
--so I have to play dirty.
AFTER YOU, MADAM.
KRASH

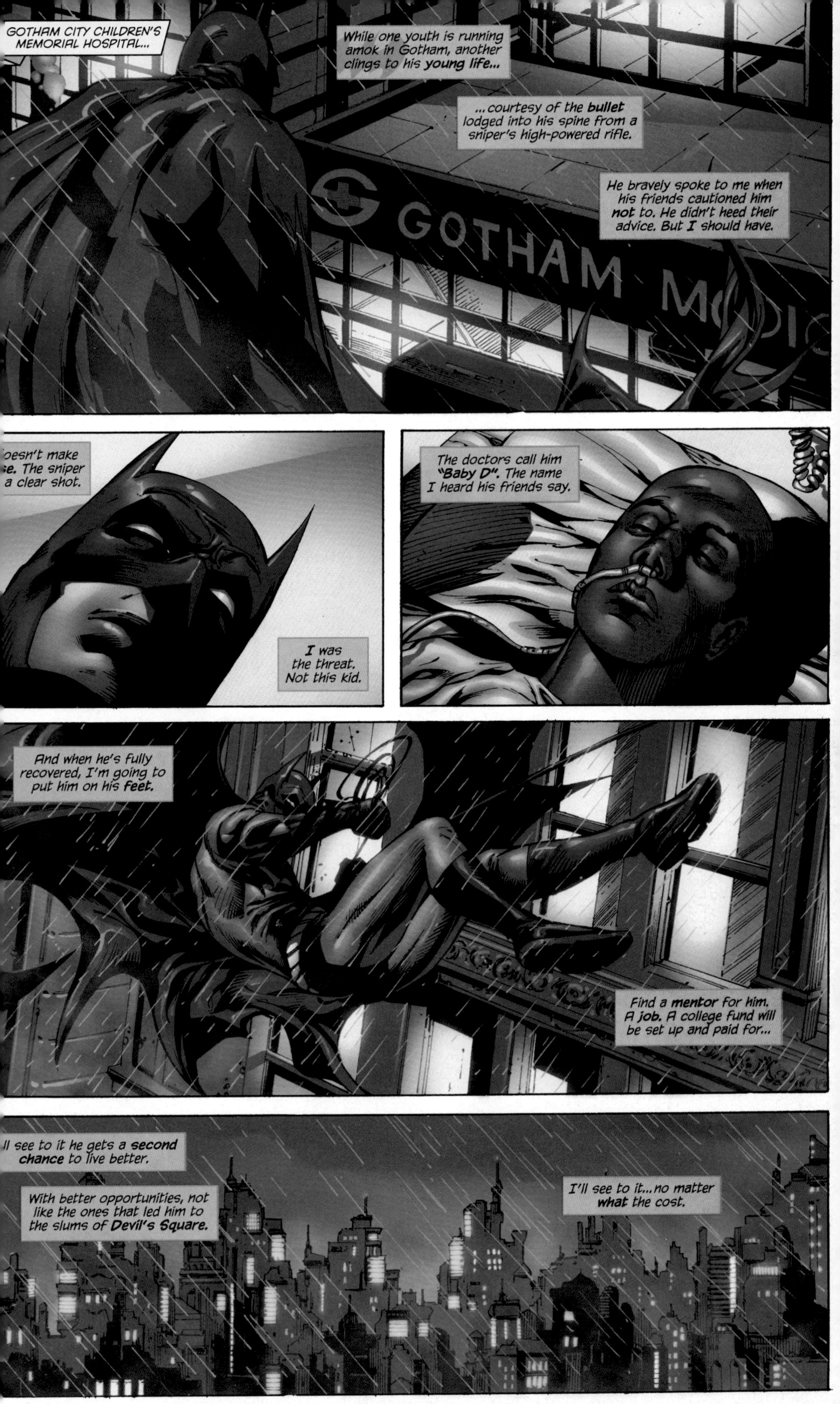
GOTHAM CITY CHILDREN'S MEMORIAL HOSPITAL...
While one youth is running amok in Gotham, another clings to his young life...
...courtesy of the bullet lodged into his spine from a sniper's high-powered rifle.
He bravely spoke to me when his friends cautioned him not to. He didn't heed their advice. But I should have.
GOTHAM M
oesn't make
e. The sniper
a clear shot.
I was the threat. Not this kid.
The doctors call him "Baby D". The name I heard his friends say.
And when he's fully recovered, I'm going to put him on his feet.
Find a mentor for him. A job. A college fund will be set up and paid for...
ll see to it he gets a second chance to live better.
With better opportunities, not like the ones that led him to the slums of Devil's Square.
I'll see to it...no matter what the cost.

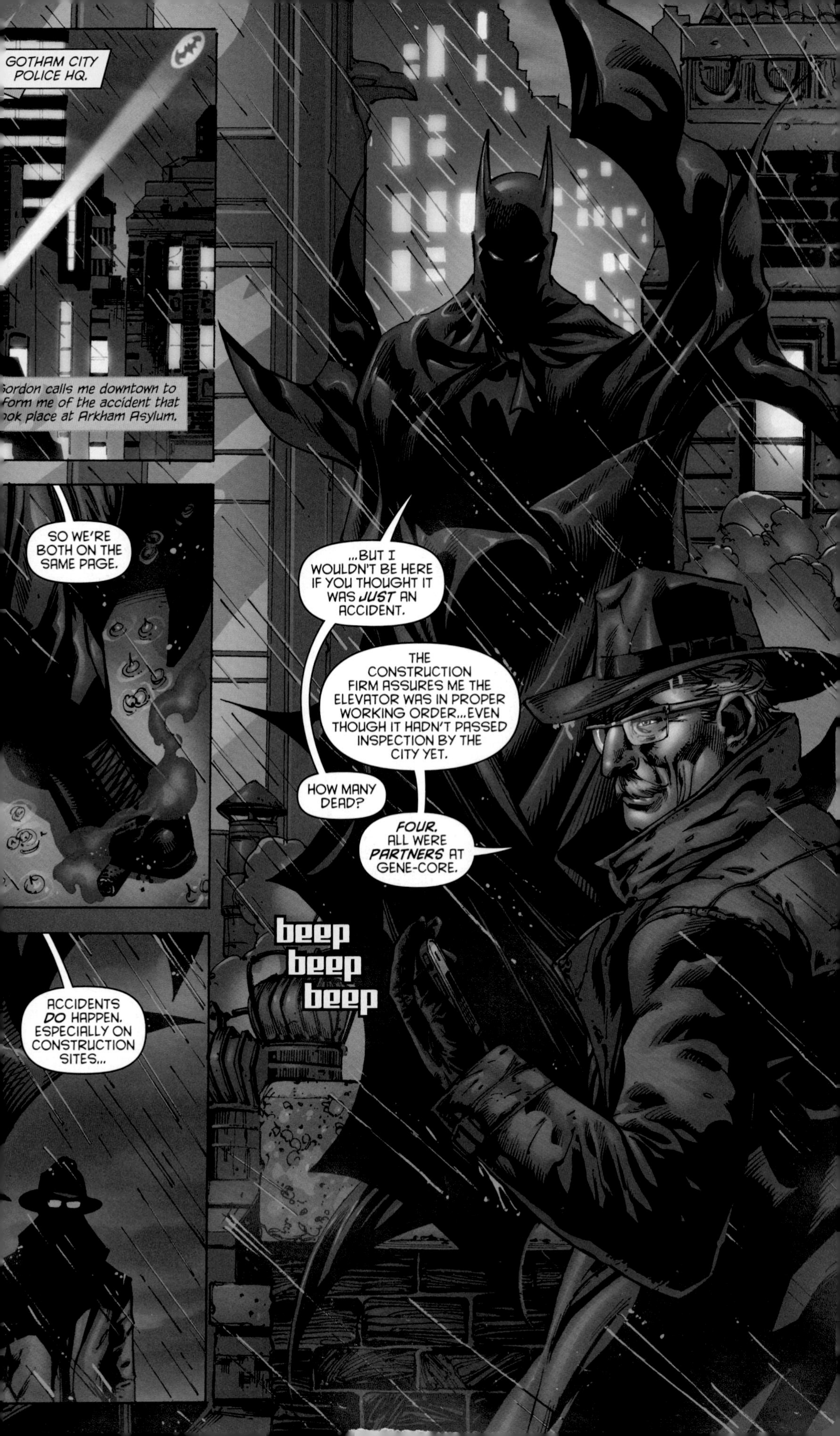
GOTHAM CITY POLICE HQ.
ordon calls me downtown to form me of the accident that ook place at Arkham Asylum.
SO WE'RE BOTH ON THE SAME PAGE.
ACCIDENTS *DO* HAPPEN. ESPECIALLY ON CONSTRUCTION SITES...
...BUT I WOULDN'T BE HERE IF YOU THOUGHT IT WAS *JUST* AN ACCIDENT.
THE CONSTRUCTION FIRM ASSURES ME THE ELEVATOR WAS IN PROPER WORKING ORDER...EVEN THOUGH IT HADN'T PASSED INSPECTION BY THE CITY YET.
HOW MANY DEAD?
FOUR. ALL WERE *PARTNERS* AT GENE-CORE.
beep beep beep

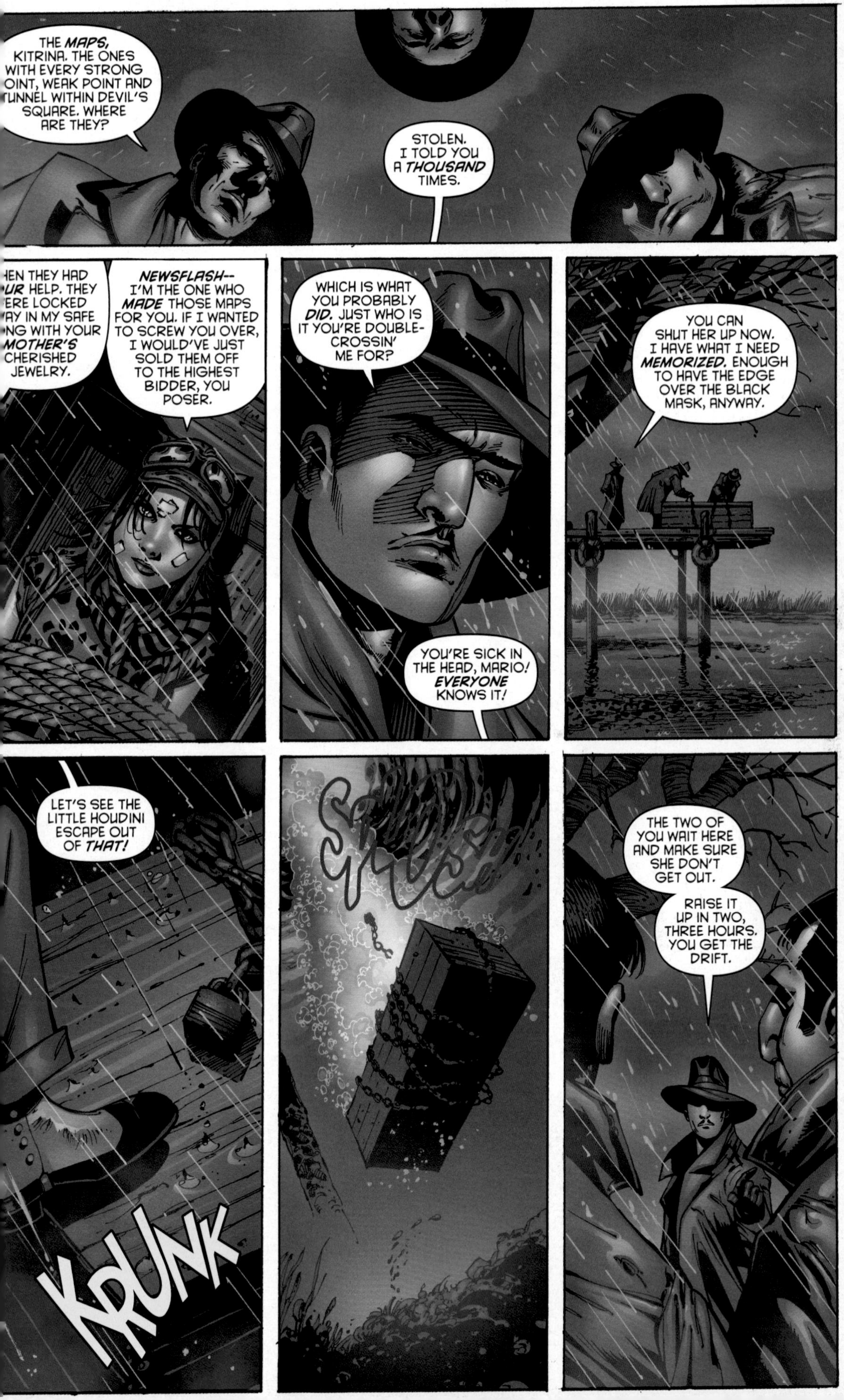
THE MAPS, KITRINA. THE ONES WITH EVERY STRONG OINT, WEAK POINT AND TUNNEL WITHIN DEVIL'S SQUARE. WHERE ARE THEY?
STOLEN. I TOLD YOU A THOUSAND TIMES.
HEN THEY HAD UR HELP. THEY ERE LOCKED AY IN MY SAFE NG WITH YOUR MOTHER'S CHERISHED JEWELRY.
NEWSFLASH-- I'M THE ONE WHO MADE THOSE MAPS FOR YOU. IF I WANTED TO SCREW YOU OVER, I WOULD'VE JUST SOLD THEM OFF TO THE HIGHEST BIDDER, YOU POSER.
WHICH IS WHAT YOU PROBABLY DID. JUST WHO IS IT YOU'RE DOUBLE-CROSSIN' ME FOR?
YOU'RE SICK IN THE HEAD, MARIO! EVERYONE KNOWS IT!
YOU CAN SHUT HER UP NOW. I HAVE WHAT I NEED MEMORIZED. ENOUGH TO HAVE THE EDGE OVER THE BLACK MASK, ANYWAY.
LET'S SEE THE LITTLE HOUDINI ESCAPE OUT OF THAT!
KRUNK
THE TWO OF YOU WAIT HERE AND MAKE SURE SHE DON'T GET OUT.
RAISE IT UP IN TWO, THREE HOURS. YOU GET THE DRIFT.

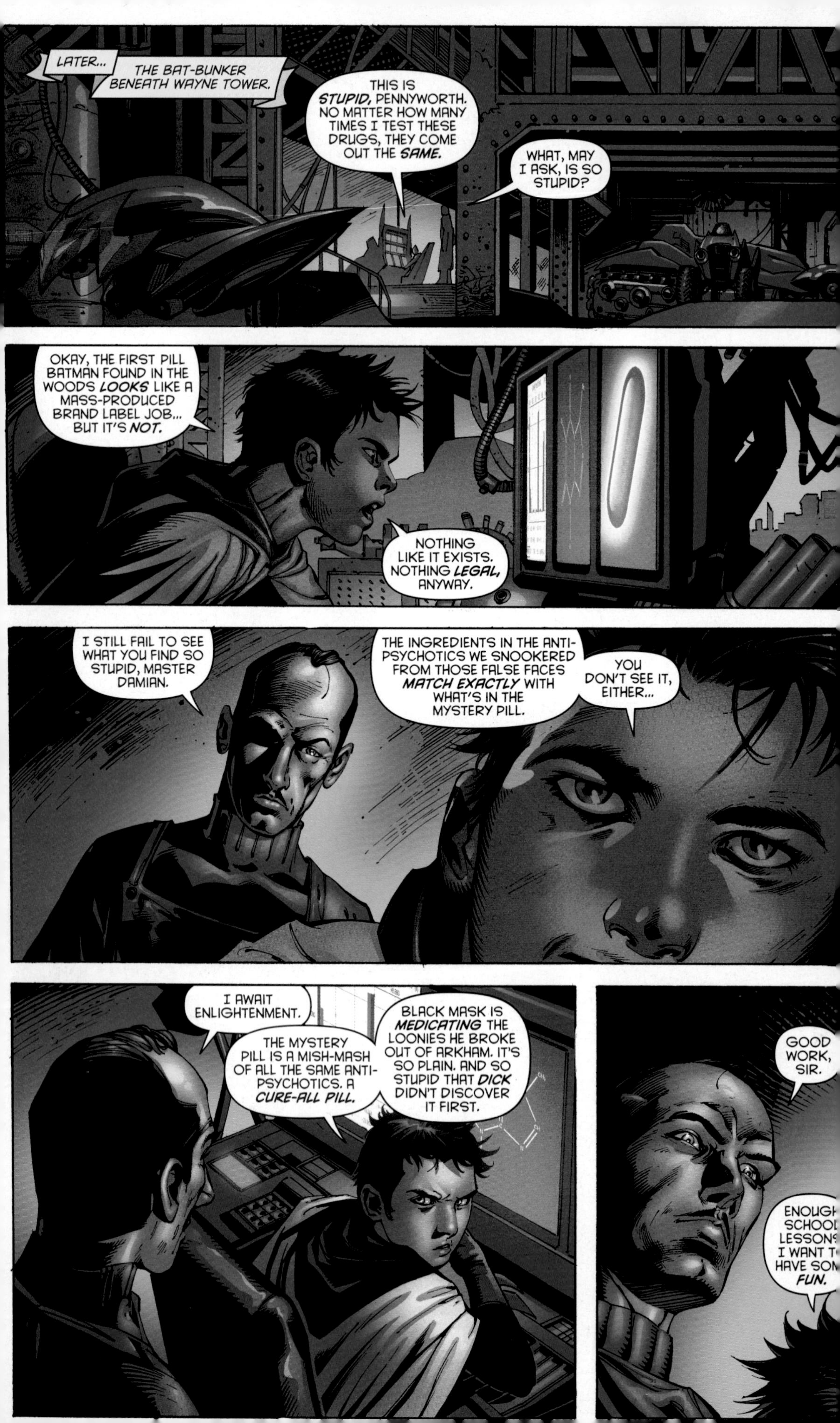
LATER...
THE BAT-BUNKER BENEATH WAYNE TOWER.
THIS IS STUPID, PENNYWORTH. NO MATTER HOW MANY TIMES I TEST THESE DRUGS, THEY COME OUT THE SAME.
WHAT, MAY I ASK, IS SO STUPID?
OKAY, THE FIRST PILL BATMAN FOUND IN THE WOODS LOOKS LIKE A MASS-PRODUCED BRAND LABEL JOB... BUT IT'S NOT.
NOTHING LIKE IT EXISTS. NOTHING LEGAL, ANYWAY.
I STILL FAIL TO SEE WHAT YOU FIND SO STUPID, MASTER DAMIAN.
THE INGREDIENTS IN THE ANTI-PSYCHOTICS WE SNOOKERED FROM THOSE FALSE FACES MATCH EXACTLY WITH WHAT'S IN THE MYSTERY PILL.
YOU DON'T SEE IT, EITHER...
I AWAIT ENLIGHTENMENT.
THE MYSTERY PILL IS A MISH-MASH OF ALL THE SAME ANTI-PSYCHOTICS. A CURE-ALL PILL.
BLACK MASK IS MEDICATING THE LOONIES HE BROKE OUT OF ARKHAM. IT'S SO PLAIN. AND SO STUPID THAT DICK DIDN'T DISCOVER IT FIRST.
GOOD WORK, SIR.

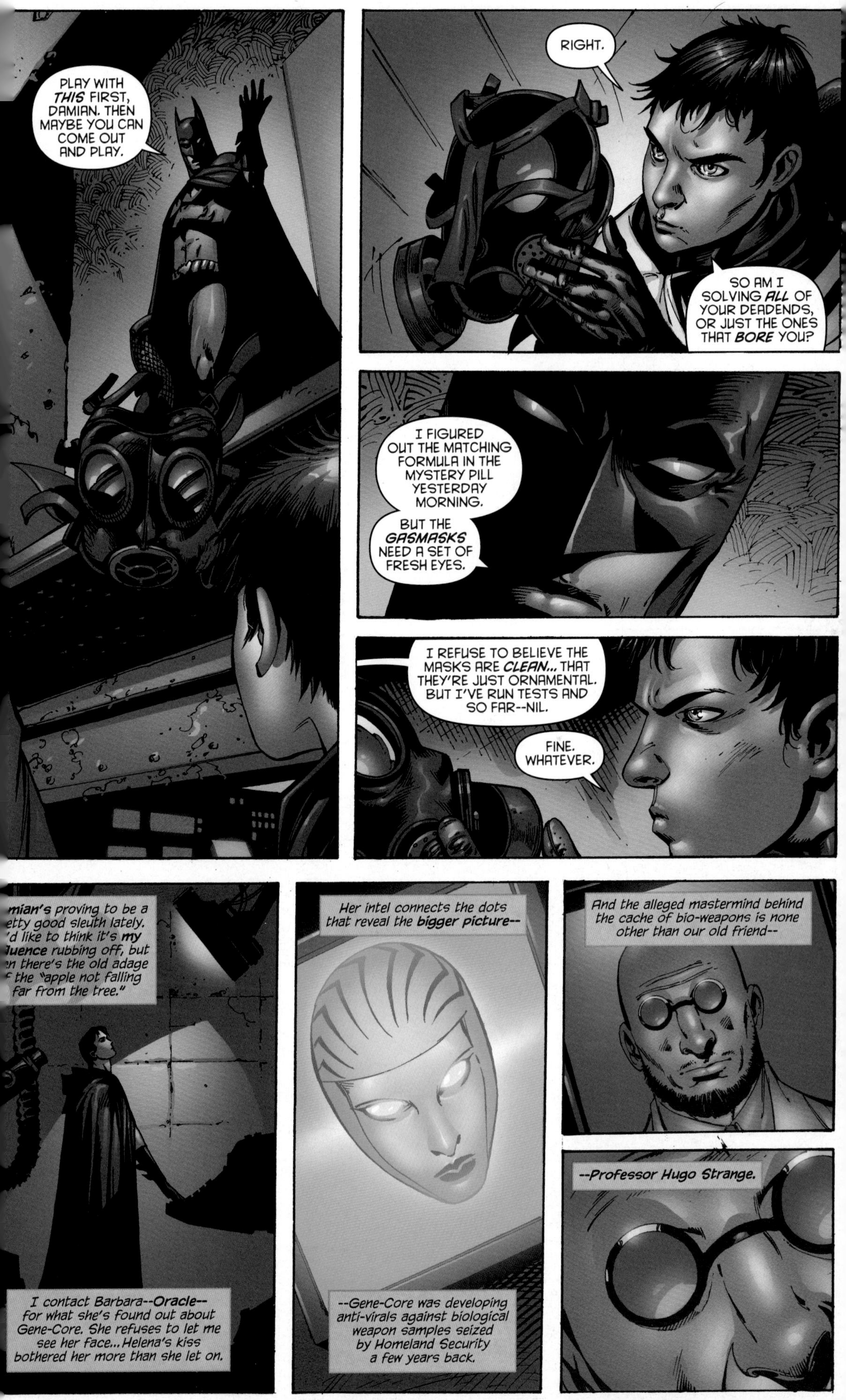
PLAY WITH *THIS* FIRST, DAMIAN. THEN MAYBE YOU CAN COME OUT AND PLAY.
RIGHT.
SO AM I SOLVING *ALL* OF YOUR DEADENDS, OR JUST THE ONES THAT *BORE* YOU?
I FIGURED OUT THE MATCHING FORMULA IN THE MYSTERY PILL YESTERDAY MORNING.
BUT THE *GASMASKS* NEED A SET OF FRESH EYES.
I REFUSE TO BELIEVE THE MASKS ARE *CLEAN...* THAT THEY'RE JUST ORNAMENTAL. BUT I'VE RUN TESTS AND SO FAR--NIL.
FINE. WHATEVER.
mian's proving to be a etty good sleuth lately. 'd like to think it's **my** luence rubbing off, but en there's the old adage the "apple not falling far from the tree."
I contact Barbara--**Oracle**-- for what she's found out about Gene-Core. She refuses to let me see her face...Helena's kiss bothered her more than she let on.
Her intel connects the dots that reveal the **bigger picture**--
--Gene-Core was developing anti-virals against biological weapon samples seized by Homeland Security a few years back.
And the alleged mastermind behind the cache of bio-weapons is none other than our old friend--
--**Professor Hugo Strange.**

HE'S THREE HOURS OVERDUE, *PROFESSOR.* DOESN'T HE KNOWS THE *CONSEQUENCES* OF NOT RETURNING IN TIME FOR HIS *SERUM?*

MAYBE YOU SHOULD HAVE OUTFITTED HIS BULLETPROOF GETUP WITH A *WATCH.*

HIS *BODY* WILL TELL HIM WHEN IT'S BEEN TOO LONG, FRIGHT. I'VE SEEN TO THAT.

HOW LONG CAN WE PLAY THESE GAMES BEFORE HE *TURNS* AGAINST US?

HE'S DEPENDENT ON US FOR HIS SURVIVAL. HE'LL PLAY UNTIL WE'VE WON.

WHATEVER WINNING EVEN MEANS.

IT'S THAT DEFEATIST ATTITUDE THAT HAS US IN THIS POSITION.

NO. IT'S BONE-HEADED *ARROGANCE* THAT HAS PUT US HERE.

HUSH.

YOU--

CARRY ON, PLEASE. THE CONVERSATION WAS TAKING A MOST *INTERESTING* TURN...

I NEED MY *SERUM.*

DR. GRUENER-- YOU MUSTN'T BE SO FRIVOLOUS WITH YOUR TIME. DON'T YOU REALIZE WHAT BLACK MASK HAS *INVESTED* IN YOU? YOU HAVE SPECIFIC--

REAPER IS MY NAME. AND YOU WILL *NOT* REPRIMAND ME OR YOU'LL FIND YOUR- SELVES LOOKING UP AT ME IN *SMALL PIECES.*

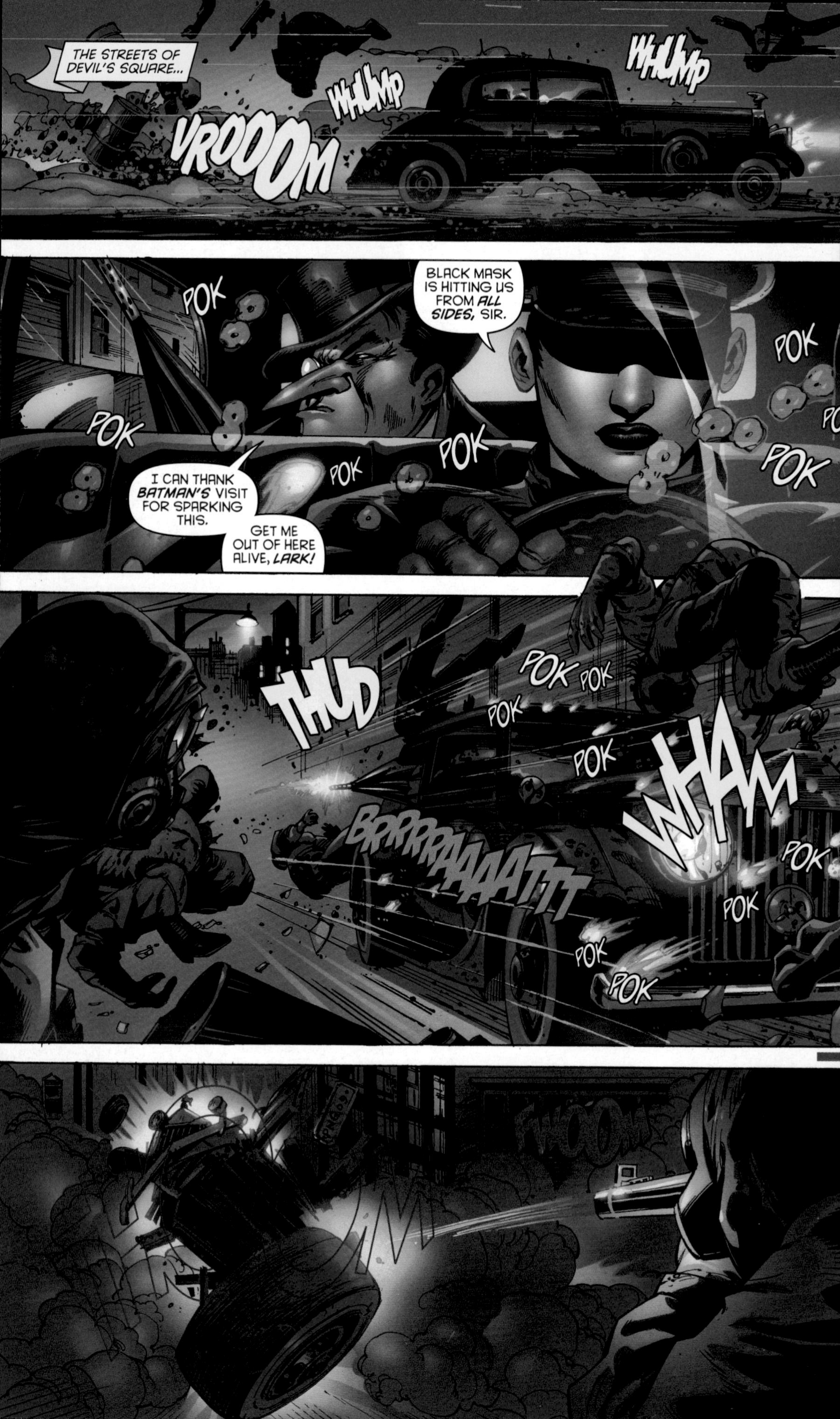
THE STREETS OF DEVIL'S SQUARE...
WHUMP
VROOOOM
WHUMP
POK
BLACK MASK IS HITTING US FROM ALL SIDES, SIR.
POK
POK
POK
POK
I CAN THANK BATMAN'S VISIT FOR SPARKING THIS.
GET ME OUT OF HERE ALIVE, LARK!
POK
THUD
POK POK
POK
POK
WHAM
BRRRRAAAATTTT
POK
POK
POK
POK

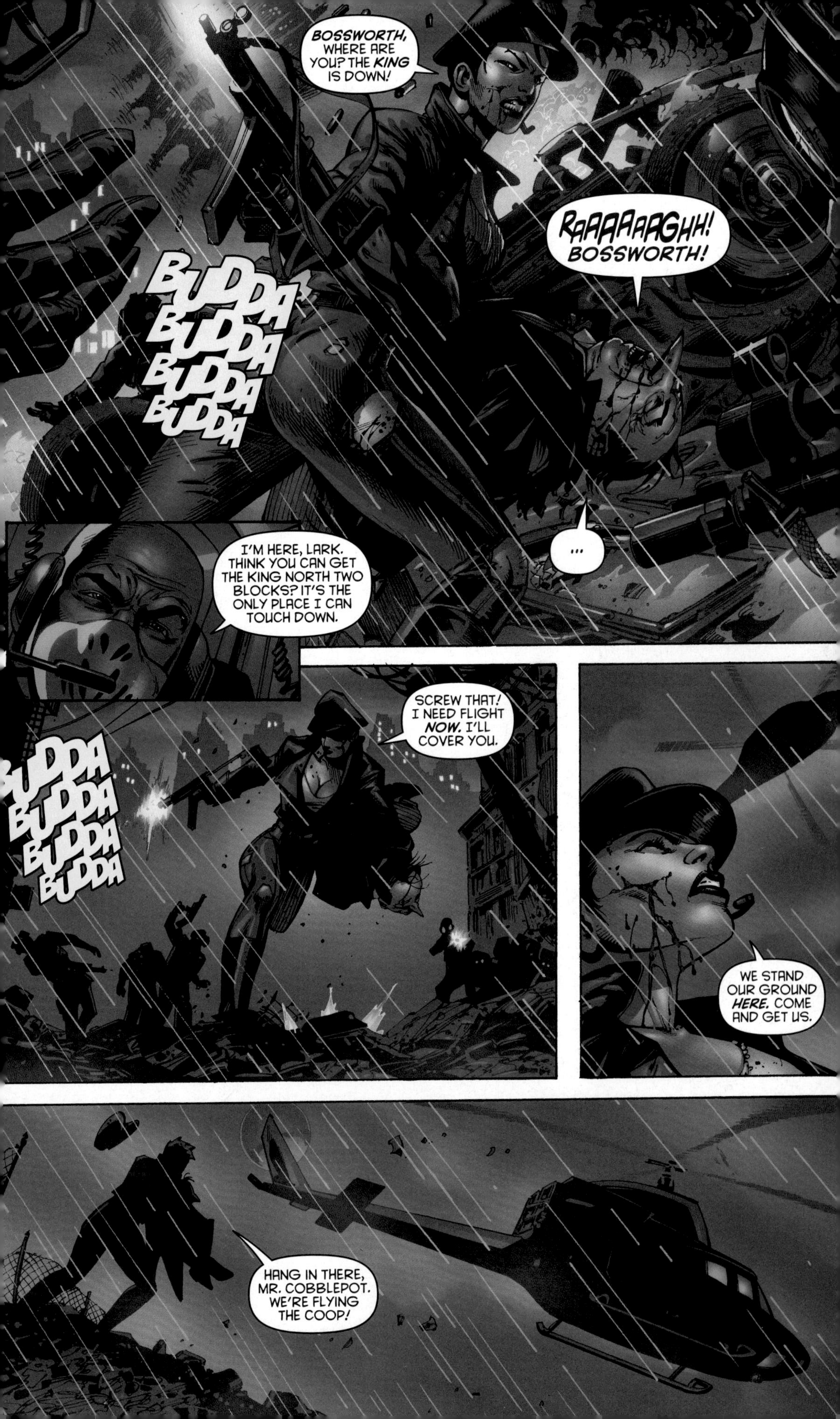
BOSSWORTH, WHERE ARE YOU? THE KING IS DOWN!
RAAAAAAAGHH! BOSSWORTH!
BUDDA BUDDA BUDDA BUDDA
...
I'M HERE, LARK. THINK YOU CAN GET THE KING NORTH TWO BLOCKS? IT'S THE ONLY PLACE I CAN TOUCH DOWN.
SCREW THAT! I NEED FLIGHT NOW. I'LL COVER YOU.
BUDDA BUDDA BUDDA BUDDA
WE STAND OUR GROUND HERE. COME AND GET US.
HANG IN THERE, MR. COBBLEPOT. WE'RE FLYING THE COOP!

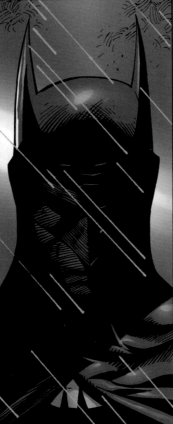

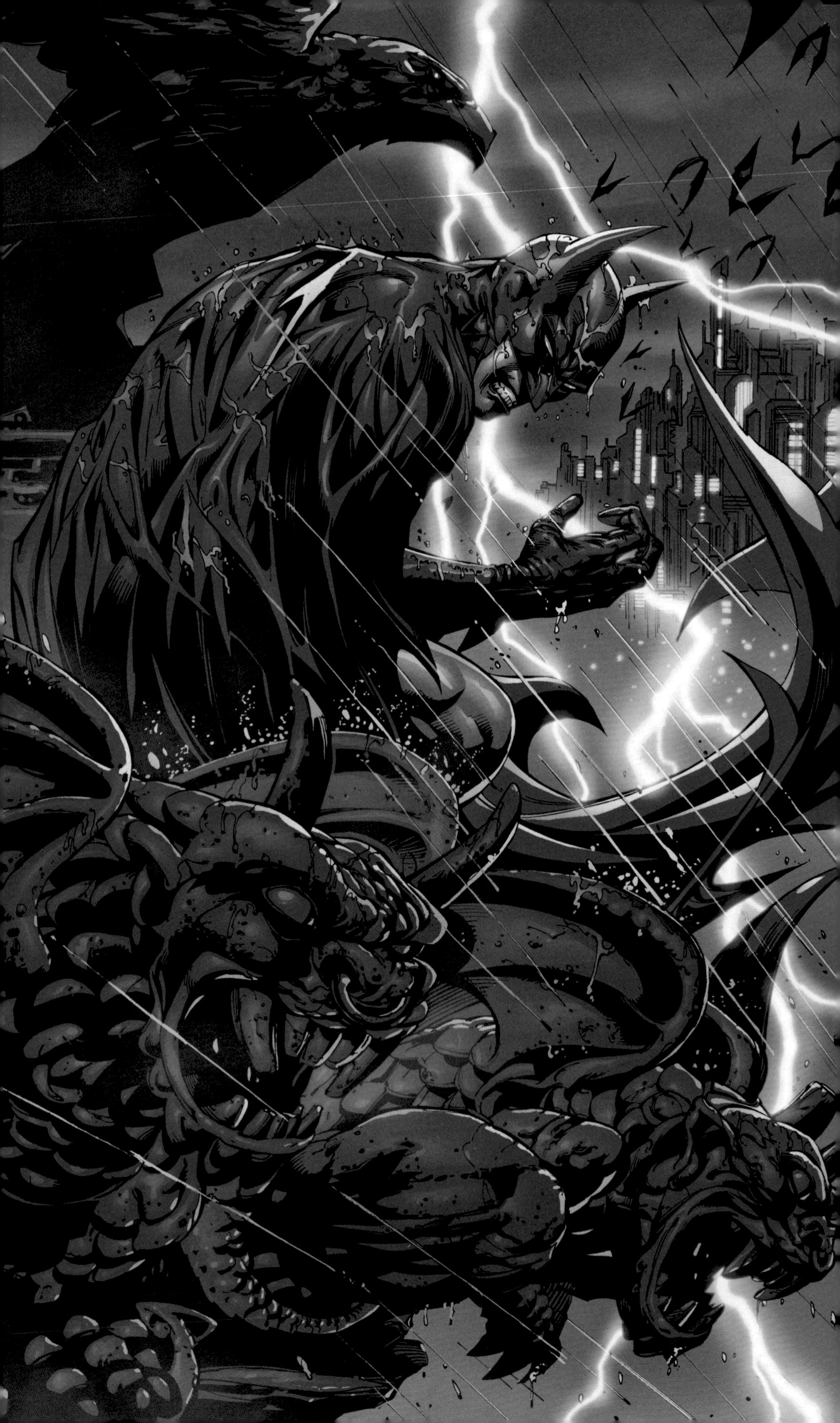

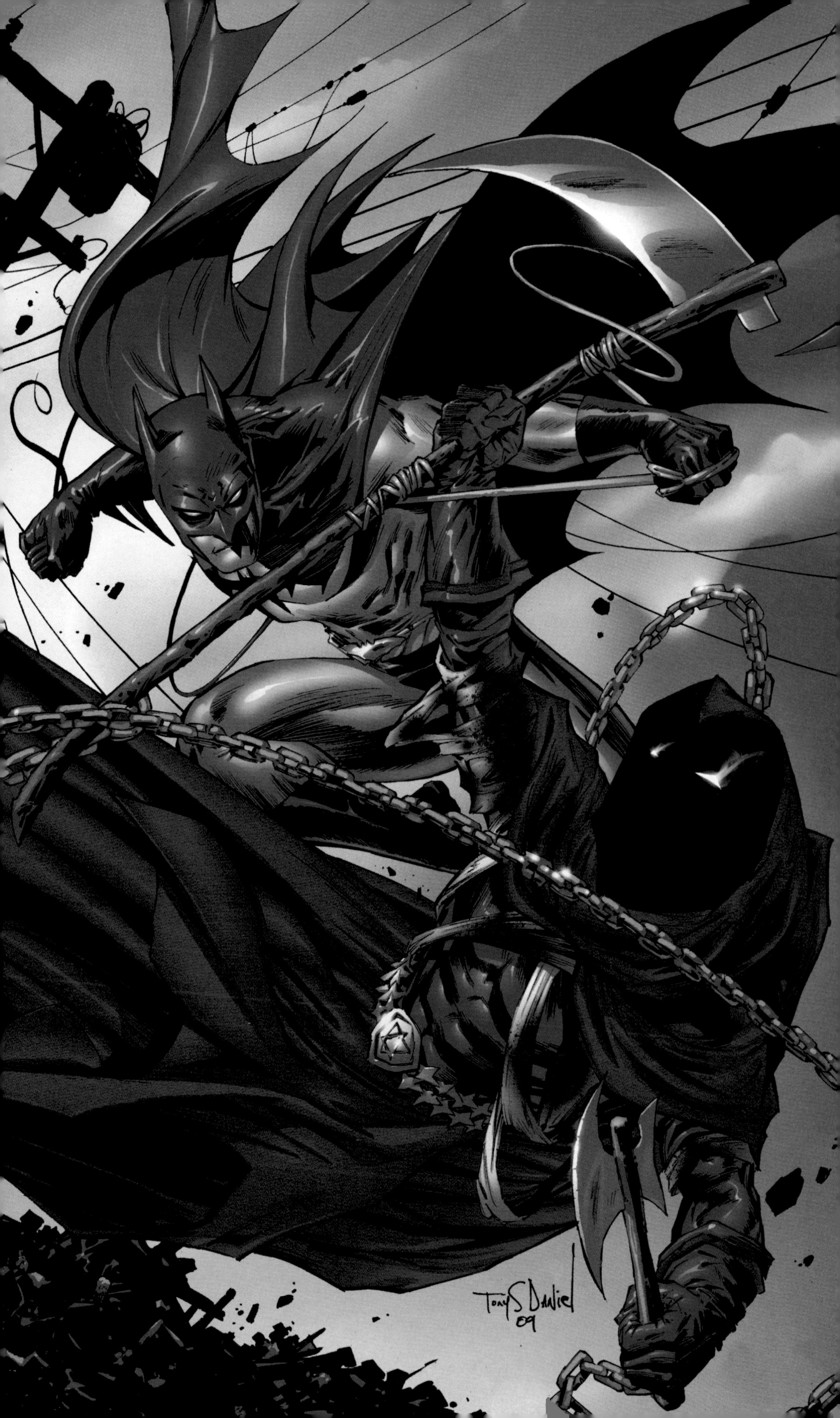
Tony S Daniel
09

"Your time is up, Falcone. Let's not keep hell waiting."

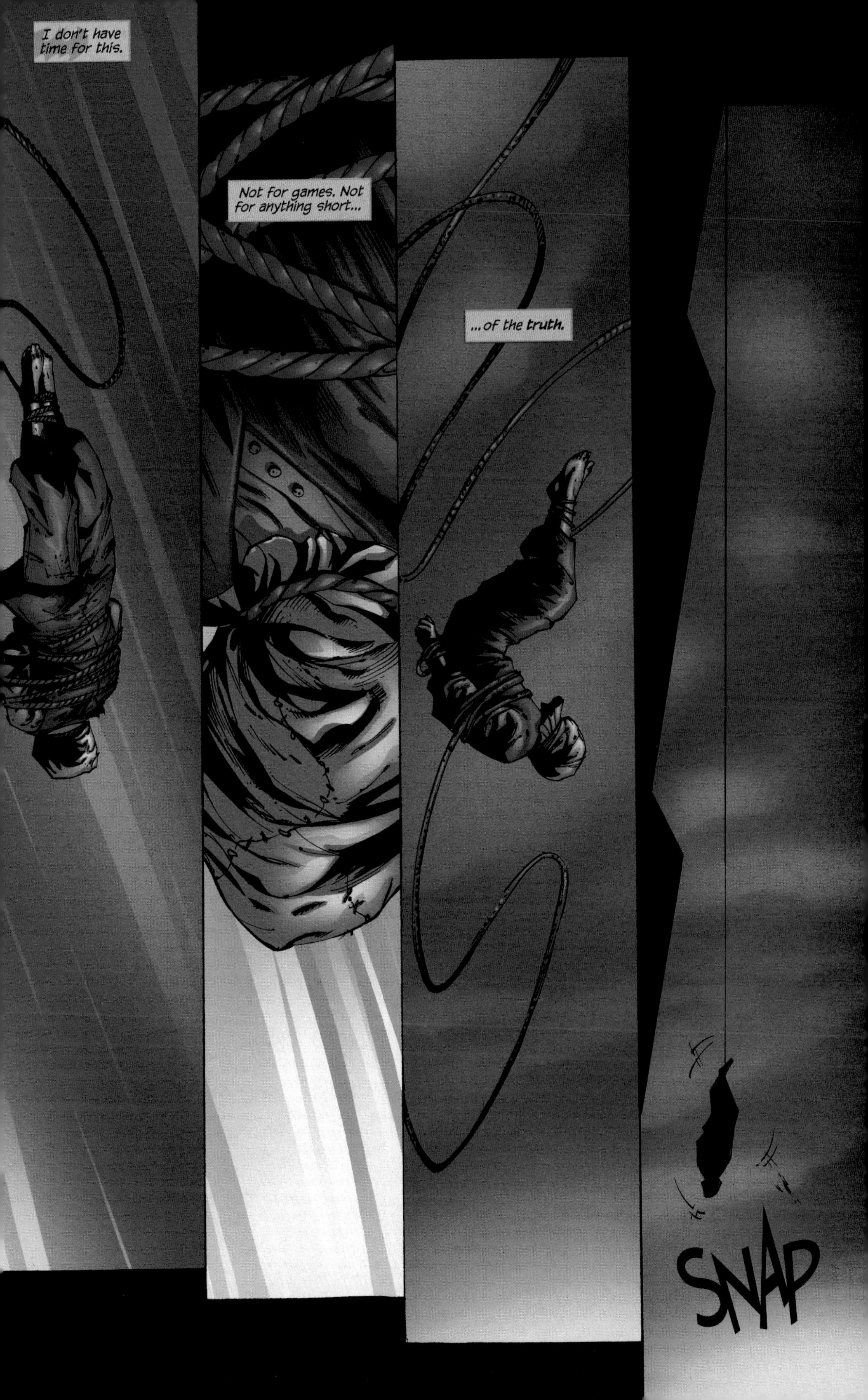

I don't have time for this.
Not for games. Not for anything short...
...of the truth.
SNAP

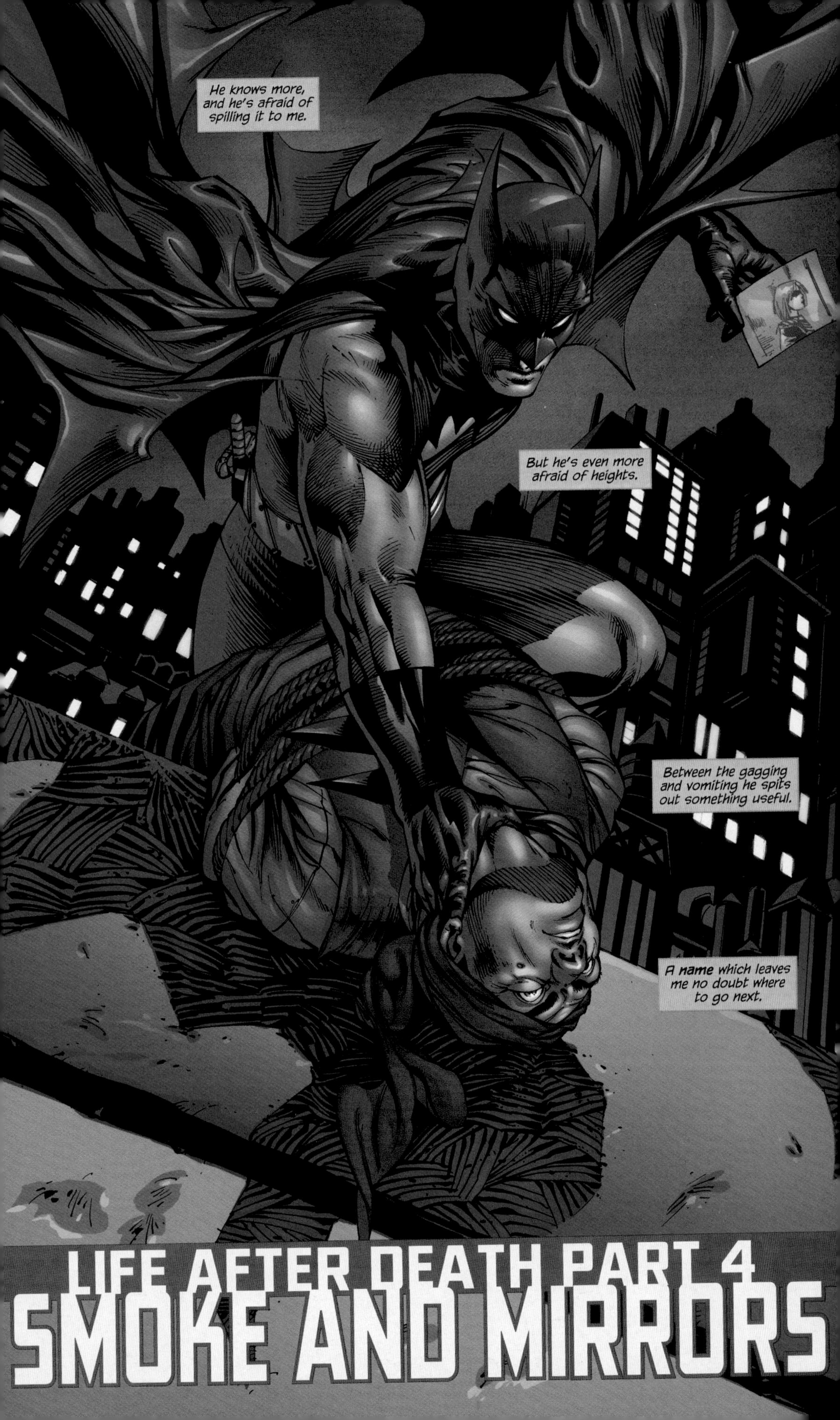

He knows more, and he's afraid of spilling it to me.
But he's even more afraid of heights.
Between the gagging and vomiting he spits out something useful.
A name which leaves me no doubt where to go next.
LIFE AFTER DEATH PART 4
SMOKE AND MIRRORS

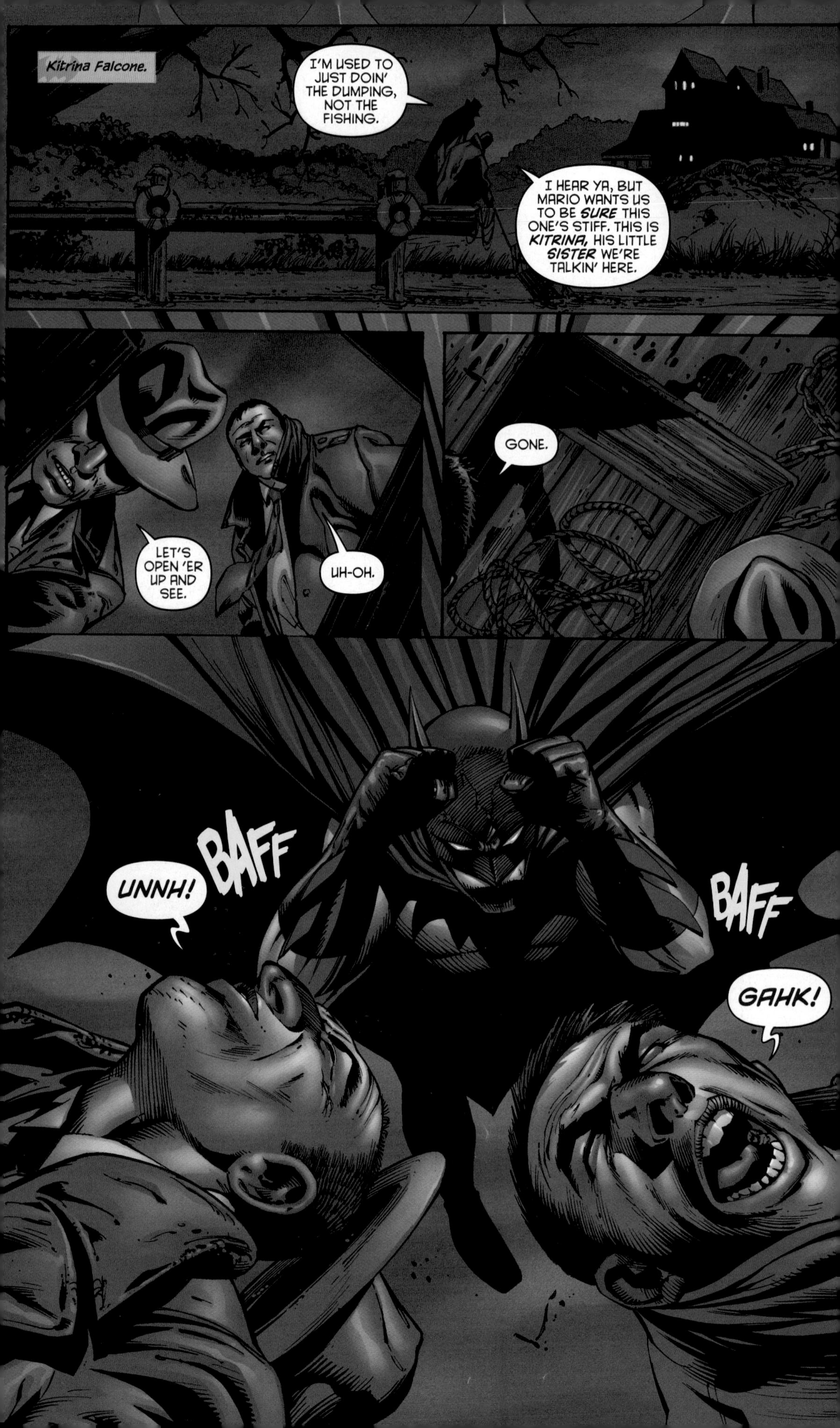
Kitrina Falcone.
I'M USED TO JUST DOIN' THE DUMPING, NOT THE FISHING.
I HEAR YA, BUT MARIO WANTS US TO BE *SURE* THIS ONE'S STIFF. THIS IS *KITRINA,* HIS LITTLE *SISTER* WE'RE TALKIN' HERE.
LET'S OPEN 'ER UP AND SEE.
UH-OH.
GONE.
UNNH!
BAFF
BAFF
GAHK!

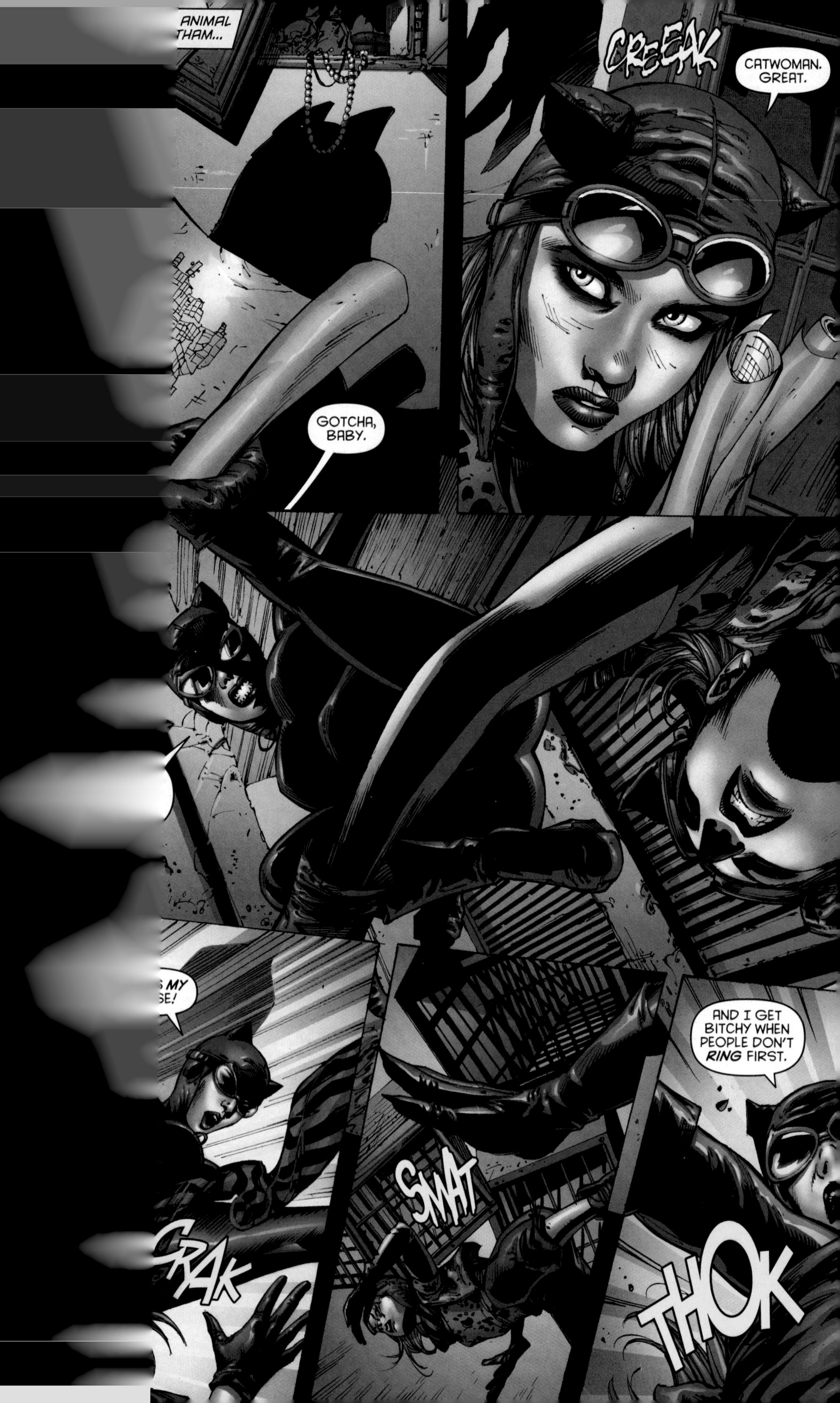
CREEAK
CATWOMAN. GREAT.
GOTCHA, BABY.
AND I GET BITCHY WHEN PEOPLE DON'T *RING* FIRST.
CRAK
SWAT
THOK

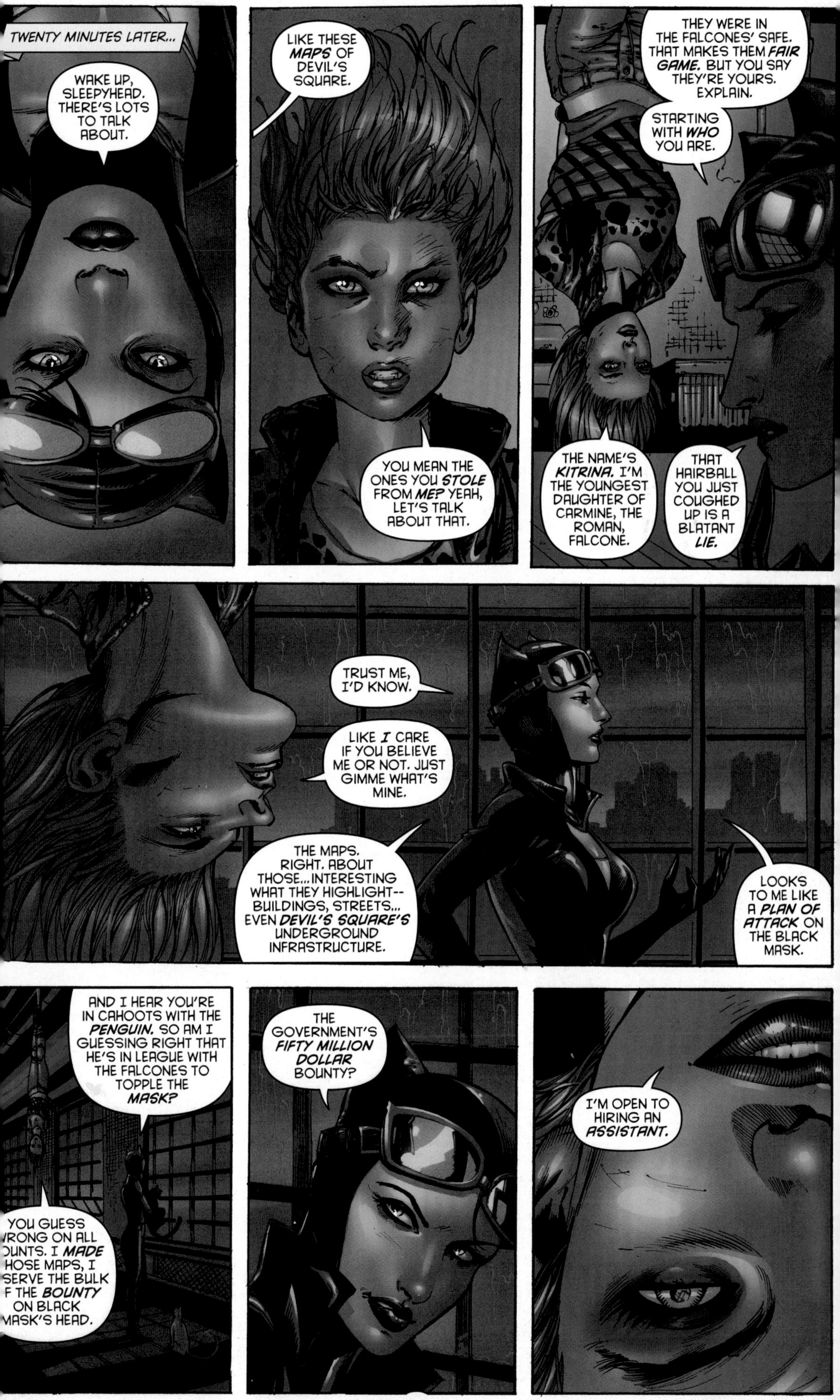

TWENTY MINUTES LATER...
WAKE UP, SLEEPYHEAD. THERE'S LOTS TO TALK ABOUT.
LIKE THESE MAPS OF DEVIL'S SQUARE.
YOU MEAN THE ONES YOU STOLE FROM ME? YEAH, LET'S TALK ABOUT THAT.
THEY WERE IN THE FALCONES' SAFE. THAT MAKES THEM FAIR GAME. BUT YOU SAY THEY'RE YOURS. EXPLAIN.
STARTING WITH WHO YOU ARE.
THE NAME'S KITRINA. I'M THE YOUNGEST DAUGHTER OF CARMINE, THE ROMAN, FALCONE.
THAT HAIRBALL YOU JUST COUGHED UP IS A BLATANT LIE.
TRUST ME, I'D KNOW.
LIKE I CARE IF YOU BELIEVE ME OR NOT. JUST GIMME WHAT'S MINE.
THE MAPS. RIGHT. ABOUT THOSE...INTERESTING WHAT THEY HIGHLIGHT-- BUILDINGS, STREETS... EVEN DEVIL'S SQUARE'S UNDERGROUND INFRASTRUCTURE.
LOOKS TO ME LIKE A PLAN OF ATTACK ON THE BLACK MASK.
AND I HEAR YOU'RE IN CAHOOTS WITH THE PENGUIN. SO AM I GUESSING RIGHT THAT HE'S IN LEAGUE WITH THE FALCONES TO TOPPLE THE MASK?
YOU GUESS RONG ON ALL OUNTS. I MADE HOSE MAPS, I SERVE THE BULK F THE BOUNTY ON BLACK MASK'S HEAD.
THE GOVERNMENT'S FIFTY MILLION DOLLAR BOUNTY?
I'M OPEN TO HIRING AN ASSISTANT.

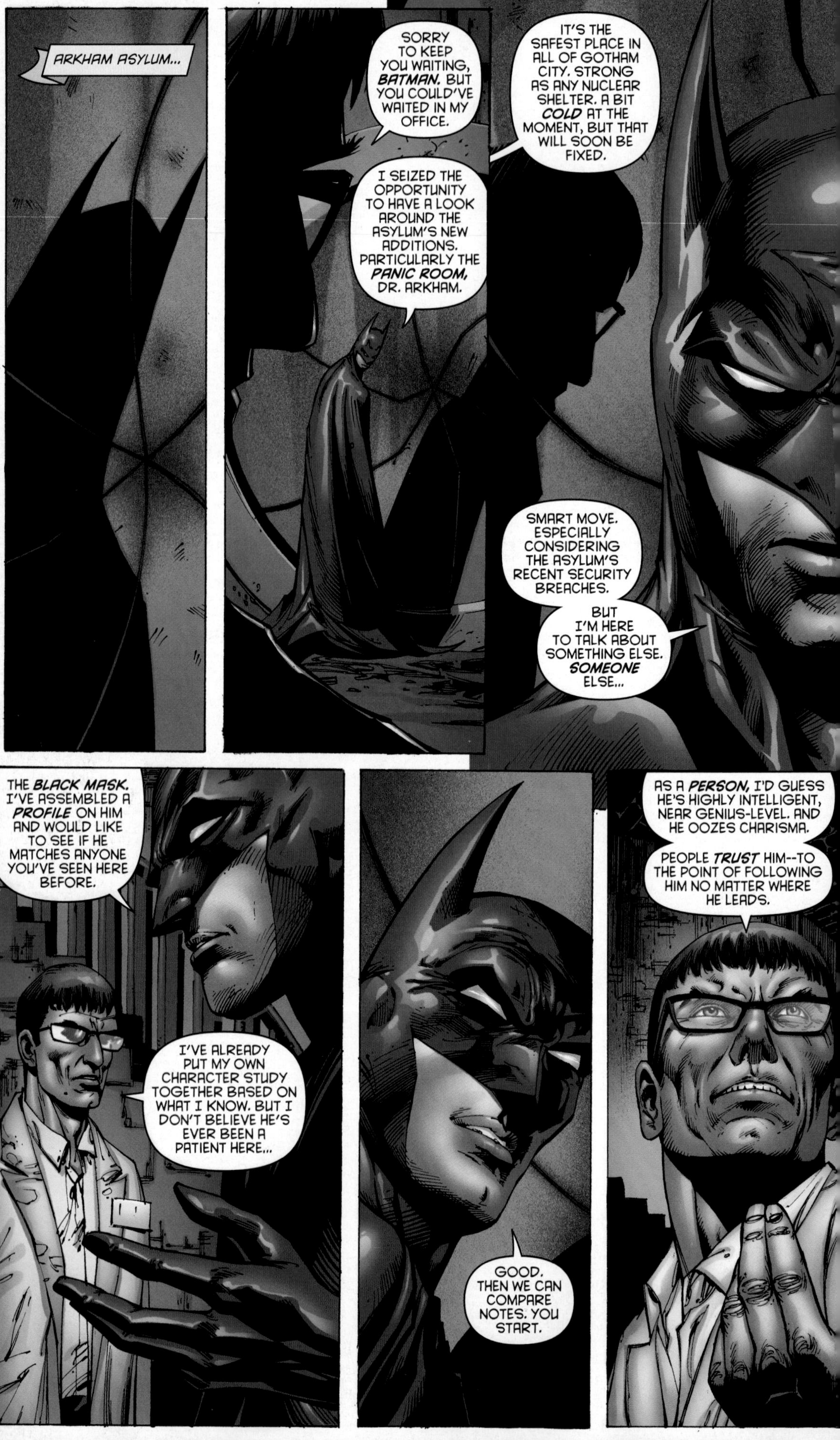
ARKHAM ASYLUM...
SORRY TO KEEP YOU WAITING, BATMAN. BUT YOU COULD'VE WAITED IN MY OFFICE.
I SEIZED THE OPPORTUNITY TO HAVE A LOOK AROUND THE ASYLUM'S NEW ADDITIONS. PARTICULARLY THE PANIC ROOM, DR. ARKHAM.
IT'S THE SAFEST PLACE IN ALL OF GOTHAM CITY. STRONG AS ANY NUCLEAR SHELTER. A BIT COLD AT THE MOMENT, BUT THAT WILL SOON BE FIXED.
SMART MOVE. ESPECIALLY CONSIDERING THE ASYLUM'S RECENT SECURITY BREACHES.
BUT I'M HERE TO TALK ABOUT SOMETHING ELSE. SOMEONE ELSE...
THE BLACK MASK. I'VE ASSEMBLED A PROFILE ON HIM AND WOULD LIKE TO SEE IF HE MATCHES ANYONE YOU'VE SEEN HERE BEFORE.
I'VE ALREADY PUT MY OWN CHARACTER STUDY TOGETHER BASED ON WHAT I KNOW. BUT I DON'T BELIEVE HE'S EVER BEEN A PATIENT HERE...
GOOD. THEN WE CAN COMPARE NOTES. YOU START.
AS A PERSON, I'D GUESS HE'S HIGHLY INTELLIGENT, NEAR GENIUS-LEVEL. AND HE OOZES CHARISMA.
PEOPLE TRUST HIM--TO THE POINT OF FOLLOWING HIM NO MATTER WHERE HE LEADS.

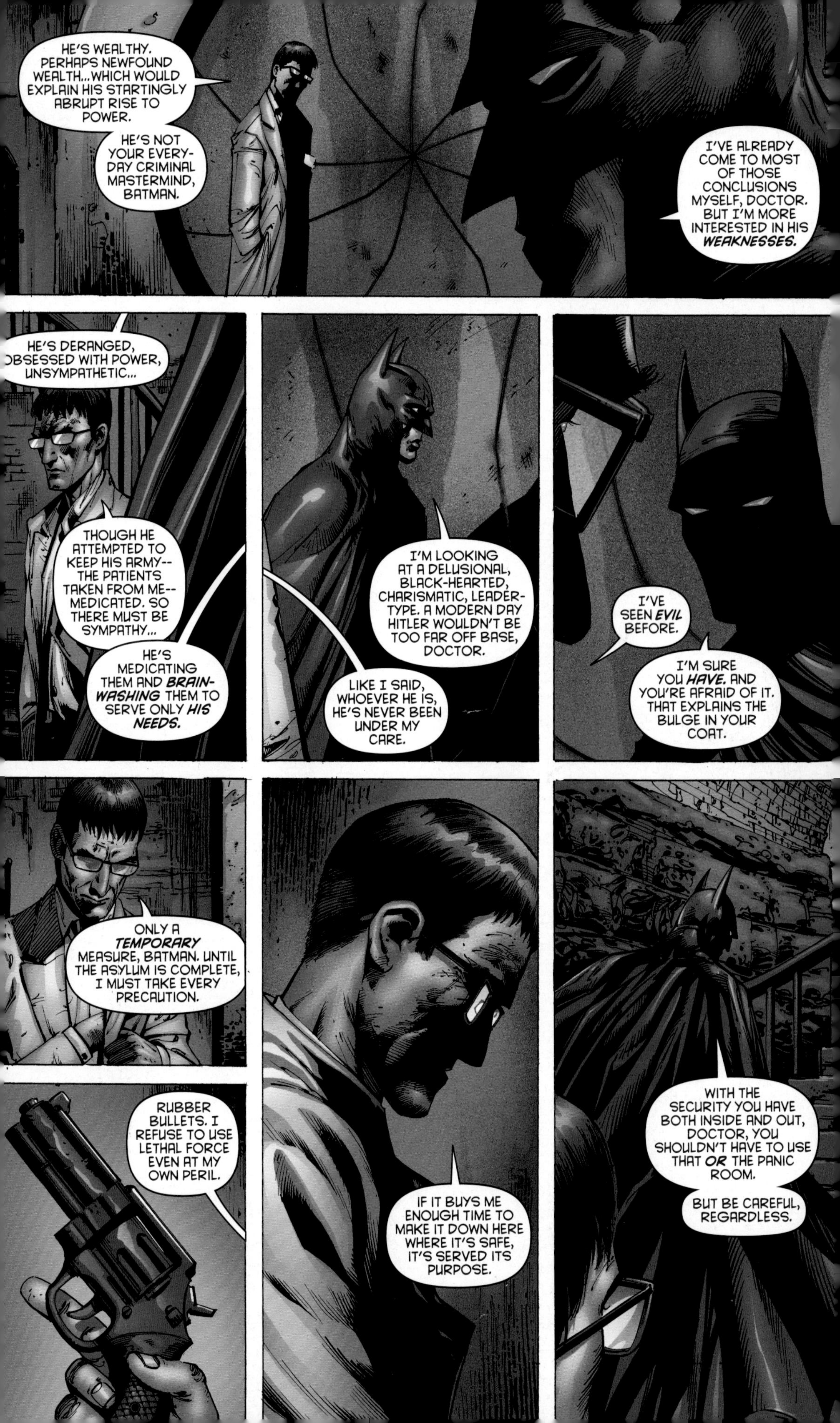
HE'S WEALTHY. PERHAPS NEWFOUND WEALTH...WHICH WOULD EXPLAIN HIS STARTINGLY ABRUPT RISE TO POWER.
HE'S NOT YOUR EVERY-DAY CRIMINAL MASTERMIND, BATMAN.
I'VE ALREADY COME TO MOST OF THOSE CONCLUSIONS MYSELF, DOCTOR. BUT I'M MORE INTERESTED IN HIS *WEAKNESSES.*
HE'S DERANGED, OBSESSED WITH POWER, UNSYMPATHETIC...
THOUGH HE ATTEMPTED TO KEEP HIS ARMY-- THE PATIENTS TAKEN FROM ME-- MEDICATED. SO THERE MUST BE SYMPATHY...
HE'S MEDICATING THEM AND *BRAIN-WASHING* THEM TO SERVE ONLY *HIS NEEDS.*
I'M LOOKING AT A DELUSIONAL, BLACK-HEARTED, CHARISMATIC, LEADER-TYPE. A MODERN DAY HITLER WOULDN'T BE TOO FAR OFF BASE, DOCTOR.
LIKE I SAID, WHOEVER HE IS, HE'S NEVER BEEN UNDER MY CARE.
I'VE SEEN *EVIL* BEFORE.
I'M SURE YOU *HAVE.* AND YOU'RE AFRAID OF IT. THAT EXPLAINS THE BULGE IN YOUR COAT.
ONLY A *TEMPORARY* MEASURE, BATMAN. UNTIL THE ASYLUM IS COMPLETE, I MUST TAKE EVERY PRECAUTION.
RUBBER BULLETS. I REFUSE TO USE LETHAL FORCE EVEN AT MY OWN PERIL.
IF IT BUYS ME ENOUGH TIME TO MAKE IT DOWN HERE WHERE IT'S SAFE, IT'S SERVED ITS PURPOSE.
WITH THE SECURITY YOU HAVE BOTH INSIDE AND OUT, DOCTOR, YOU SHOULDN'T HAVE TO USE THAT *OR* THE PANIC ROOM.
BUT BE CAREFUL, REGARDLESS.

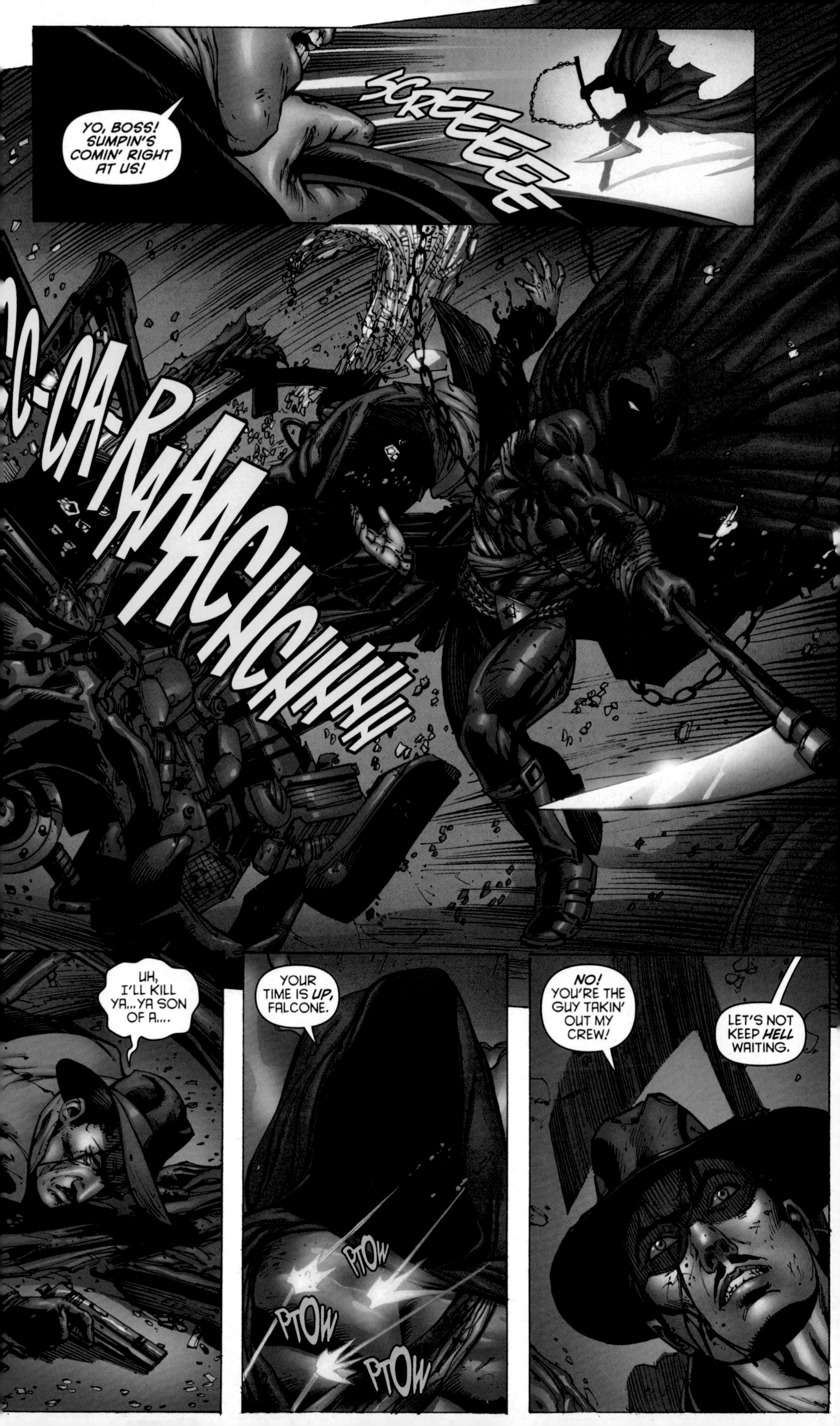
YO, BOSS! SUMPIN'S COMIN' RIGHT AT US!
SCREEEEE
CC-CA-RAAACHCHCHHH
UH, I'LL KILL YA...YA SON OF A....
YOUR TIME IS *UP*, FALCONE.
PTOW
PTOW
PTOW
NO! YOU'RE THE GUY TAKIN' OUT MY CREW!
LET'S NOT KEEP *HELL* WAITING.

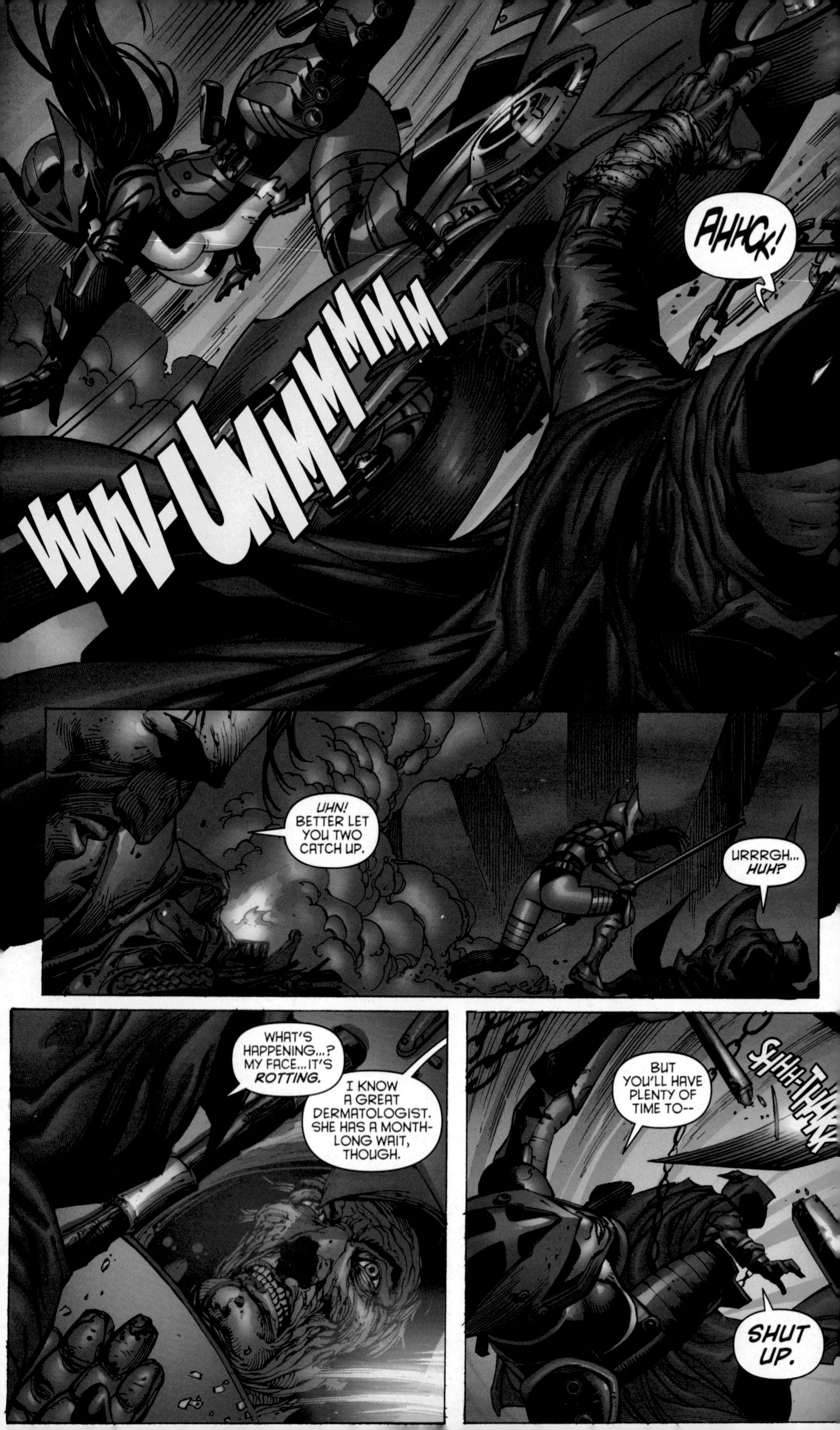
AHHCK!
VVVV-UMMMMMMM
UHN! BETTER LET YOU TWO CATCH UP.
URRRGH... HUH?
WHAT'S HAPPENING...? MY FACE...IT'S ROTTING.
I KNOW A GREAT DERMATOLOGIST. SHE HAS A MONTH-LONG WAIT, THOUGH.
BUT YOU'LL HAVE PLENTY OF TIME TO--
SHHH-THHAKK
SHUT UP.

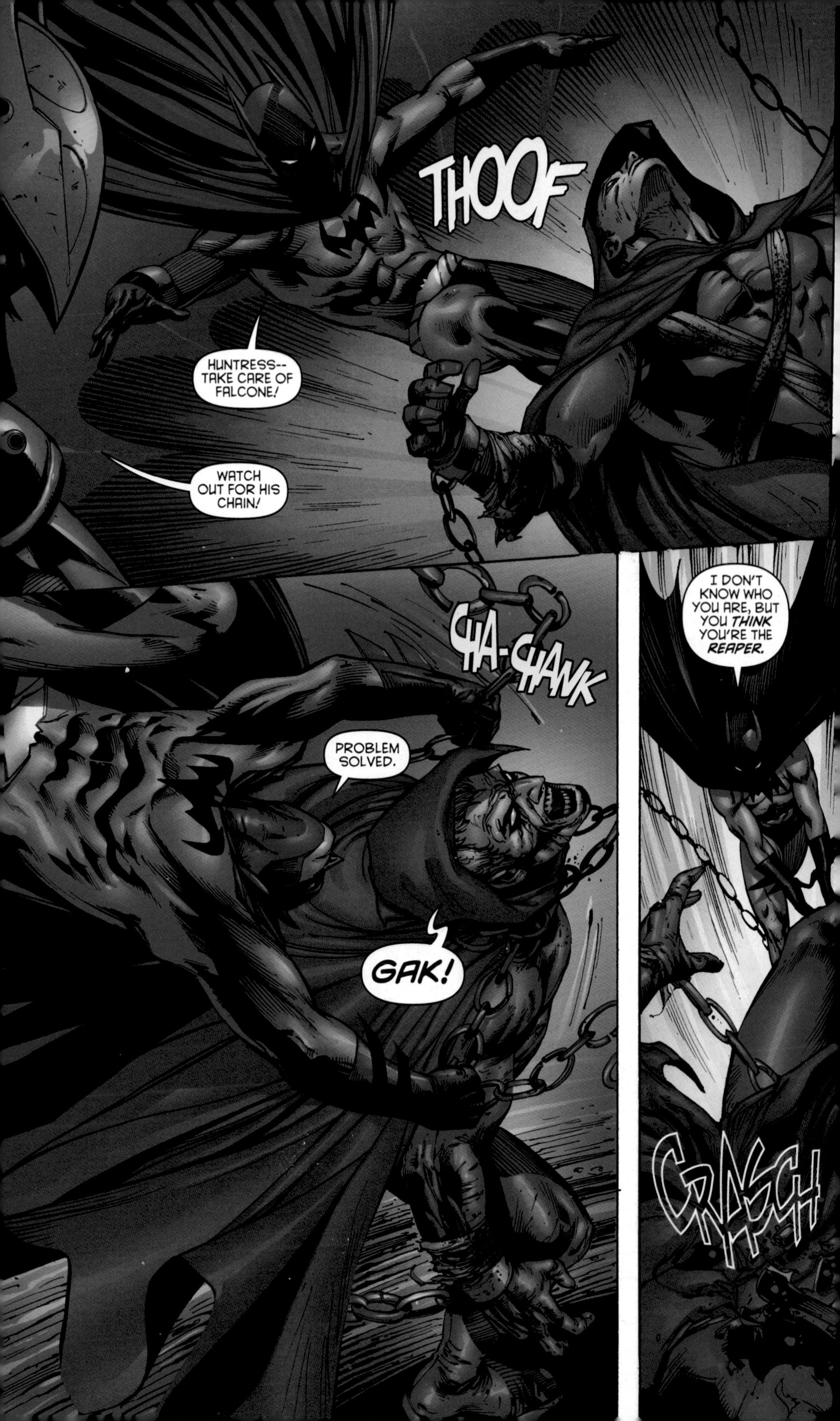
THOOF
HUNTRESS-- TAKE CARE OF FALCONE!
WATCH OUT FOR HIS CHAIN!
CHA-CHANK
PROBLEM SOLVED.
GAK!
I DON'T KNOW WHO YOU ARE, BUT YOU *THINK* YOU'RE THE *REAPER.*
CRASCH

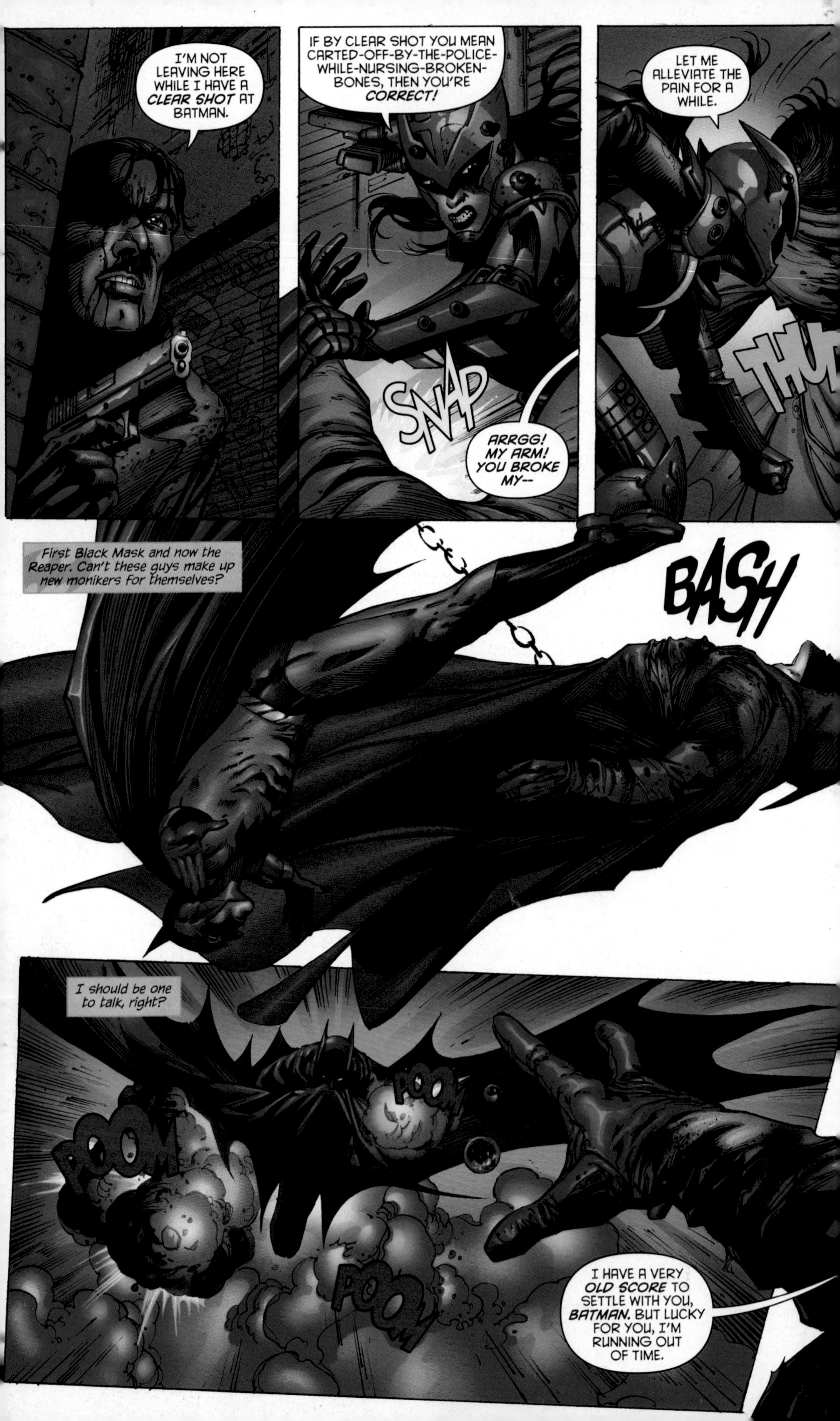
I'M NOT LEAVING HERE WHILE I HAVE A CLEAR SHOT AT BATMAN.
IF BY CLEAR SHOT YOU MEAN CARTED-OFF-BY-THE-POLICE-WHILE-NURSING-BROKEN-BONES, THEN YOU'RE CORRECT!
SNAP
ARRGG! MY ARM! YOU BROKE MY--
LET ME ALLEVIATE THE PAIN FOR A WHILE.
First Black Mask and now the Reaper. Can't these guys make up new monikers for themselves?
BASH
I should be one to talk, right?
POOM
POOM
POOM
I HAVE A VERY OLD SCORE TO SETTLE WITH YOU, BATMAN. BUT LUCKY FOR YOU, I'M RUNNING OUT OF TIME.

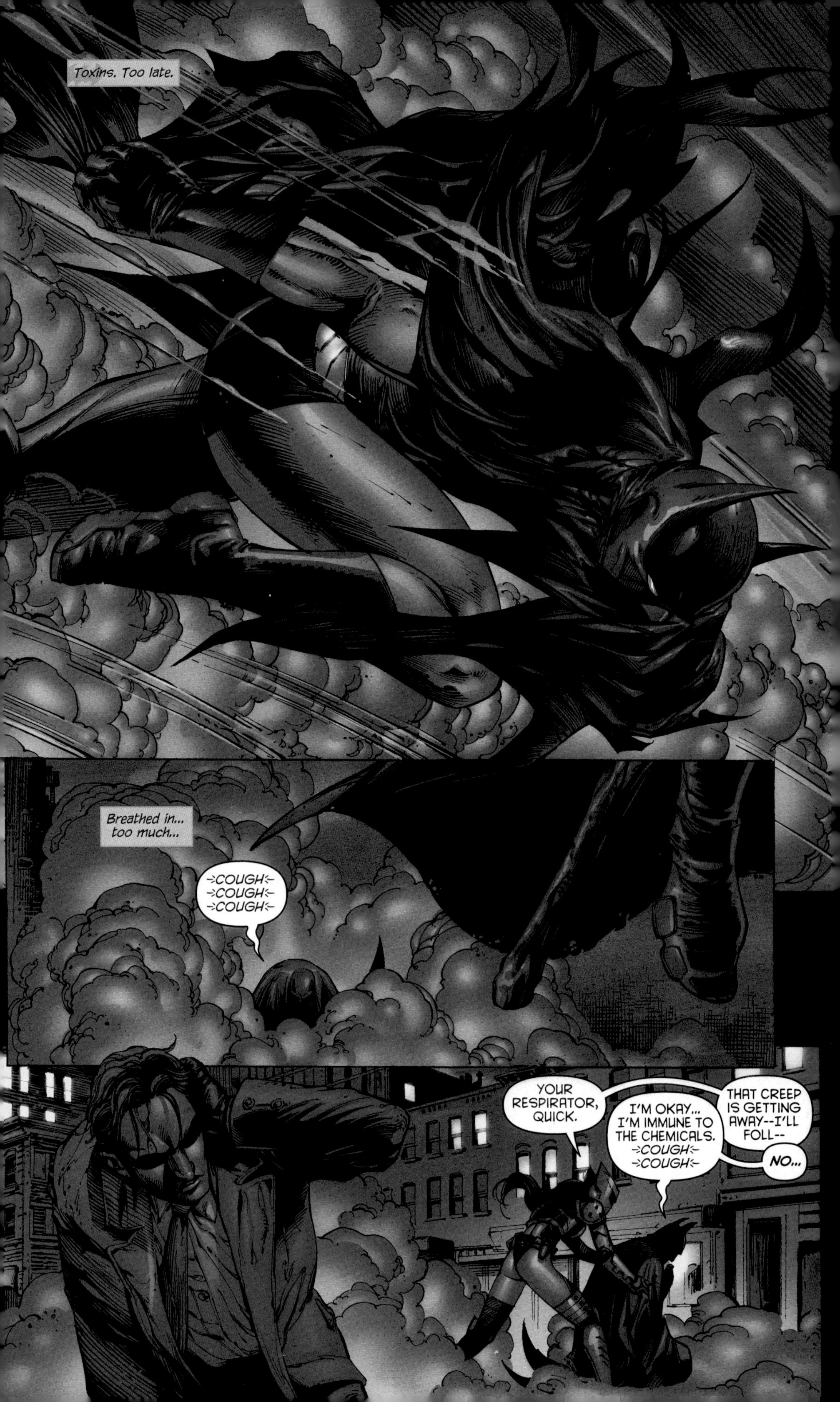
Toxins. Too late.
Breathed in... too much...
~COUGH~ ~COUGH~ ~COUGH~
YOUR RESPIRATOR, QUICK.
I'M OKAY... I'M IMMUNE TO THE CHEMICALS. ~COUGH~ ~COUGH~
THAT CREEP IS GETTING AWAY--I'LL FOLL--
NO...

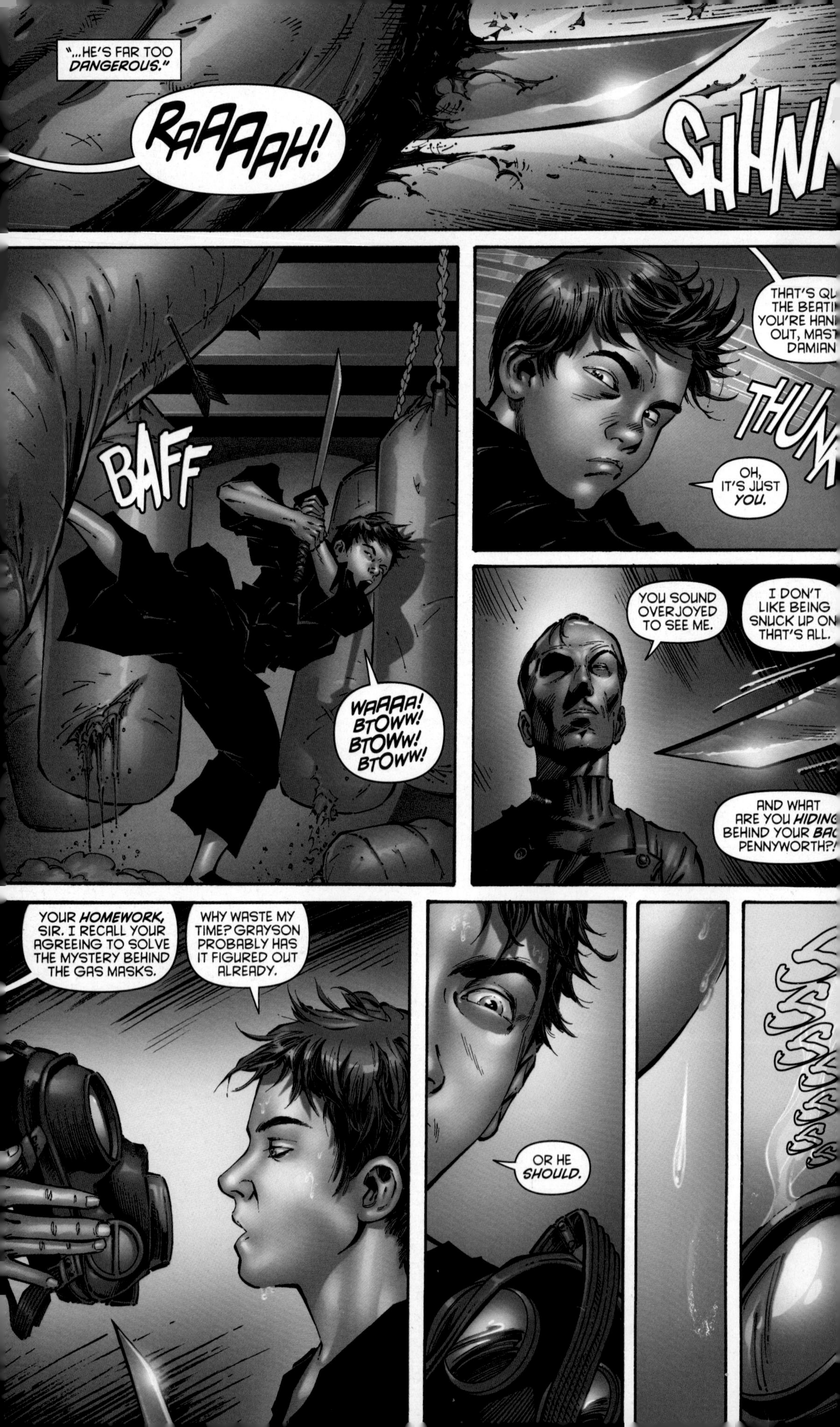

"...HE'S FAR TOO *DANGEROUS.*"
RAAAAAH!
SHHN
BAFF
WAAAA! BTOWW! BTOWW! BTOWW!
THAT'S QU THE BEATI YOU'RE HAN OUT, MAST DAMIAN
THUNK
OH, IT'S JUST *YOU.*
YOU SOUND OVERJOYED TO SEE ME.
I DON'T LIKE BEING SNUCK UP ON THAT'S ALL.
AND WHAT ARE YOU *HIDING* BEHIND YOUR *BAC* PENNYWORTH?!
YOUR *HOMEWORK,* SIR. I RECALL YOUR AGREEING TO SOLVE THE MYSTERY BEHIND THE GAS MASKS.
WHY WASTE MY TIME? GRAYSON PROBABLY HAS IT FIGURED OUT ALREADY.
OR HE *SHOULD.*

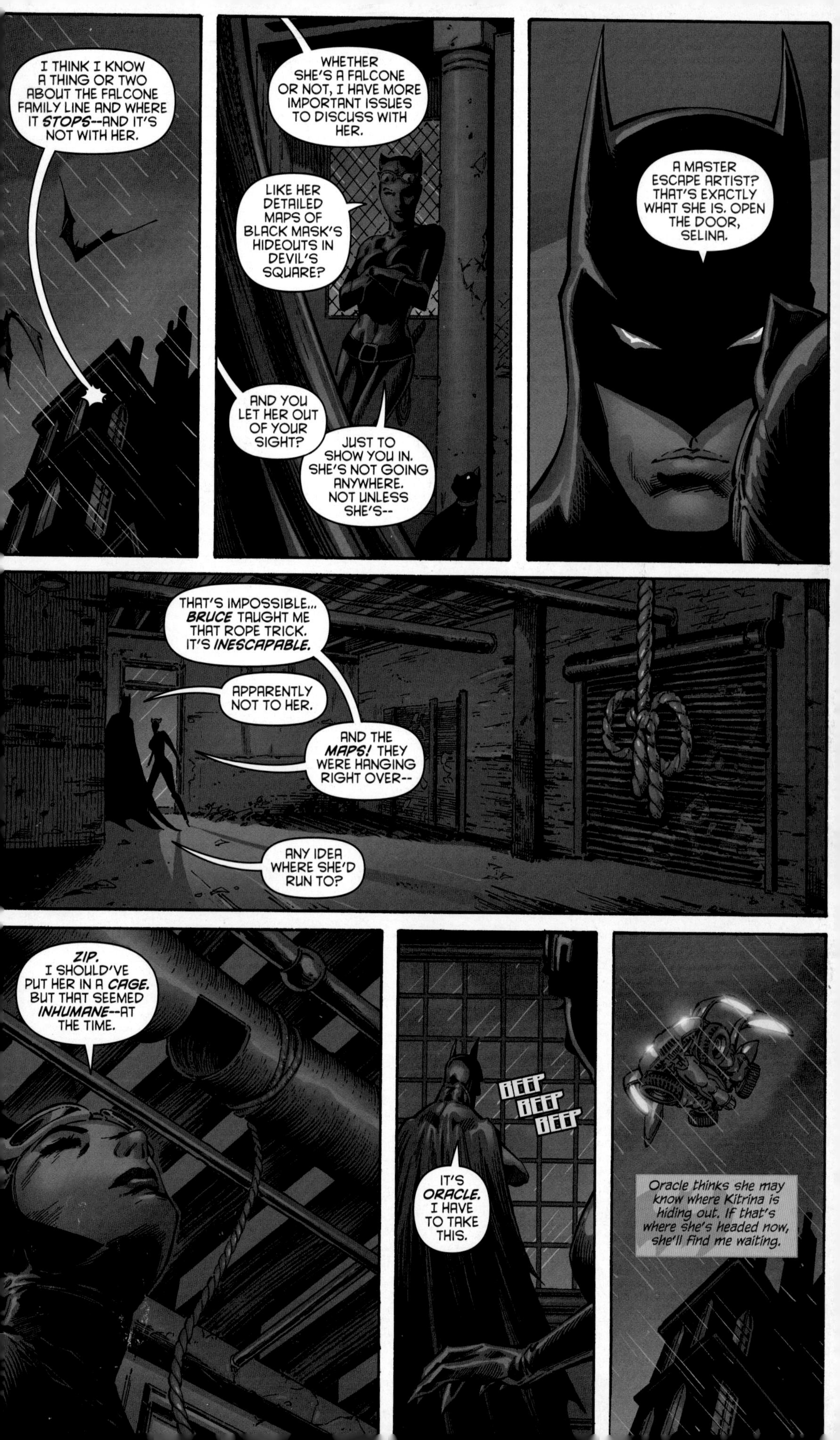
I THINK I KNOW A THING OR TWO ABOUT THE FALCONE FAMILY LINE AND WHERE IT STOPS--AND IT'S NOT WITH HER.
WHETHER SHE'S A FALCONE OR NOT, I HAVE MORE IMPORTANT ISSUES TO DISCUSS WITH HER.
LIKE HER DETAILED MAPS OF BLACK MASK'S HIDEOUTS IN DEVIL'S SQUARE?
AND YOU LET HER OUT OF YOUR SIGHT?
JUST TO SHOW YOU IN. SHE'S NOT GOING ANYWHERE. NOT UNLESS SHE'S--
A MASTER ESCAPE ARTIST? THAT'S EXACTLY WHAT SHE IS. OPEN THE DOOR, SELINA.
THAT'S IMPOSSIBLE... BRUCE TAUGHT ME THAT ROPE TRICK. IT'S INESCAPABLE.
APPARENTLY NOT TO HER.
AND THE MAPS! THEY WERE HANGING RIGHT OVER--
ANY IDEA WHERE SHE'D RUN TO?
ZIP. I SHOULD'VE PUT HER IN A CAGE. BUT THAT SEEMED INHUMANE--AT THE TIME.
BEEP BEEP BEEP
IT'S ORACLE. I HAVE TO TAKE THIS.
Oracle thinks she may know where Kitrina is hiding out. If that's where she's headed now, she'll find me waiting.

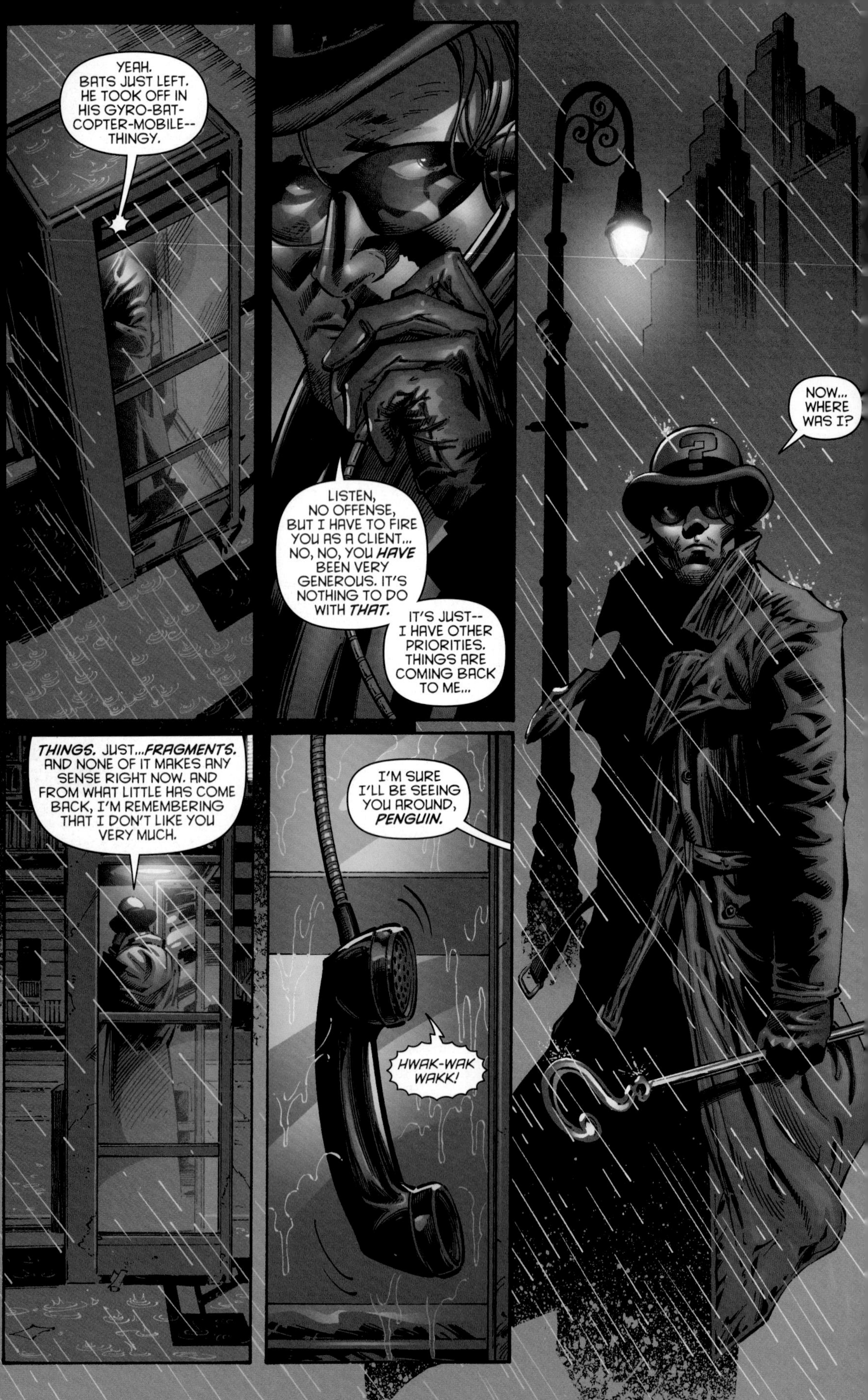
YEAH. BATS JUST LEFT. HE TOOK OFF IN HIS GYRO-BAT-COPTER-MOBILE--THINGY.
LISTEN, NO OFFENSE, BUT I HAVE TO FIRE YOU AS A CLIENT... NO, NO, YOU *HAVE* BEEN VERY GENEROUS. IT'S NOTHING TO DO WITH *THAT.*
IT'S JUST--I HAVE OTHER PRIORITIES. THINGS ARE COMING BACK TO ME...
NOW... WHERE WAS I?
THINGS. JUST...*FRAGMENTS.* AND NONE OF IT MAKES ANY SENSE RIGHT NOW. AND FROM WHAT LITTLE HAS COME BACK, I'M REMEMBERING THAT I DON'T LIKE YOU VERY MUCH.
I'M SURE I'LL BE SEEING YOU AROUND, *PENGUIN.*
HWAK-WAK WAKK!

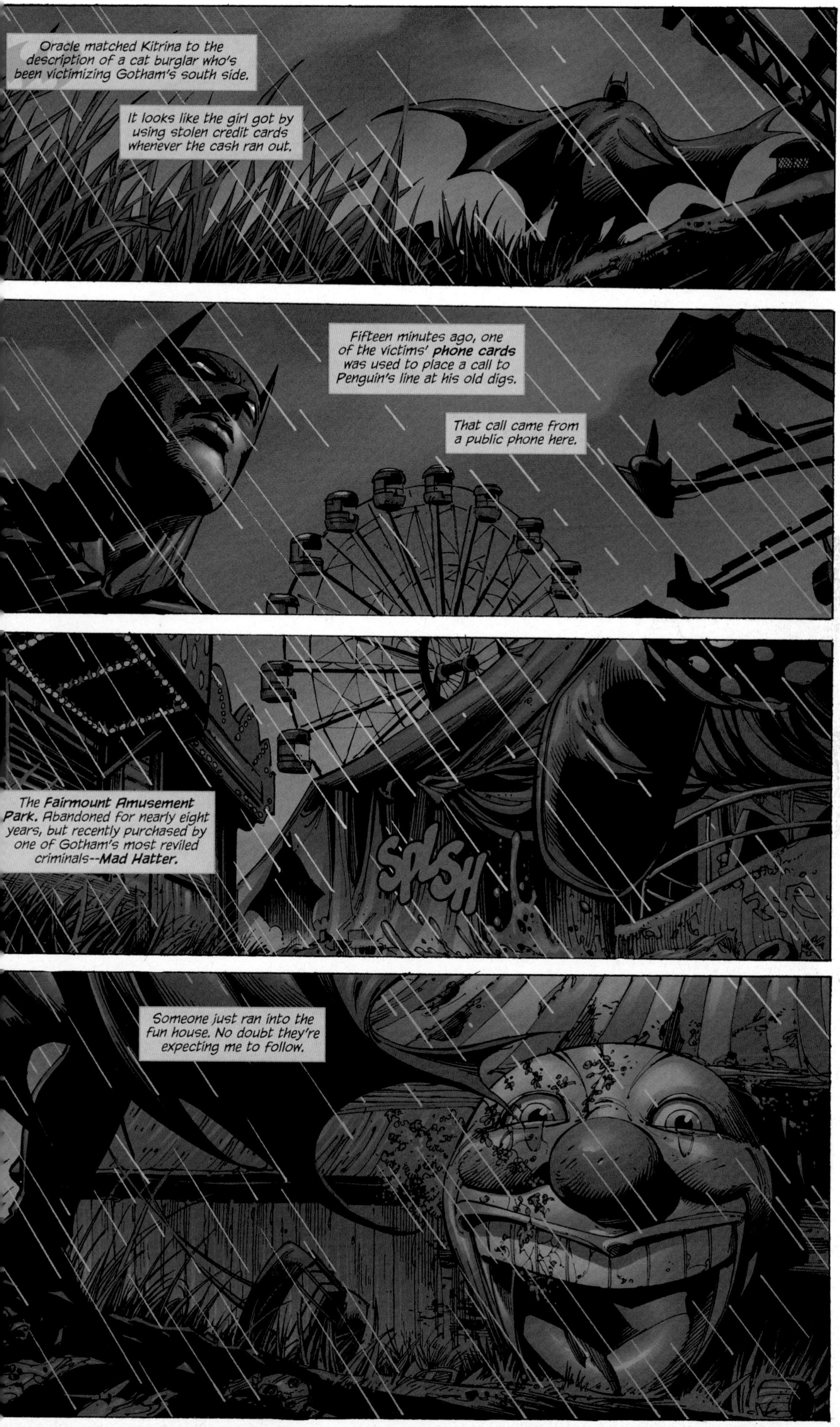
Oracle matched Kitrina to the description of a cat burglar who's been victimizing Gotham's south side.
It looks like the girl got by using stolen credit cards whenever the cash ran out.
Fifteen minutes ago, one of the victims' phone cards was used to place a call to Penguin's line at his old digs.
That call came from a public phone here.
The Fairmount Amusement Park. Abandoned for nearly eight years, but recently purchased by one of Gotham's most reviled criminals--Mad Hatter.
SPLSH
Someone just ran into the fun house. No doubt they're expecting me to follow.

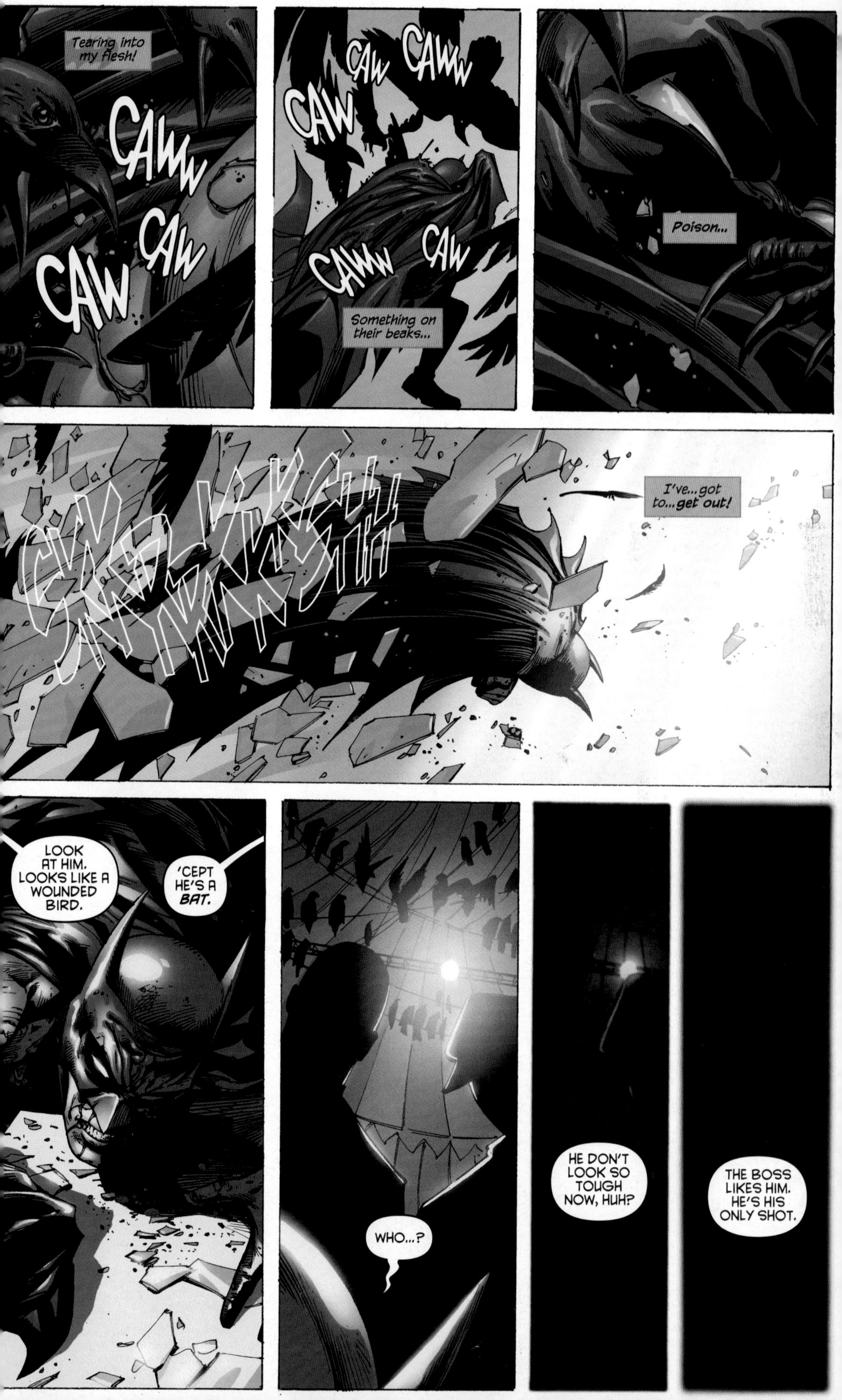
Tearing into my flesh!
CAWW
CAW
CAW
CAW
CAW
CAWW
CAWW
CAW
Something on their beaks...
Poison...
I've...got to...get out!
LOOK AT HIM. LOOKS LIKE A WOUNDED BIRD.
'CEPT HE'S A BAT.
WHO...?
HE DON'T LOOK SO TOUGH NOW, HUH?
THE BOSS LIKES HIM. HE'S HIS ONLY SHOT.

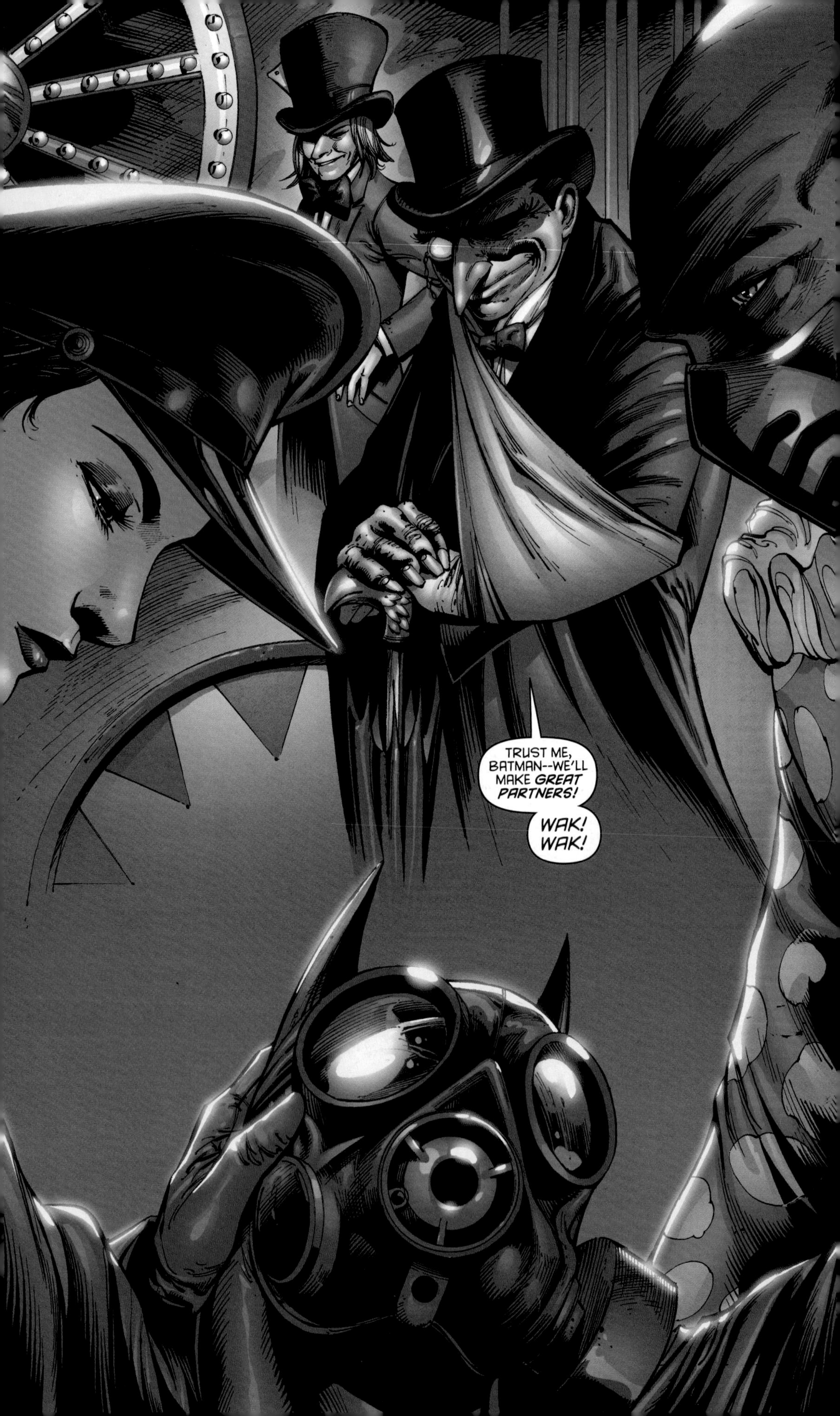
TRUST ME, BATMAN--WE'LL MAKE *GREAT PARTNERS!*
WAK! WAK!

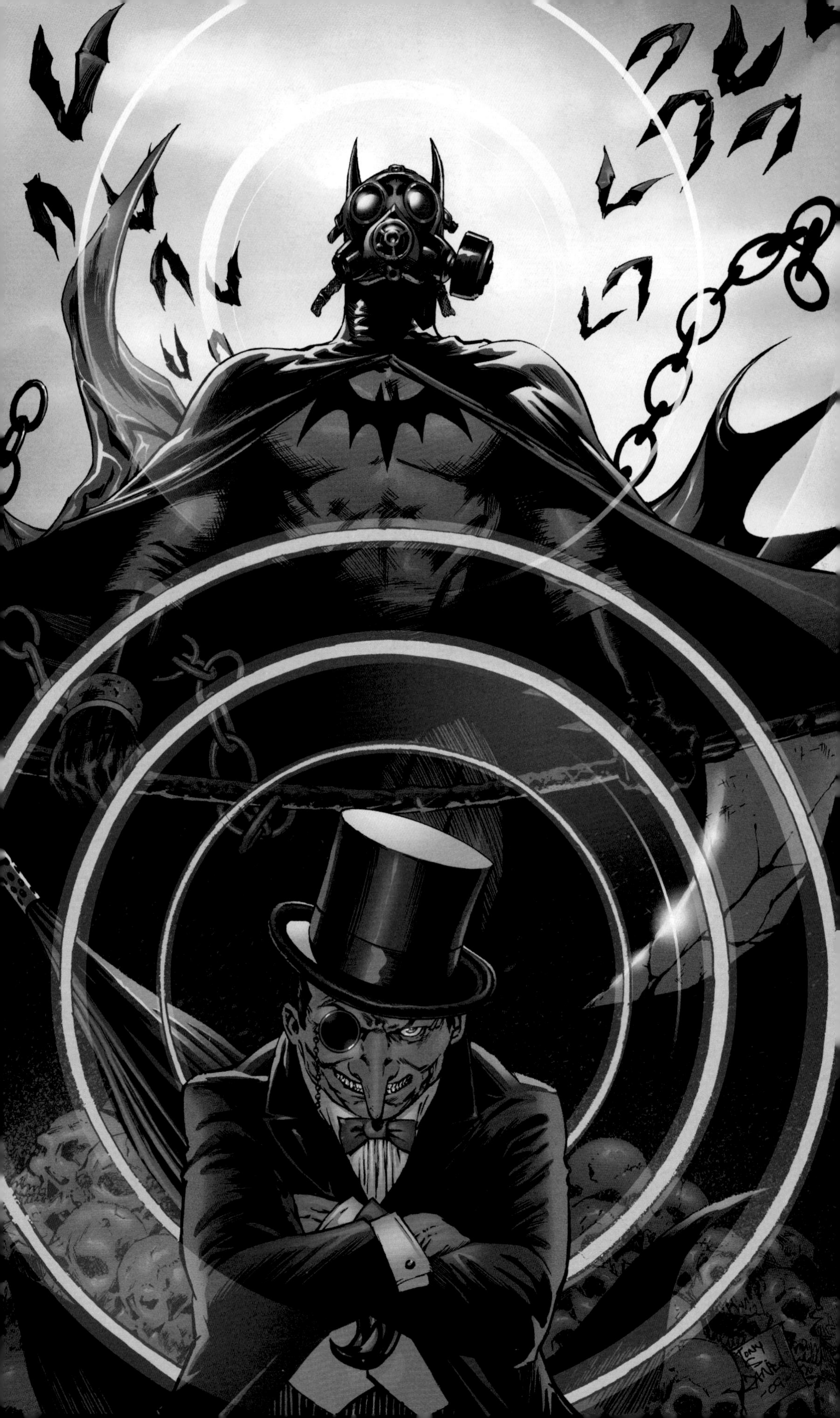

"You shouldn't feel any remorse for what you have to do to survive here."

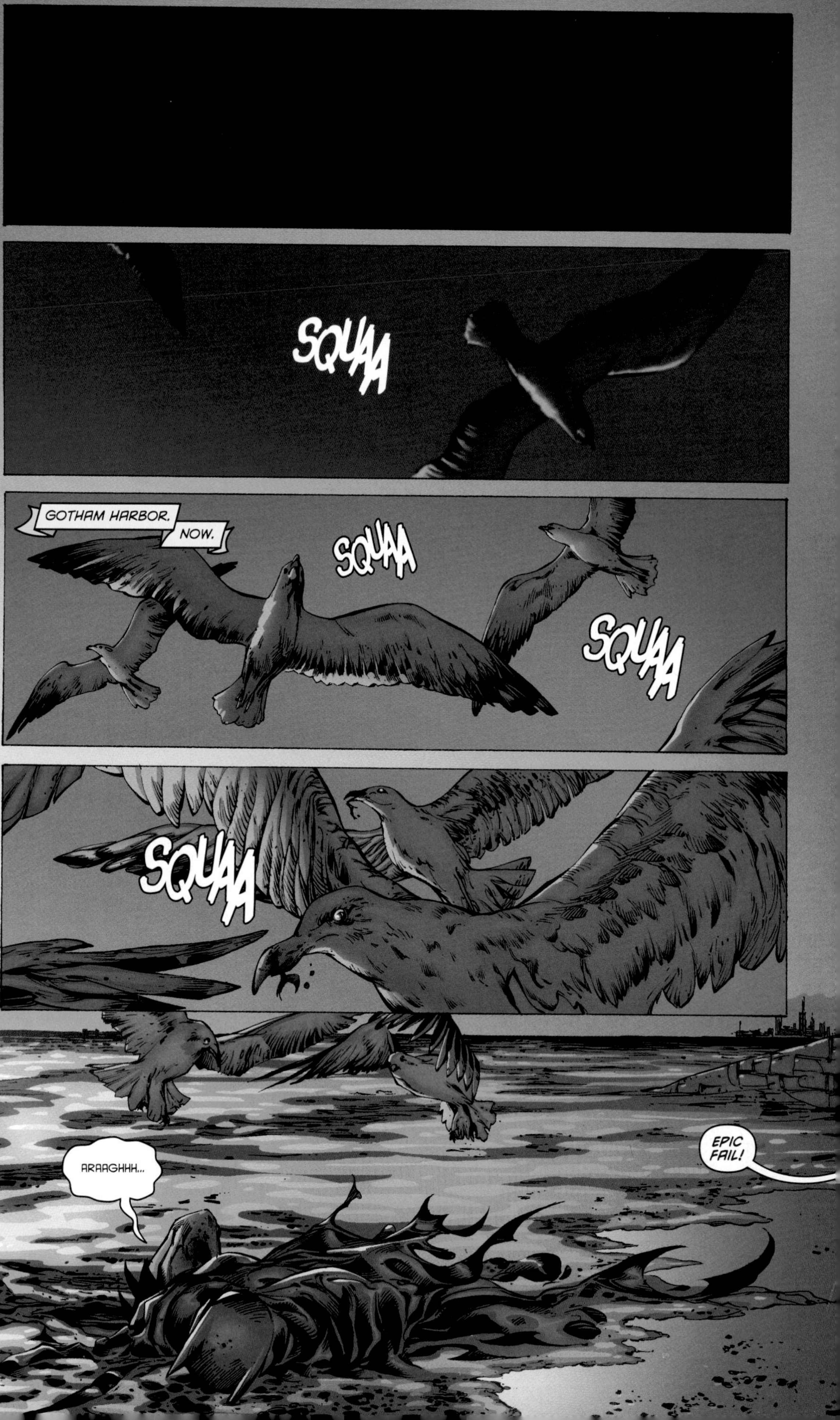
SQUAA
GOTHAM HARBOR.
NOW.
SQUAA
SQUAA
SQUAA
ARAAGHHH...
EPIC FAIL!

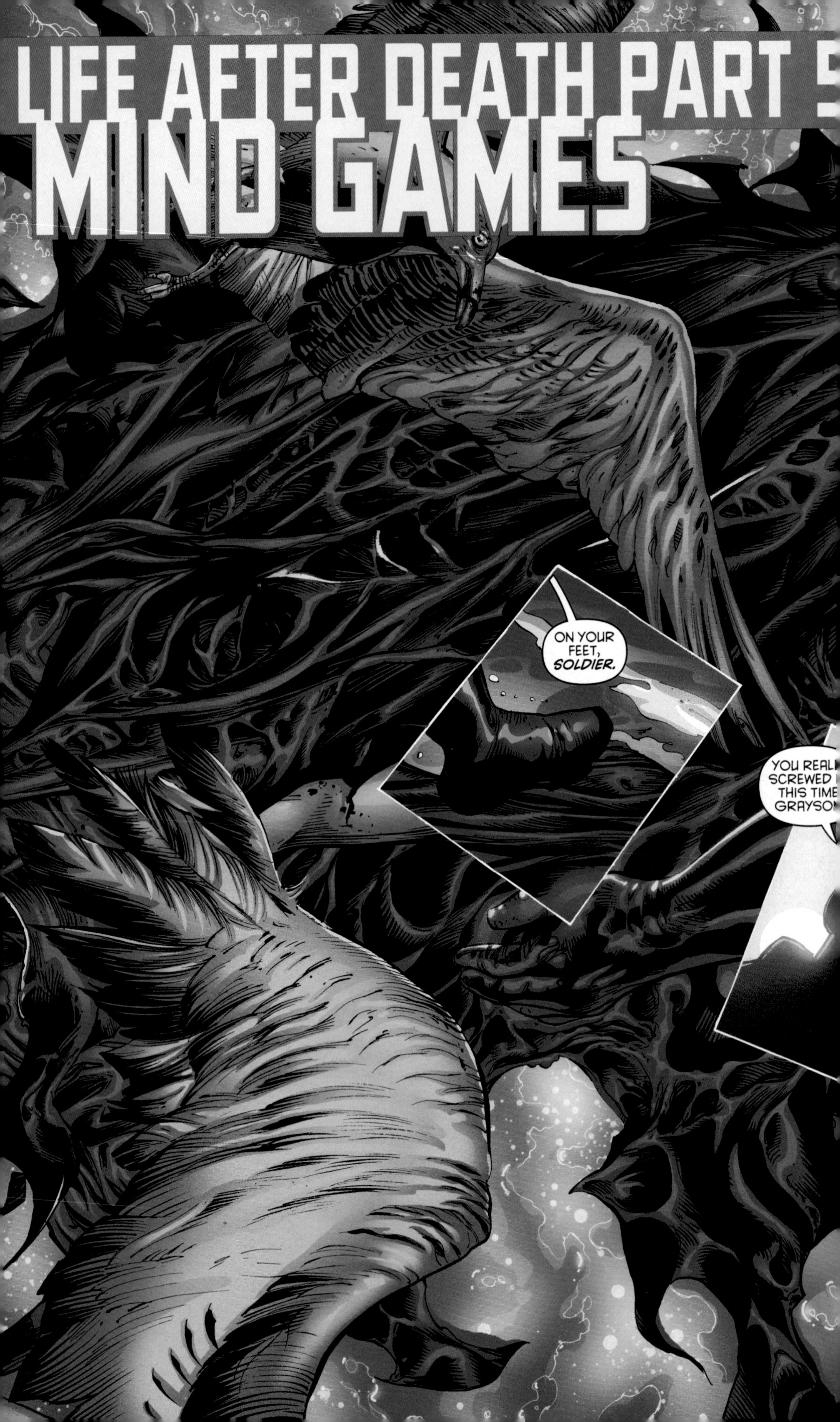

LIFE AFTER DEATH PART 5
MIND GAMES
ON YOUR FEET, SOLDIER.

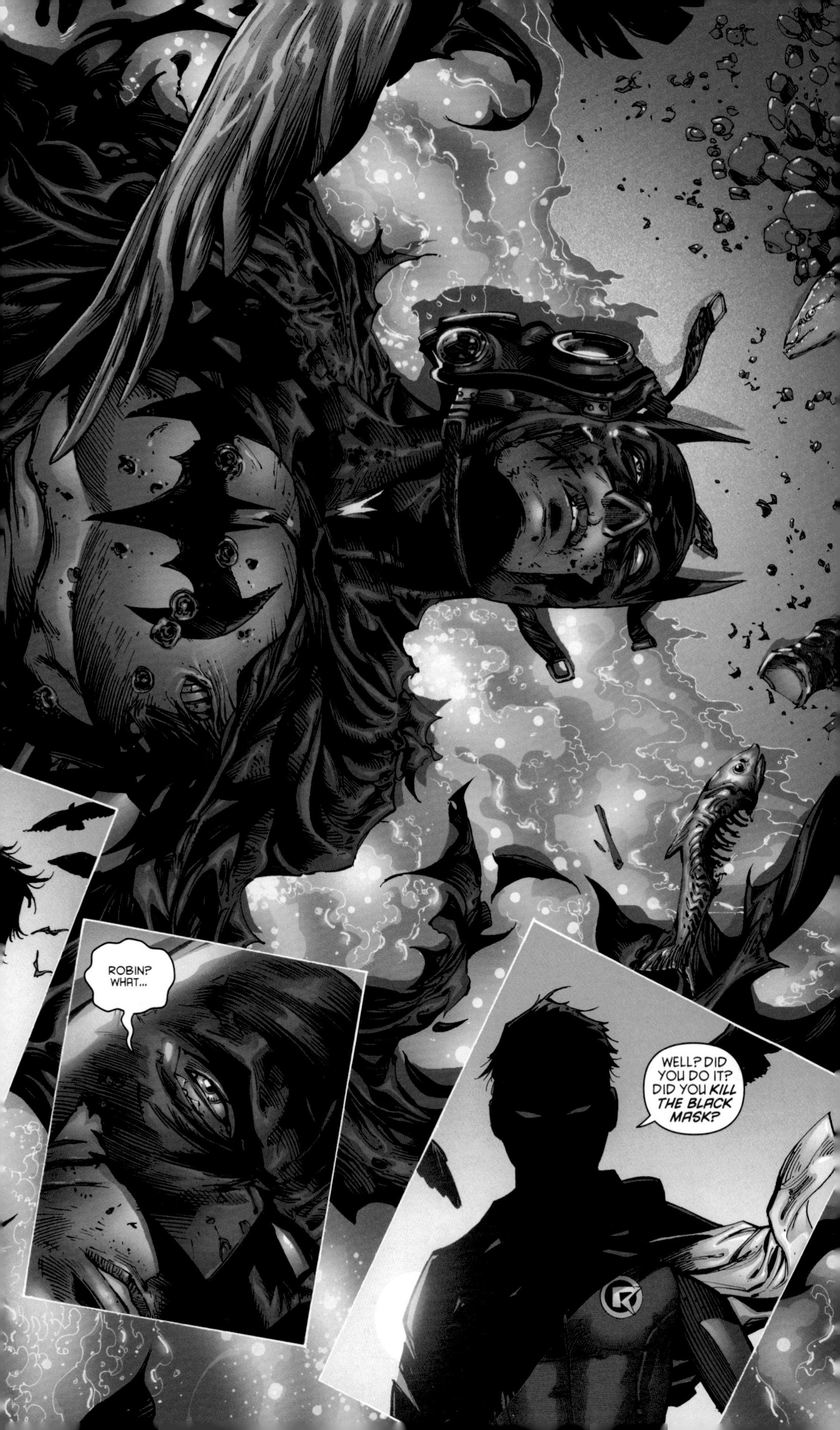
ROBIN? WHAT...
WELL? DID YOU DO IT? DID YOU KILL THE BLACK MASK?

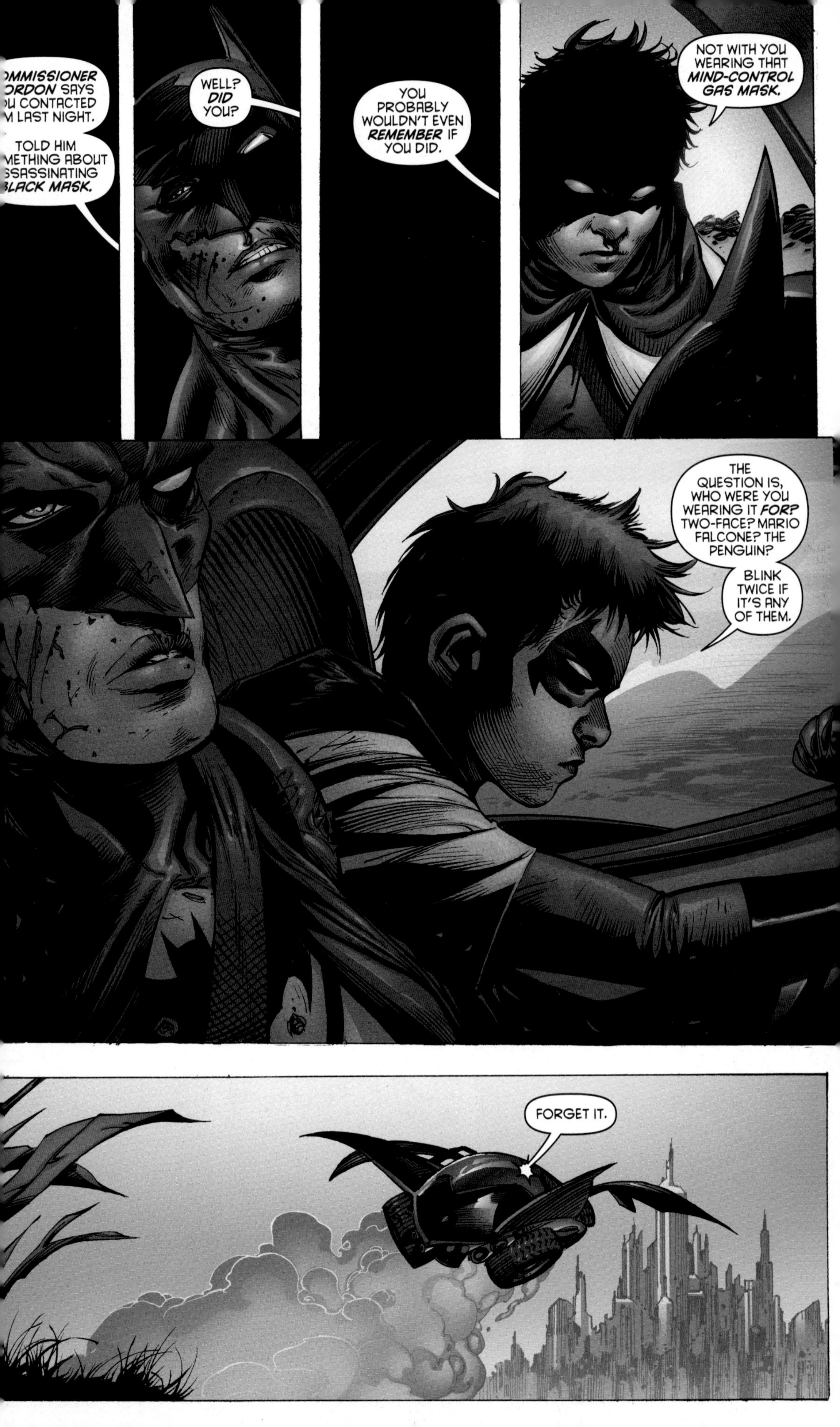
OMMISSIONER ORDON SAYS OU CONTACTED M LAST NIGHT.
TOLD HIM METHING ABOUT SSASSINATING BLACK MASK.
WELL? DID YOU?
YOU PROBABLY WOULDN'T EVEN REMEMBER IF YOU DID.
NOT WITH YOU WEARING THAT MIND-CONTROL GAS MASK.
THE QUESTION IS, WHO WERE YOU WEARING IT FOR? TWO-FACE? MARIO FALCONE? THE PENGUIN?
BLINK TWICE IF IT'S ANY OF THEM.
FORGET IT.

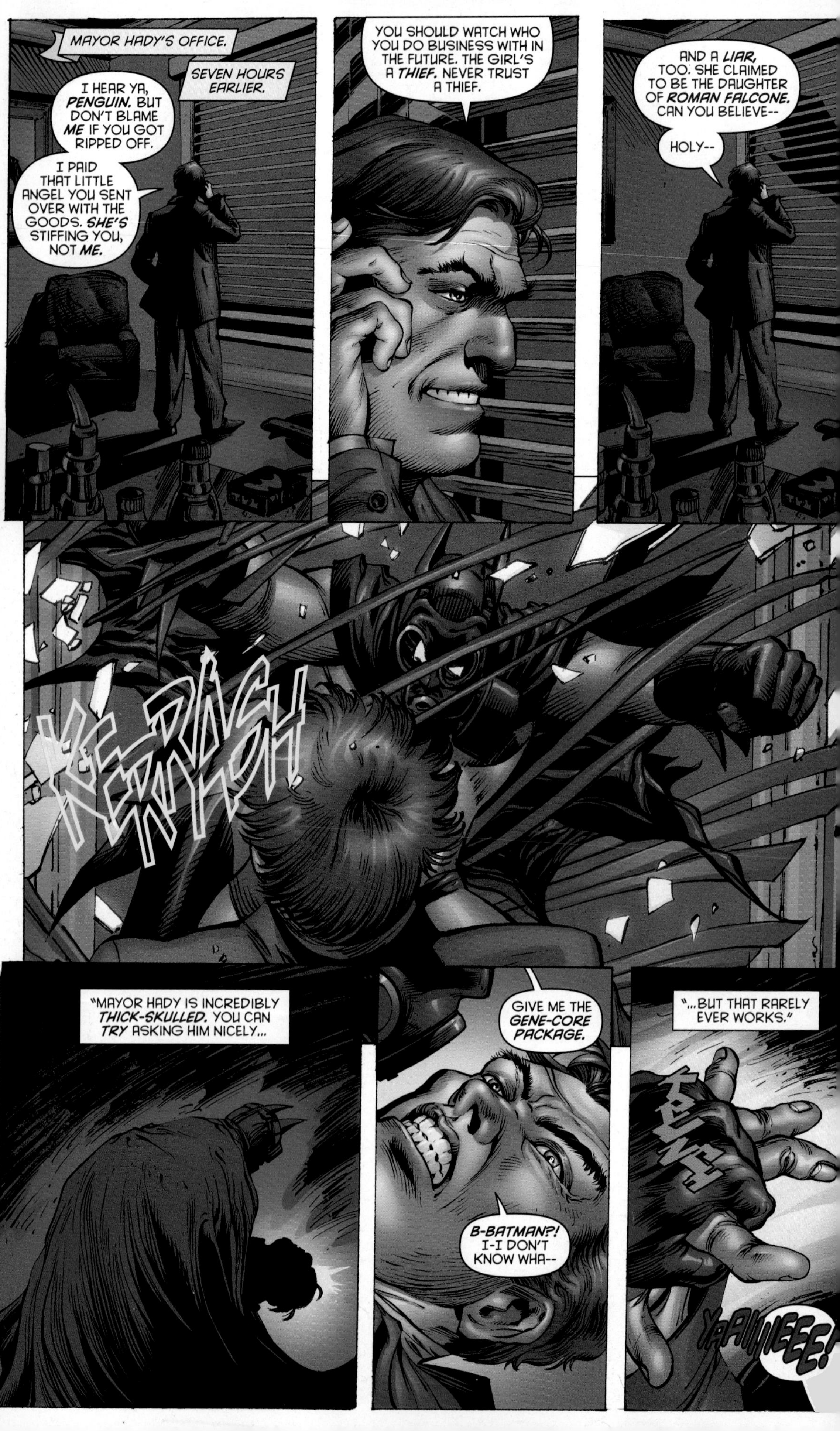
MAYOR HADY'S OFFICE.
SEVEN HOURS EARLIER.
I HEAR YA, *PENGUIN.* BUT DON'T BLAME *ME* IF YOU GOT RIPPED OFF.
I PAID THAT LITTLE ANGEL YOU SENT OVER WITH THE GOODS. *SHE'S* STIFFING YOU, NOT *ME.*
YOU SHOULD WATCH WHO YOU DO BUSINESS WITH IN THE FUTURE. THE GIRL'S A *THIEF.* NEVER TRUST A THIEF.
AND A *LIAR,* TOO. SHE CLAIMED TO BE THE DAUGHTER OF *ROMAN FALCONE.* CAN YOU BELIEVE--
HOLY--
KE-RASH
"MAYOR HADY IS INCREDIBLY *THICK-SKULLED.* YOU CAN *TRY* ASKING HIM NICELY...
GIVE ME THE *GENE-CORE PACKAGE.*
B-BATMAN?! I-I DON'T KNOW WHA--
"...BUT THAT RARELY EVER WORKS."
YAAIIIEEE!

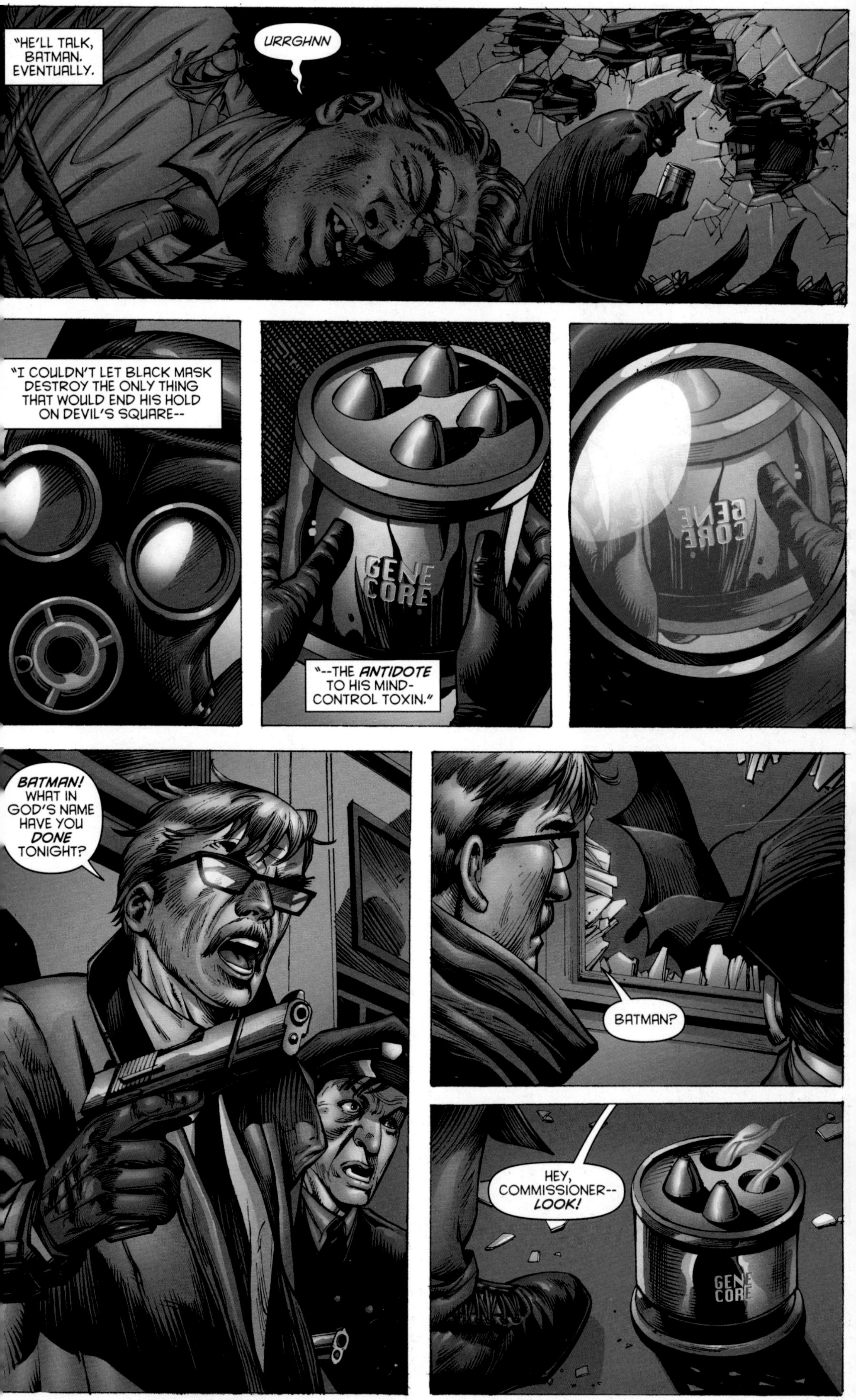
"HE'LL TALK, BATMAN. EVENTUALLY.
URRGHNN
"I COULDN'T LET BLACK MASK DESTROY THE ONLY THING THAT WOULD END HIS HOLD ON DEVIL'S SQUARE--
GENE CORE
"--THE ANTIDOTE TO HIS MIND-CONTROL TOXIN."
BATMAN! WHAT IN GOD'S NAME HAVE YOU DONE TONIGHT?
BATMAN?
HEY, COMMISSIONER-- LOOK!
GENE CORE

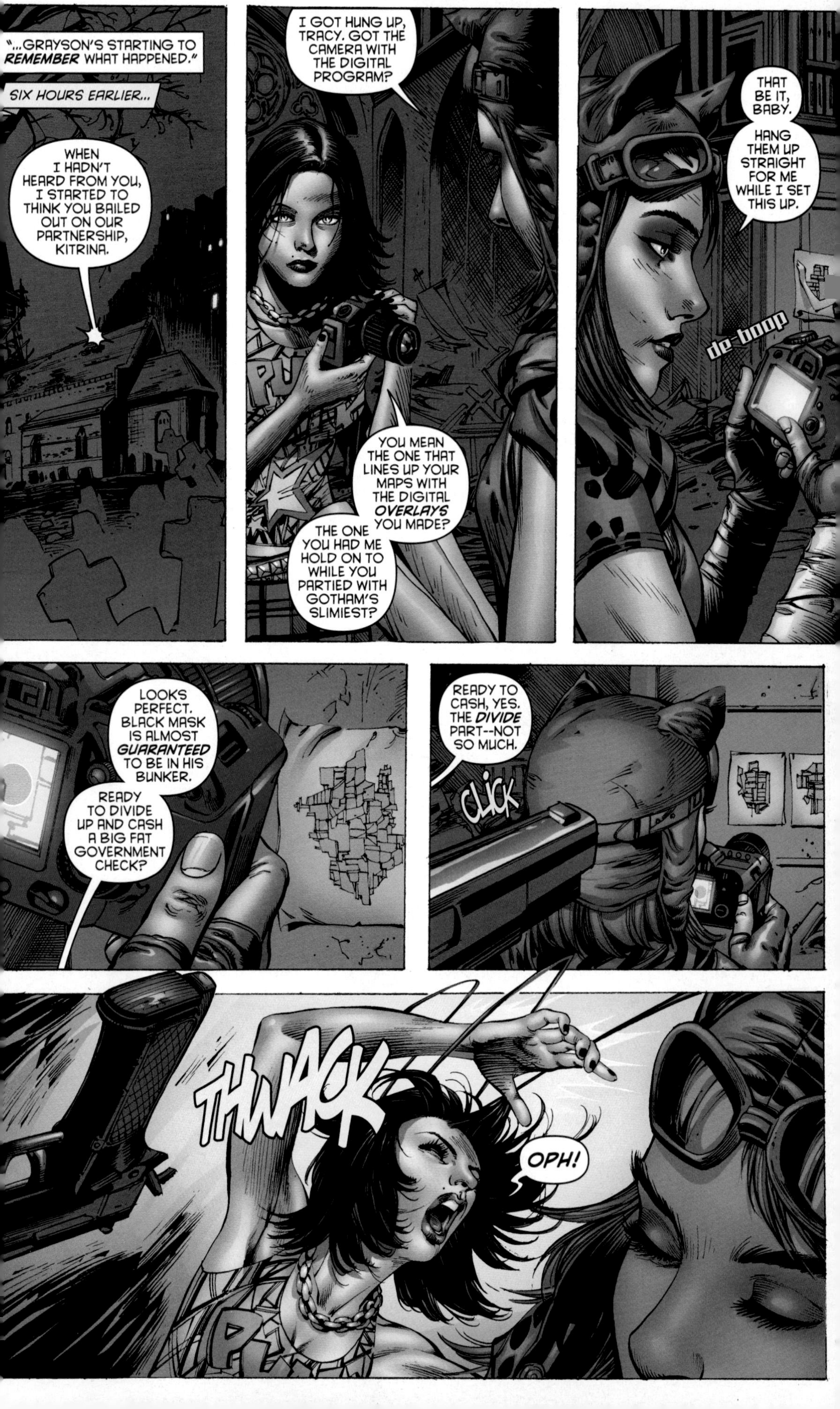
"...GRAYSON'S STARTING TO REMEMBER WHAT HAPPENED."
SIX HOURS EARLIER...
WHEN I HADN'T HEARD FROM YOU, I STARTED TO THINK YOU BAILED OUT ON OUR PARTNERSHIP, KITRINA.
I GOT HUNG UP, TRACY. GOT THE CAMERA WITH THE DIGITAL PROGRAM?
YOU MEAN THE ONE THAT LINES UP YOUR MAPS WITH THE DIGITAL OVERLAYS YOU MADE?
THE ONE YOU HAD ME HOLD ON TO WHILE YOU PARTIED WITH GOTHAM'S SLIMIEST?
THAT BE IT, BABY.
HANG THEM UP STRAIGHT FOR ME WHILE I SET THIS UP.
de-boop
LOOKS PERFECT. BLACK MASK IS ALMOST GUARANTEED TO BE IN HIS BUNKER.
READY TO DIVIDE UP AND CASH A BIG FAT GOVERNMENT CHECK?
READY TO CASH, YES. THE DIVIDE PART--NOT SO MUCH.
CLICK
THWACK
OPH!

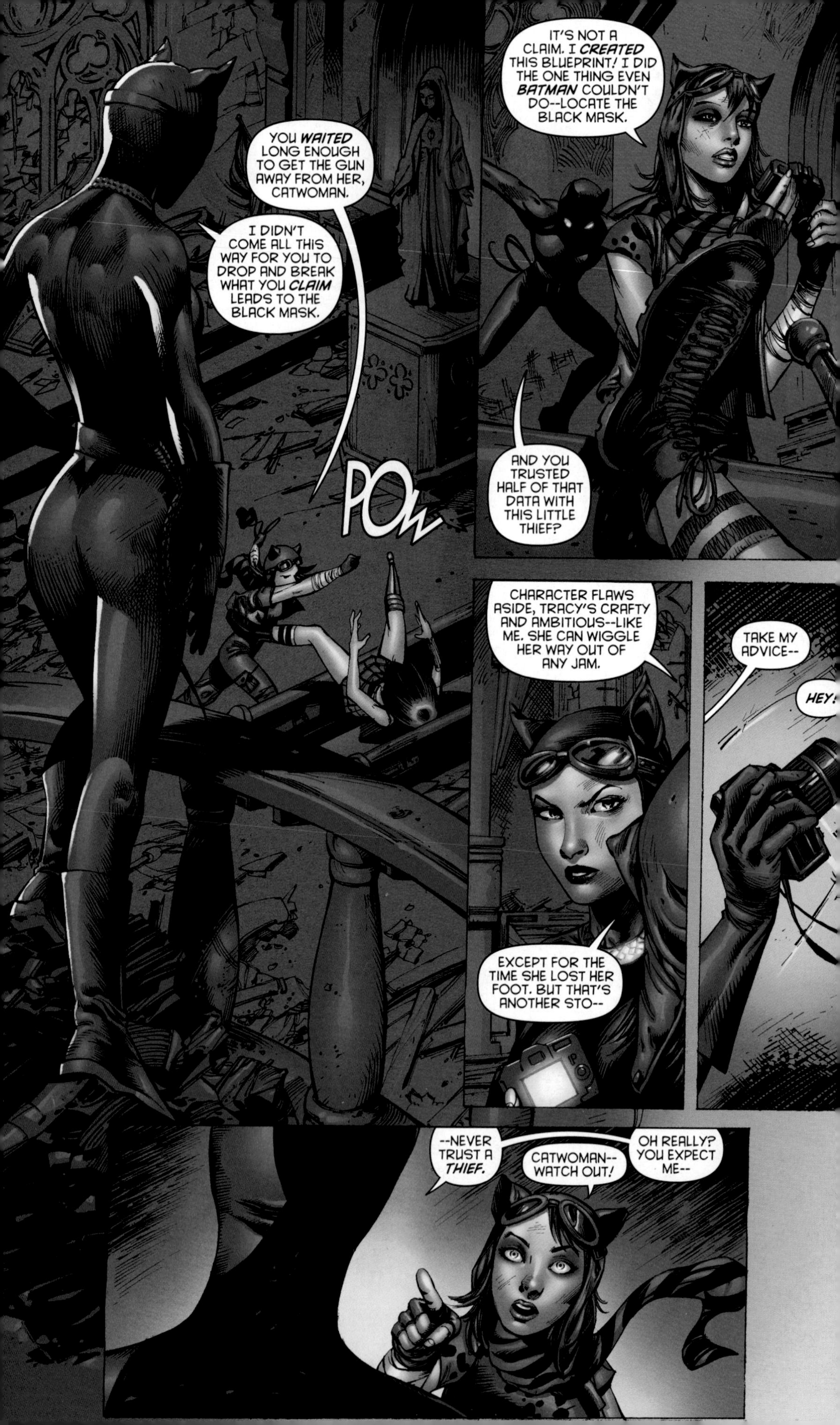
YOU WAITED LONG ENOUGH TO GET THE GUN AWAY FROM HER, CATWOMAN.
I DIDN'T COME ALL THIS WAY FOR YOU TO DROP AND BREAK WHAT YOU CLAIM LEADS TO THE BLACK MASK.
POW
IT'S NOT A CLAIM. I CREATED THIS BLUEPRINT! I DID THE ONE THING EVEN BATMAN COULDN'T DO--LOCATE THE BLACK MASK.
AND YOU TRUSTED HALF OF THAT DATA WITH THIS LITTLE THIEF?
CHARACTER FLAWS ASIDE, TRACY'S CRAFTY AND AMBITIOUS--LIKE ME. SHE CAN WIGGLE HER WAY OUT OF ANY JAM.
EXCEPT FOR THE TIME SHE LOST HER FOOT. BUT THAT'S ANOTHER STO--
TAKE MY ADVICE--
HEY!
--NEVER TRUST A THIEF.
CATWOMAN-- WATCH OUT!
OH REALLY? YOU EXPECT ME--

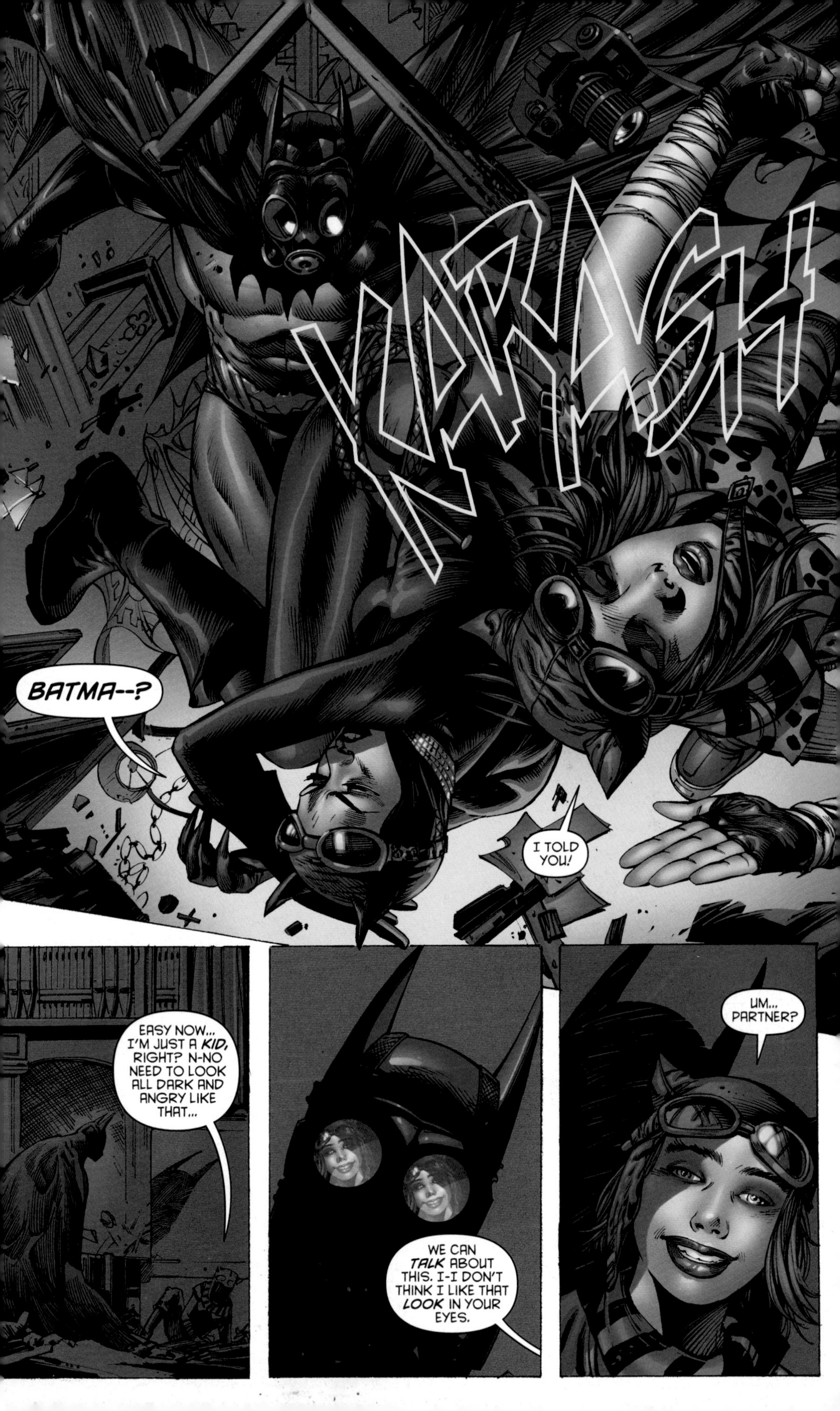
KRASH
BATMA--?
I TOLD YOU!
EASY NOW... I'M JUST A KID, RIGHT? N-NO NEED TO LOOK ALL DARK AND ANGRY LIKE THAT...
WE CAN TALK ABOUT THIS. I-I DON'T THINK I LIKE THAT LOOK IN YOUR EYES.
UM... PARTNER?

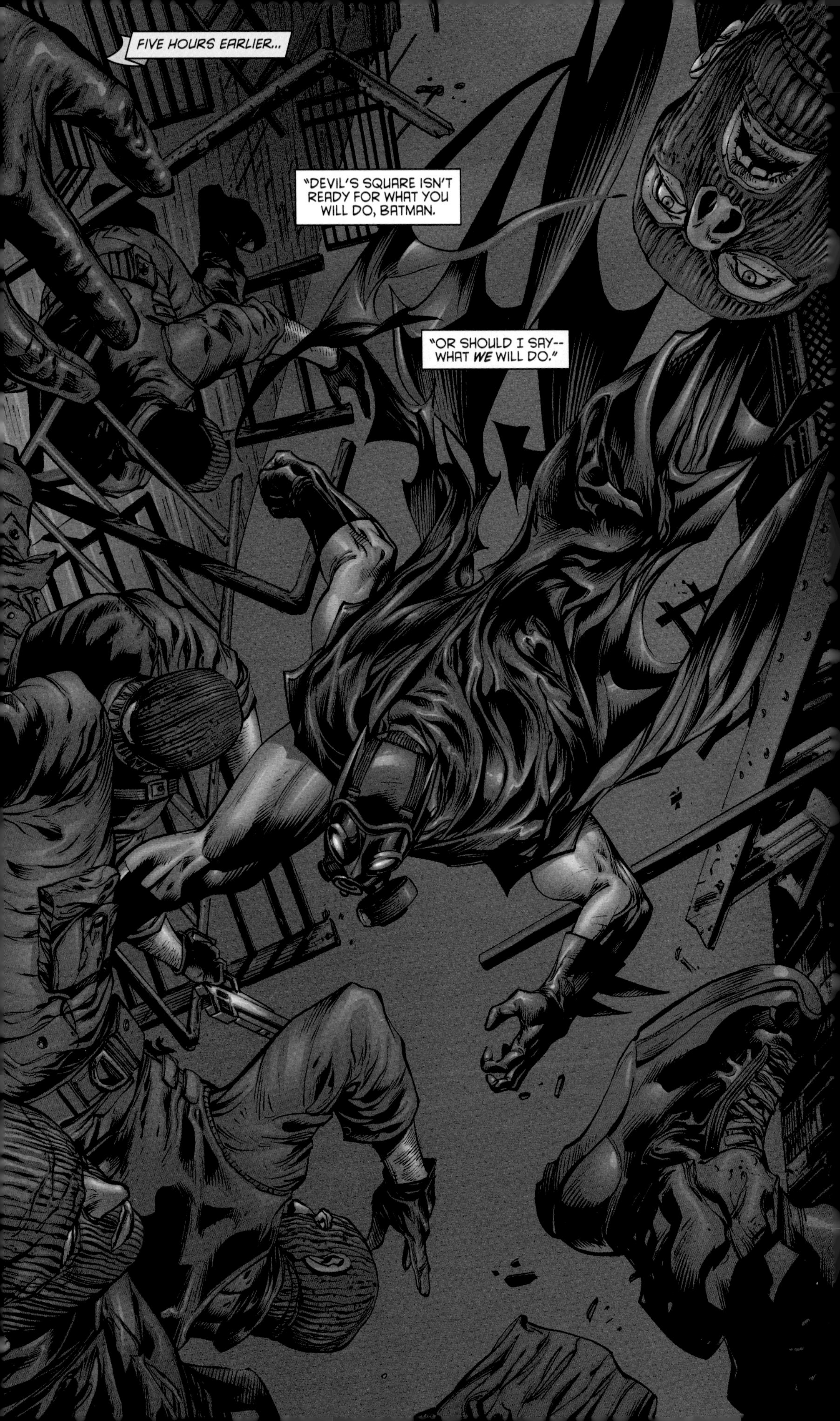
FIVE HOURS EARLIER...
"DEVIL'S SQUARE ISN'T READY FOR WHAT YOU WILL DO, BATMAN.
"OR SHOULD I SAY-- WHAT *WE* WILL DO."

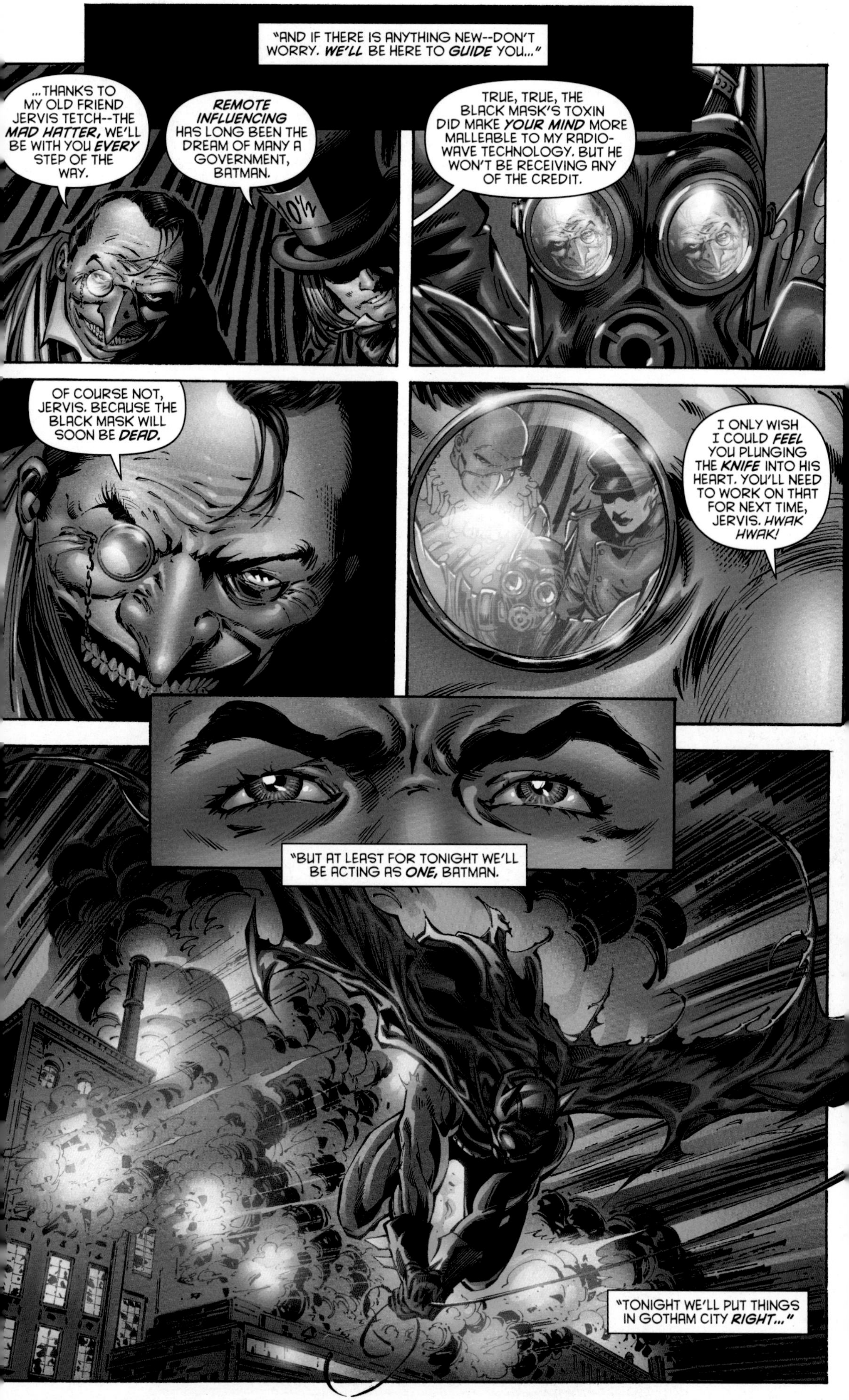
"AND IF THERE IS ANYTHING NEW--DON'T WORRY. *WE'LL* BE HERE TO *GUIDE* YOU..."
...THANKS TO MY OLD FRIEND JERVIS TETCH--THE *MAD HATTER,* WE'LL BE WITH YOU *EVERY* STEP OF THE WAY.
REMOTE INFLUENCING HAS LONG BEEN THE DREAM OF MANY A GOVERNMENT, BATMAN.
10/6
TRUE, TRUE, THE BLACK MASK'S TOXIN DID MAKE *YOUR MIND* MORE MALLEABLE TO MY RADIO-WAVE TECHNOLOGY. BUT HE WON'T BE RECEIVING ANY OF THE CREDIT.
OF COURSE NOT, JERVIS. BECAUSE THE BLACK MASK WILL SOON BE *DEAD.*
I ONLY WISH I COULD *FEEL* YOU PLUNGING THE *KNIFE* INTO HIS HEART. YOU'LL NEED TO WORK ON THAT FOR NEXT TIME, JERVIS. *HWAK HWAK!*
"BUT AT LEAST FOR TONIGHT WE'LL BE ACTING AS *ONE,* BATMAN.
"TONIGHT WE'LL PUT THINGS IN GOTHAM CITY *RIGHT...*"

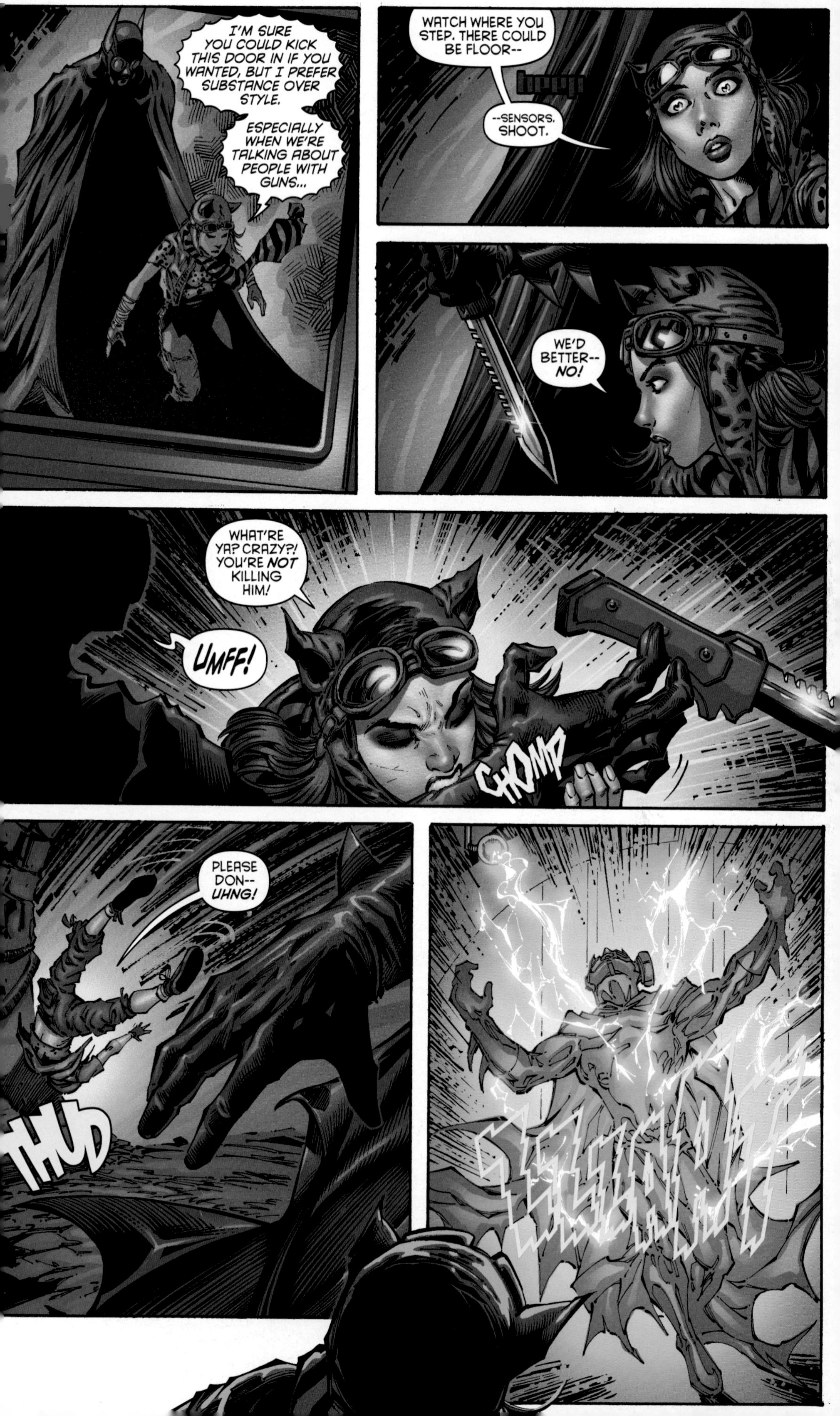
I'M SURE YOU COULD KICK THIS DOOR IN IF YOU WANTED, BUT I PREFER SUBSTANCE OVER STYLE.
ESPECIALLY WHEN WE'RE TALKING ABOUT PEOPLE WITH GUNS...
WATCH WHERE YOU STEP. THERE COULD BE FLOOR--
beep
--SENSORS. SHOOT.
WE'D BETTER-- NO!
WHAT'RE YA? CRAZY?! YOU'RE NOT KILLING HIM!
UMFF!
CHOMP
PLEASE DON-- UHNG!
THUD

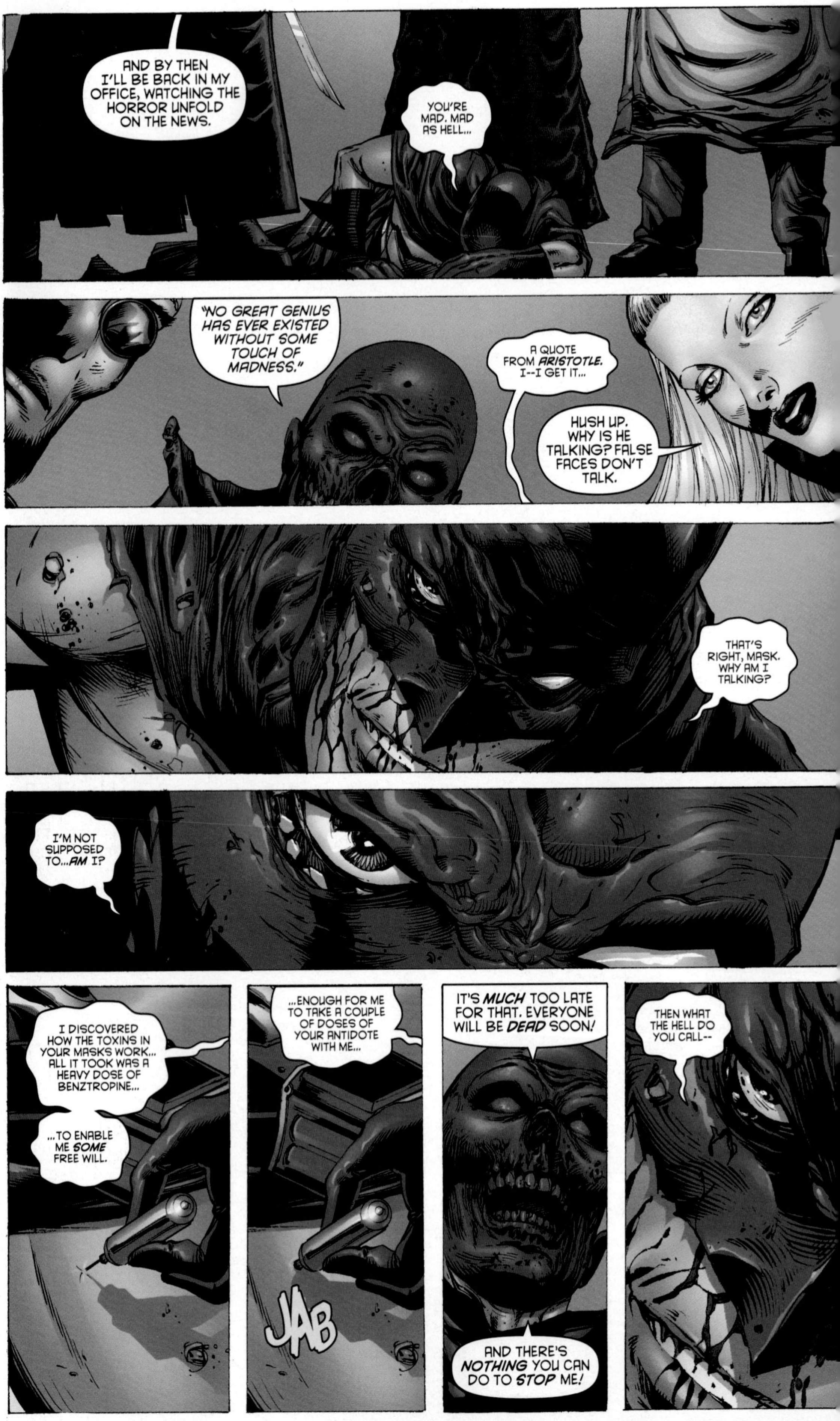
AND BY THEN I'LL BE BACK IN MY OFFICE, WATCHING THE HORROR UNFOLD ON THE NEWS.
YOU'RE MAD. MAD AS HELL...
"NO GREAT GENIUS HAS EVER EXISTED WITHOUT SOME TOUCH OF MADNESS."
A QUOTE FROM ARISTOTLE. I--I GET IT...
HUSH UP. WHY IS HE TALKING? FALSE FACES DON'T TALK.
THAT'S RIGHT, MASK. WHY AM I TALKING?
I'M NOT SUPPOSED TO...AM I?
I DISCOVERED HOW THE TOXINS IN YOUR MASKS WORK... ALL IT TOOK WAS A HEAVY DOSE OF BENZTROPINE...
...TO ENABLE ME SOME FREE WILL.
...ENOUGH FOR ME TO TAKE A COUPLE OF DOSES OF YOUR ANTIDOTE WITH ME...
JAB
IT'S MUCH TOO LATE FOR THAT. EVERYONE WILL BE DEAD SOON!
AND THERE'S NOTHING YOU CAN DO TO STOP ME!
THEN WHAT THE HELL DO YOU CALL--

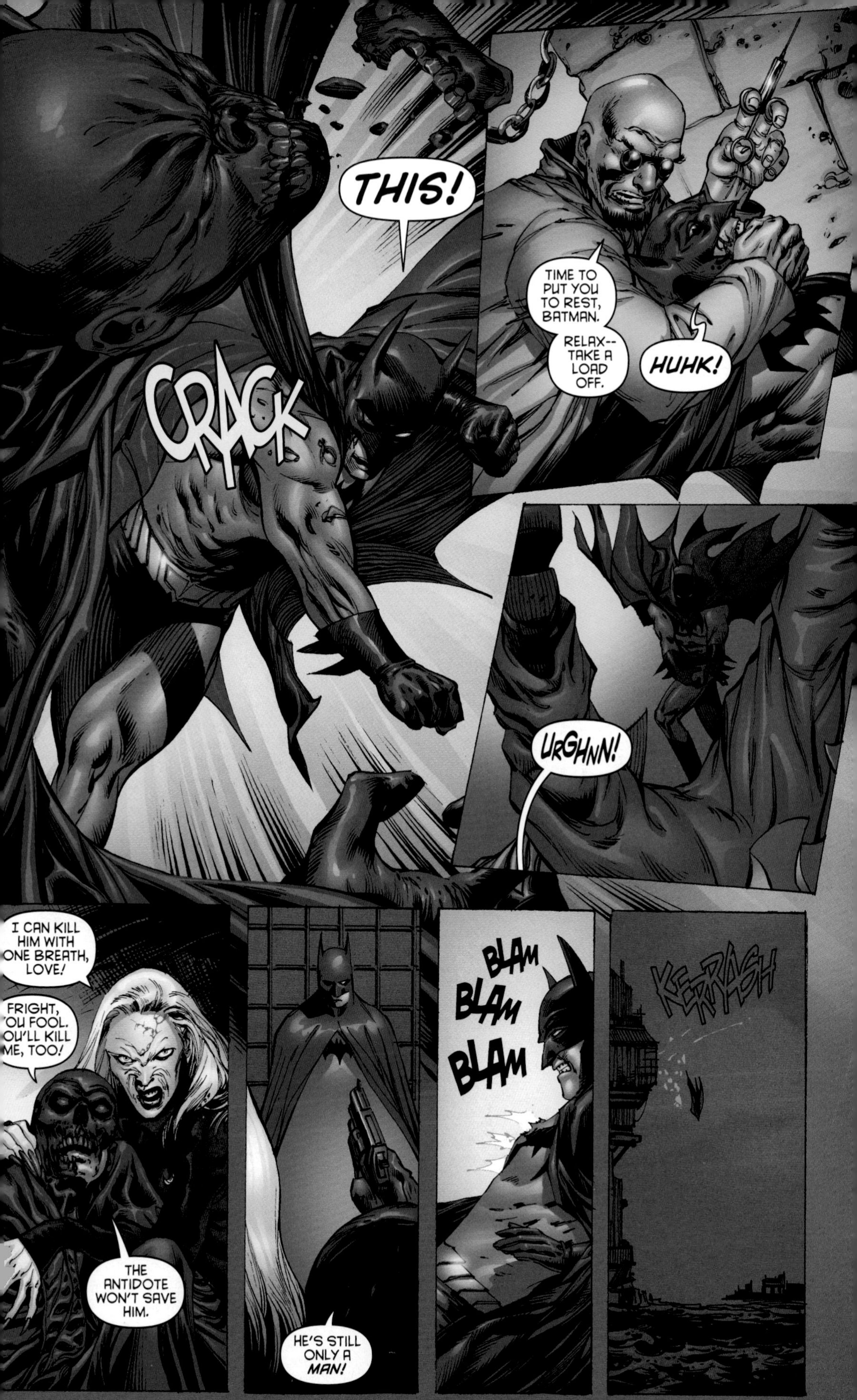
THIS!
CRACK
TIME TO PUT YOU TO REST, BATMAN.
RELAX-- TAKE A LOAD OFF.
HUHK!
URGHNN!
I CAN KILL HIM WITH ONE BREATH, LOVE!
FRIGHT, OU FOOL. OU'LL KILL ME, TOO!
THE ANTIDOTE WON'T SAVE HIM.
HE'S STILL ONLY A MAN!
BLAM
BLAM
BLAM
KERRASH

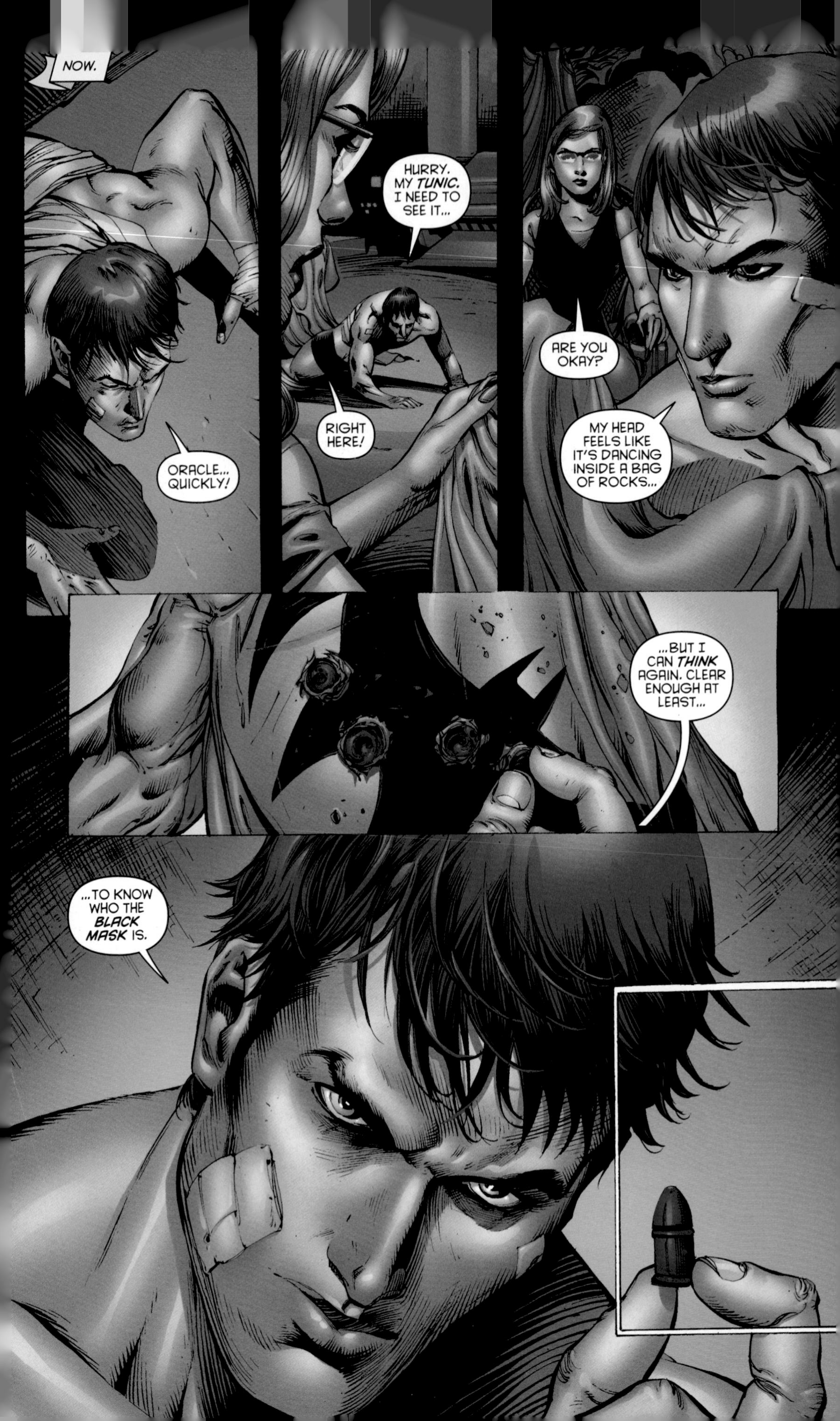

NOW.
ORACLE... QUICKLY!
HURRY. MY TUNIC. I NEED TO SEE IT...
RIGHT HERE!
ARE YOU OKAY?
MY HEAD FEELS LIKE IT'S DANCING INSIDE A BAG OF ROCKS...
...BUT I CAN THINK AGAIN. CLEAR ENOUGH AT LEAST...
...TO KNOW WHO THE BLACK MASK IS.

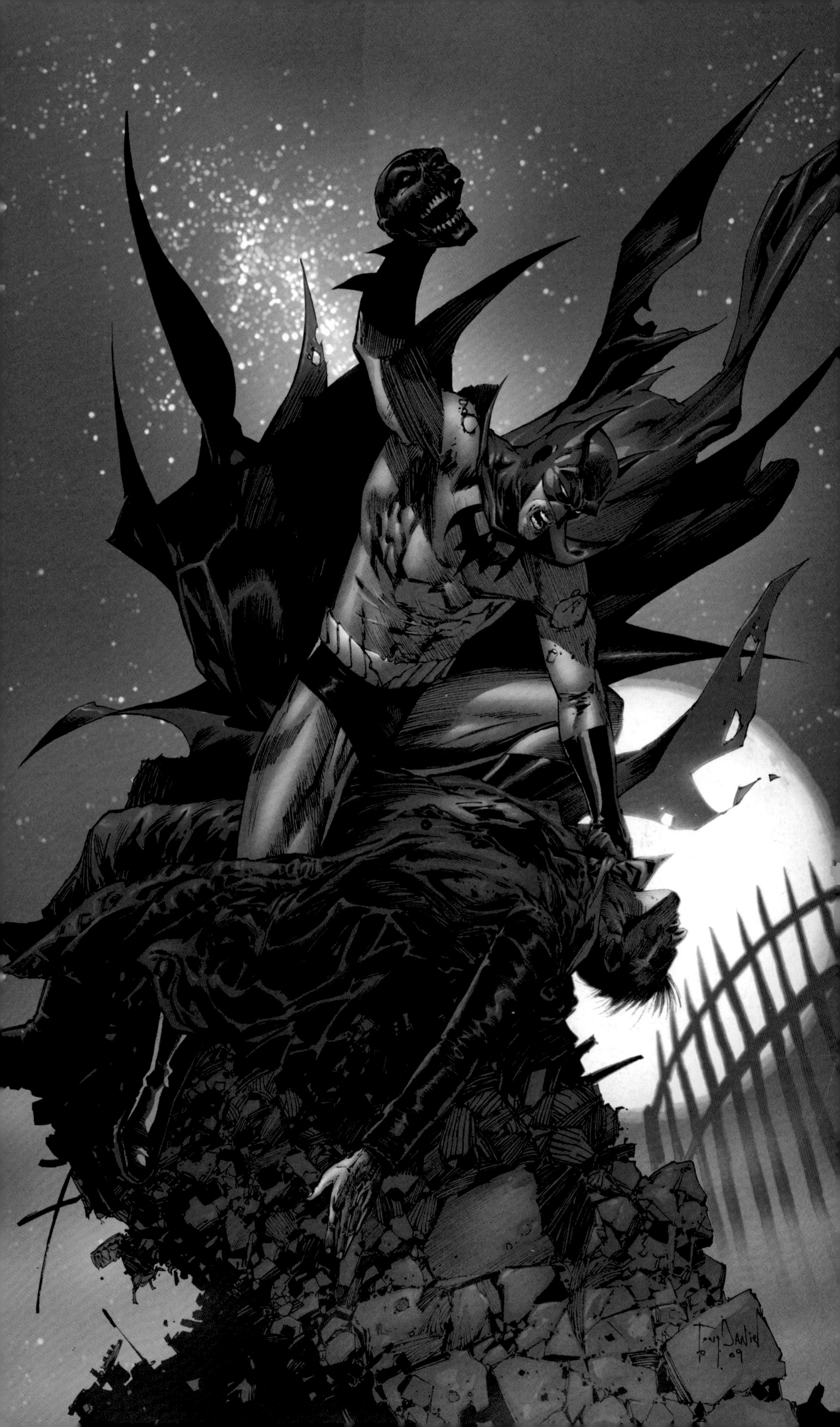

"I cannot be stopped. I always go on."

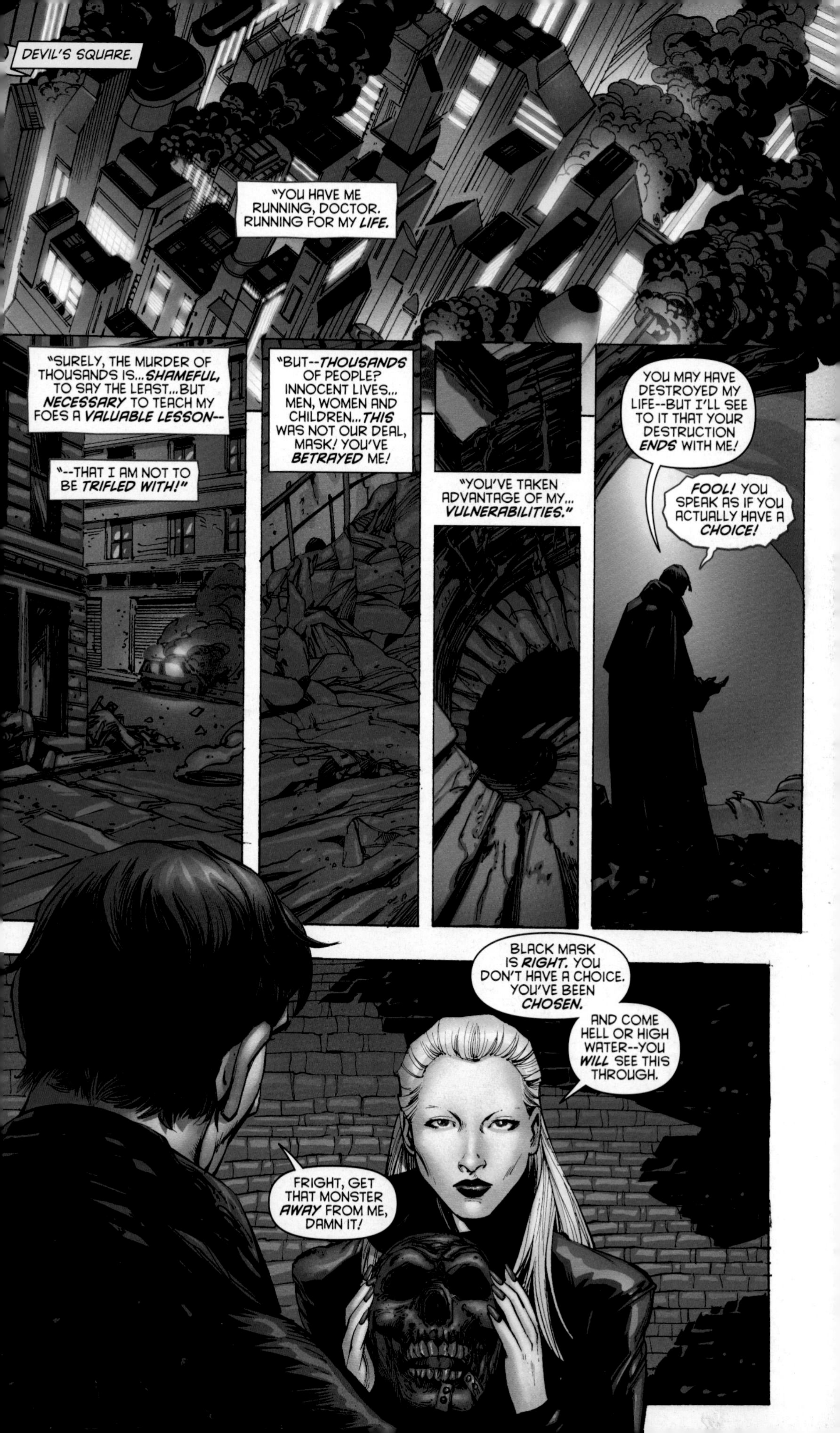

DEVIL'S SQUARE.
"YOU HAVE ME RUNNING, DOCTOR. RUNNING FOR MY LIFE.
"SURELY, THE MURDER OF THOUSANDS IS...SHAMEFUL, TO SAY THE LEAST...BUT NECESSARY TO TEACH MY FOES A VALUABLE LESSON--
"--THAT I AM NOT TO BE TRIFLED WITH!"
"BUT--THOUSANDS OF PEOPLE? INNOCENT LIVES... MEN, WOMEN AND CHILDREN...THIS WAS NOT OUR DEAL, MASK! YOU'VE BETRAYED ME!
"YOU'VE TAKEN ADVANTAGE OF MY... VULNERABILITIES."
YOU MAY HAVE DESTROYED MY LIFE--BUT I'LL SEE TO IT THAT YOUR DESTRUCTION ENDS WITH ME!
FOOL! YOU SPEAK AS IF YOU ACTUALLY HAVE A CHOICE!
FRIGHT, GET THAT MONSTER AWAY FROM ME, DAMN IT!
BLACK MASK IS RIGHT. YOU DON'T HAVE A CHOICE. YOU'VE BEEN CHOSEN.
AND COME HELL OR HIGH WATER--YOU WILL SEE THIS THROUGH.

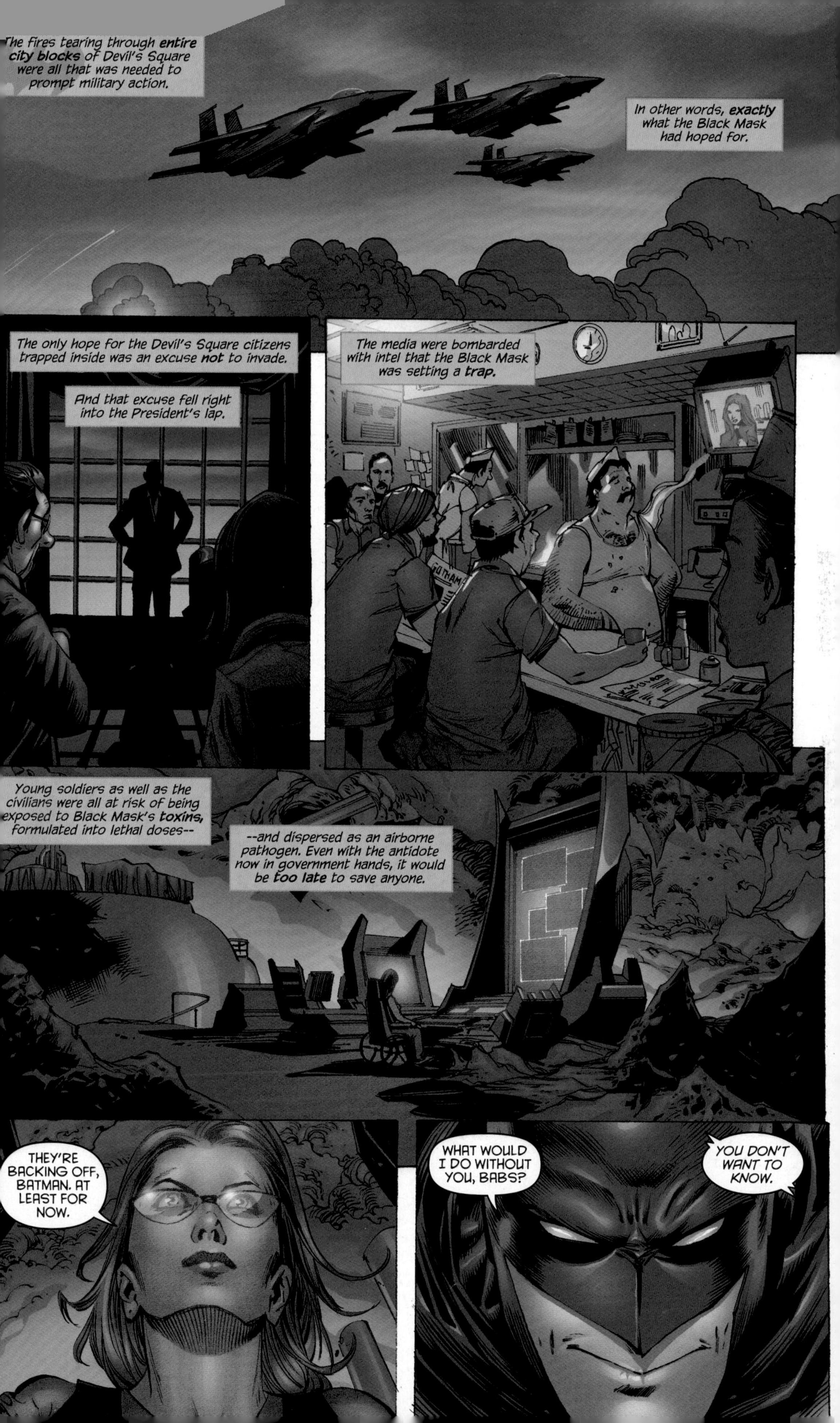

The fires tearing through entire city blocks of Devil's Square were all that was needed to prompt military action.
In other words, exactly what the Black Mask had hoped for.
The only hope for the Devil's Square citizens trapped inside was an excuse not to invade.
And that excuse fell right into the President's lap.
The media were bombarded with intel that the Black Mask was setting a trap.
Young soldiers as well as the civilians were all at risk of being exposed to Black Mask's toxins, formulated into lethal doses--
--and dispersed as an airborne pathogen. Even with the antidote now in government hands, it would be too late to save anyone.
THEY'RE BACKING OFF, BATMAN. AT LEAST FOR NOW.
WHAT WOULD I DO WITHOUT YOU, BABS?
YOU DON'T WANT TO KNOW.

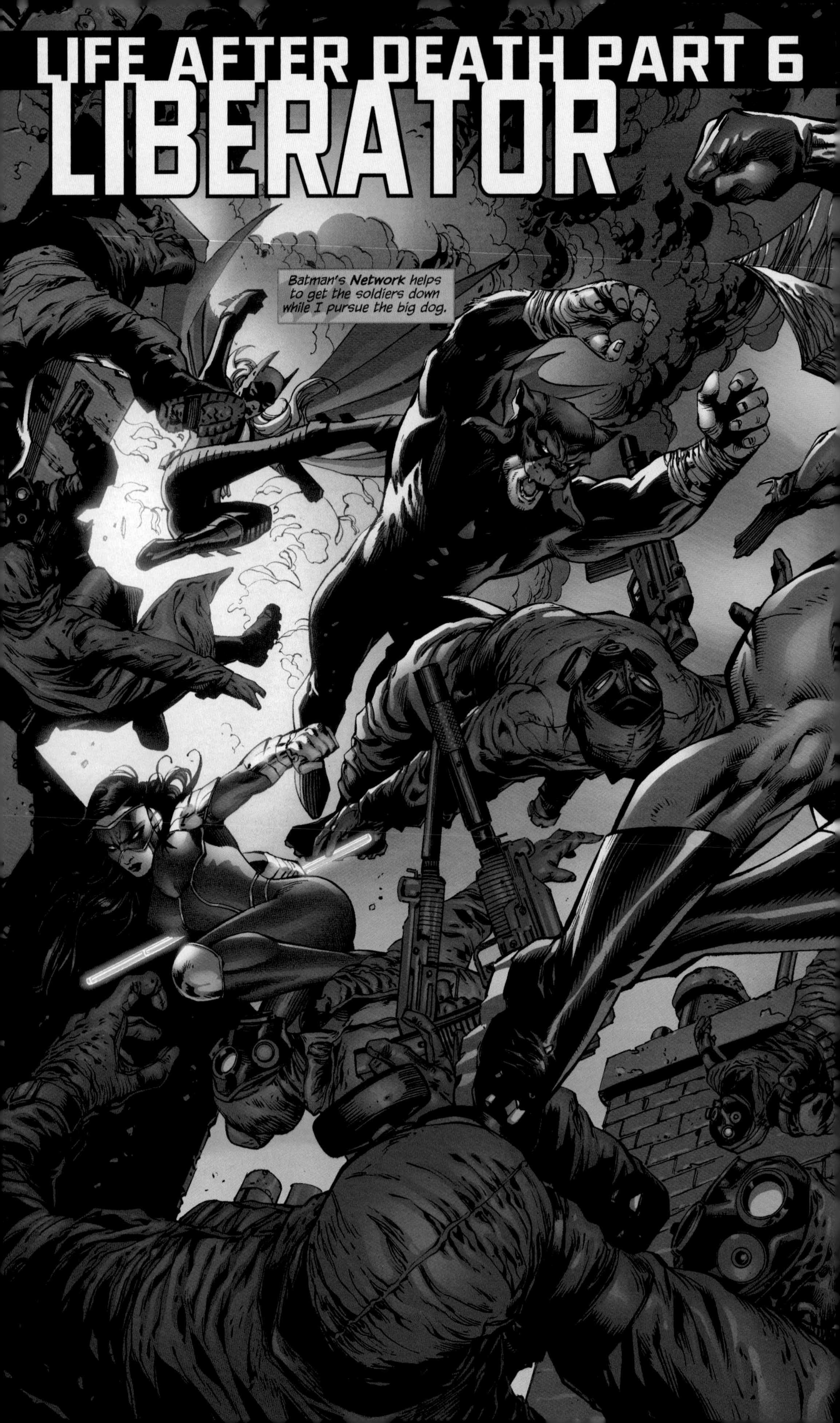
LIFE AFTER DEATH PART 6
LIBERATOR
Batman's **Network** helps to get the soldiers down while I pursue the big dog.

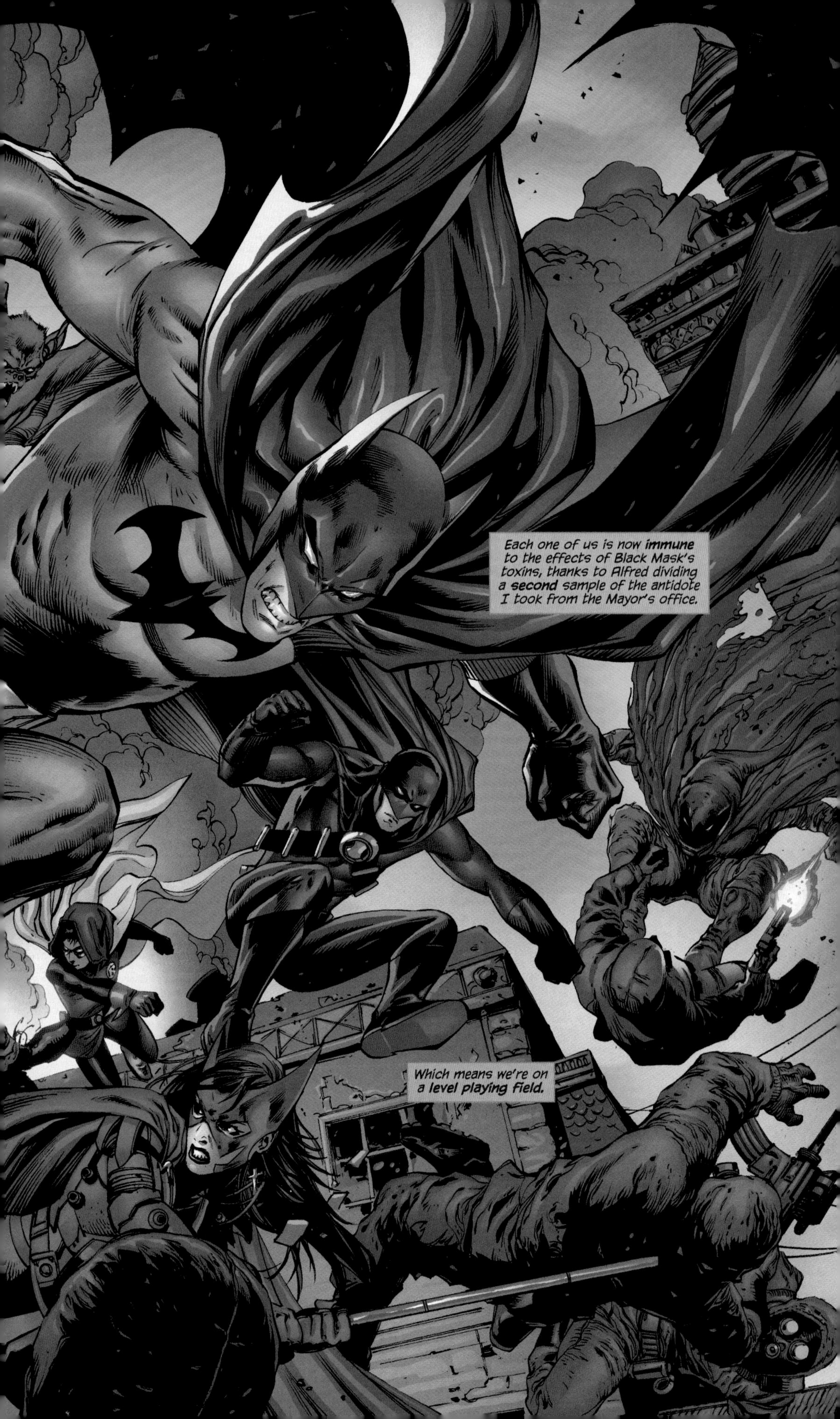

Each one of us is now **immune** to the effects of Black Mask's toxins, thanks to Alfred dividing a **second** sample of the antidote I took from the Mayor's office.
Which means we're on a **level playing field.**

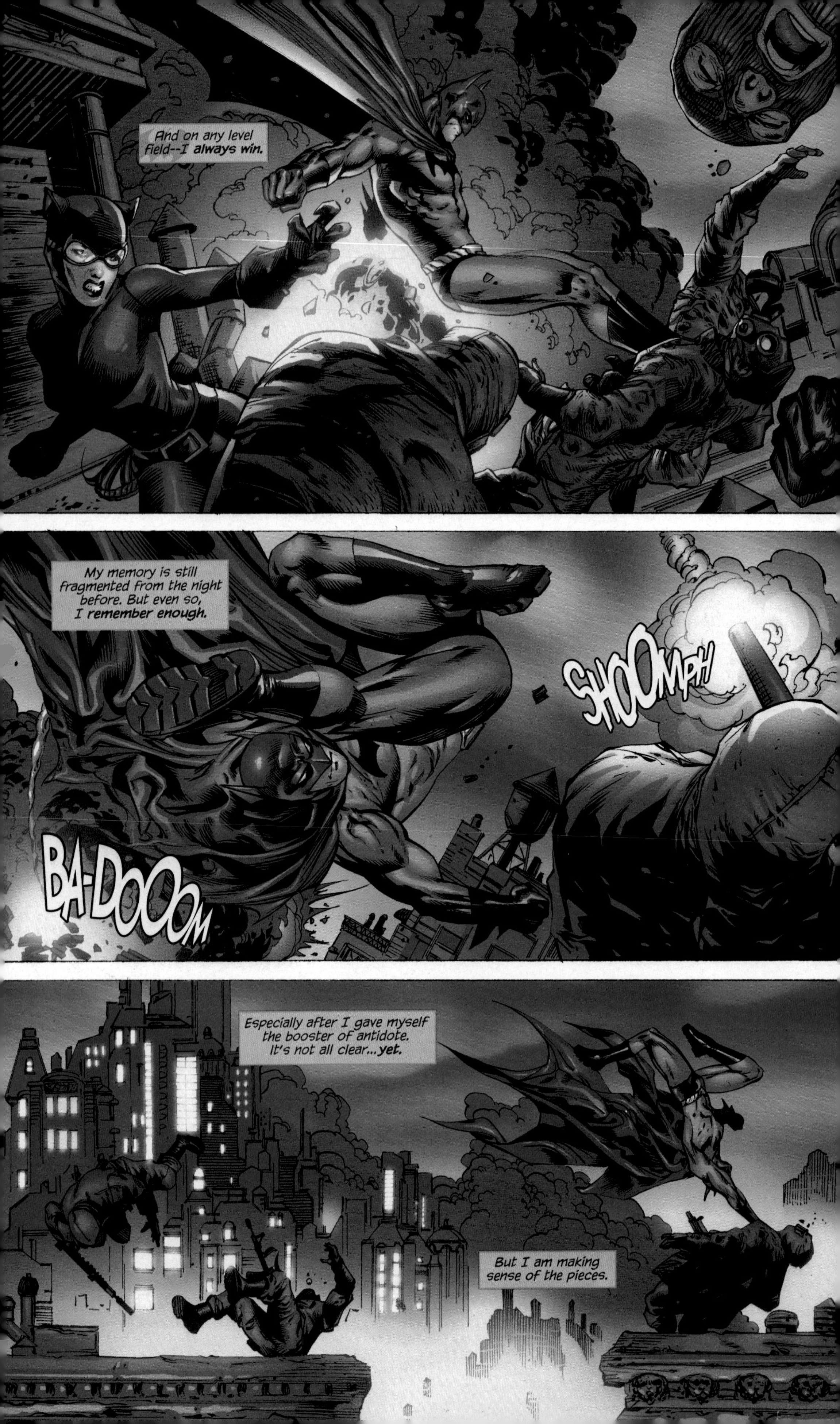
And on any level field--I always win.
My memory is still fragmented from the night before. But even so, I remember enough.
SHOOMPH
BA-DOOOM
Especially after I gave myself the booster of antidote. It's not all clear...yet.
But I am making sense of the pieces.

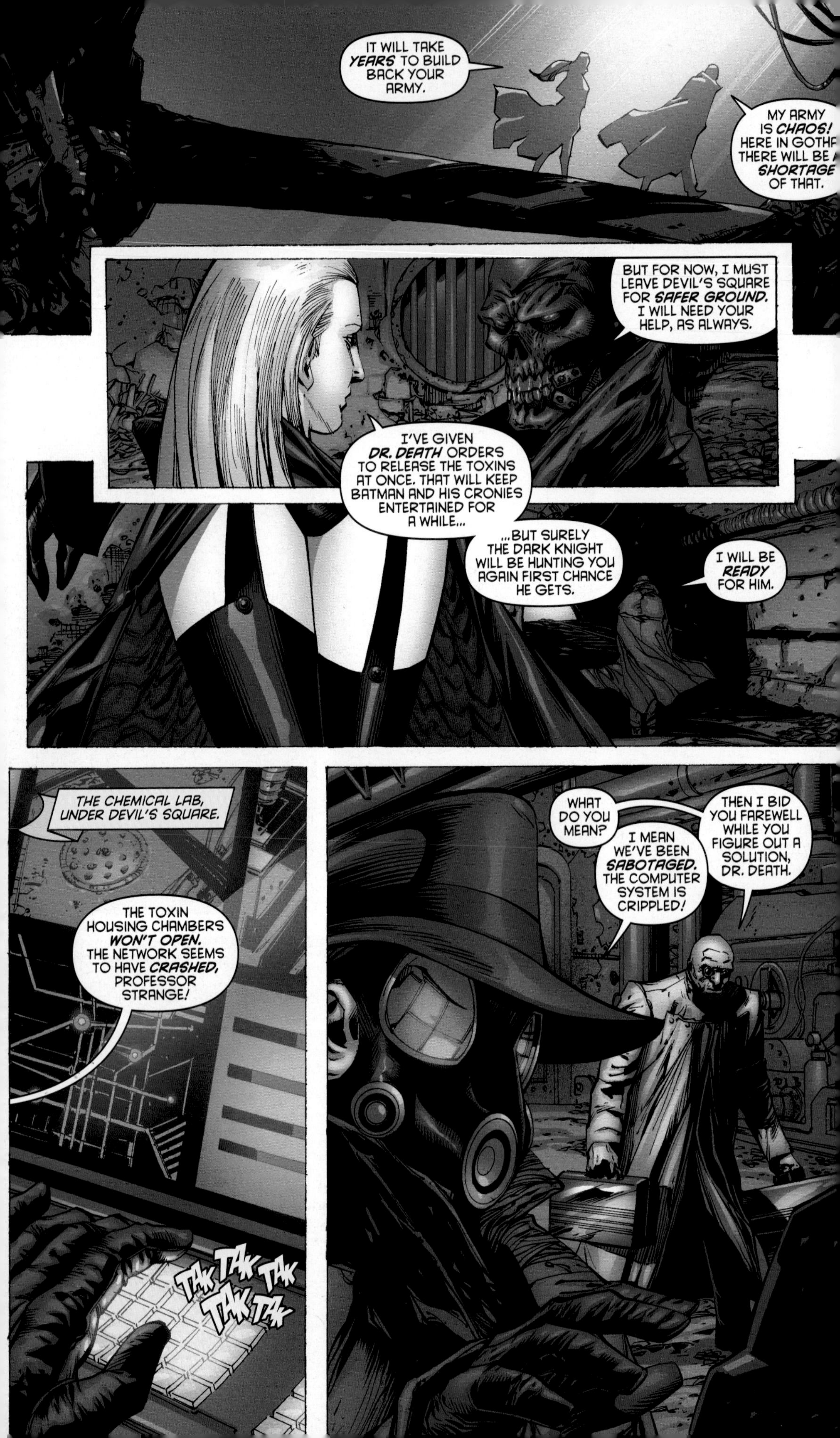
IT WILL TAKE *YEARS* TO BUILD BACK YOUR ARMY.
MY ARMY IS *CHAOS!* HERE IN GOTHA THERE WILL BE A *SHORTAGE* OF THAT.
BUT FOR NOW, I MUST LEAVE DEVIL'S SQUARE FOR *SAFER GROUND.* I WILL NEED YOUR HELP, AS ALWAYS.
I'VE GIVEN *DR. DEATH* ORDERS TO RELEASE THE TOXINS AT ONCE. THAT WILL KEEP BATMAN AND HIS CRONIES ENTERTAINED FOR A WHILE...
...BUT SURELY THE DARK KNIGHT WILL BE HUNTING YOU AGAIN FIRST CHANCE HE GETS.
I WILL BE *READY* FOR HIM.
THE CHEMICAL LAB, UNDER DEVIL'S SQUARE.
THE TOXIN HOUSING CHAMBERS *WON'T OPEN.* THE NETWORK SEEMS TO HAVE *CRASHED,* PROFESSOR STRANGE!
TAK TAK TAK TAK TAK
WHAT DO YOU MEAN?
I MEAN WE'VE BEEN *SABOTAGED.* THE COMPUTER SYSTEM IS CRIPPLED!
THEN I BID YOU FAREWELL WHILE YOU FIGURE OUT A SOLUTION, DR. DEATH.

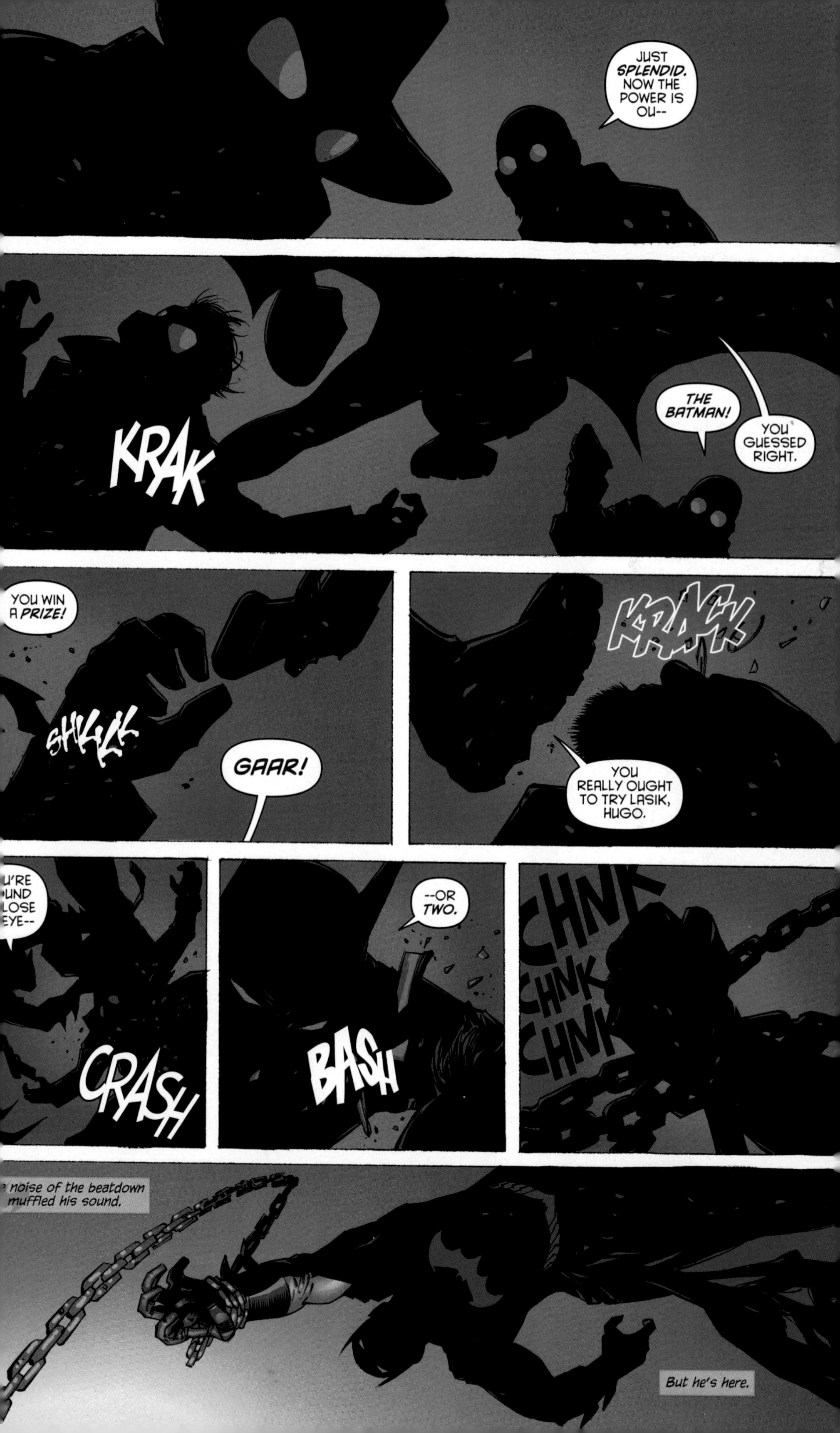
JUST SPLENDID. NOW THE POWER IS OU--
KRAK
THE BATMAN!
YOU GUESSED RIGHT.
YOU WIN A PRIZE!
SHKLK
GAAR!
KRACK
YOU REALLY OUGHT TO TRY LASIK, HUGO.
U'RE UND LOSE EYE--
CRASH
--OR TWO.
BASH
CHNK CHNK CHNK
noise of the beatdown muffled his sound.
But he's here.

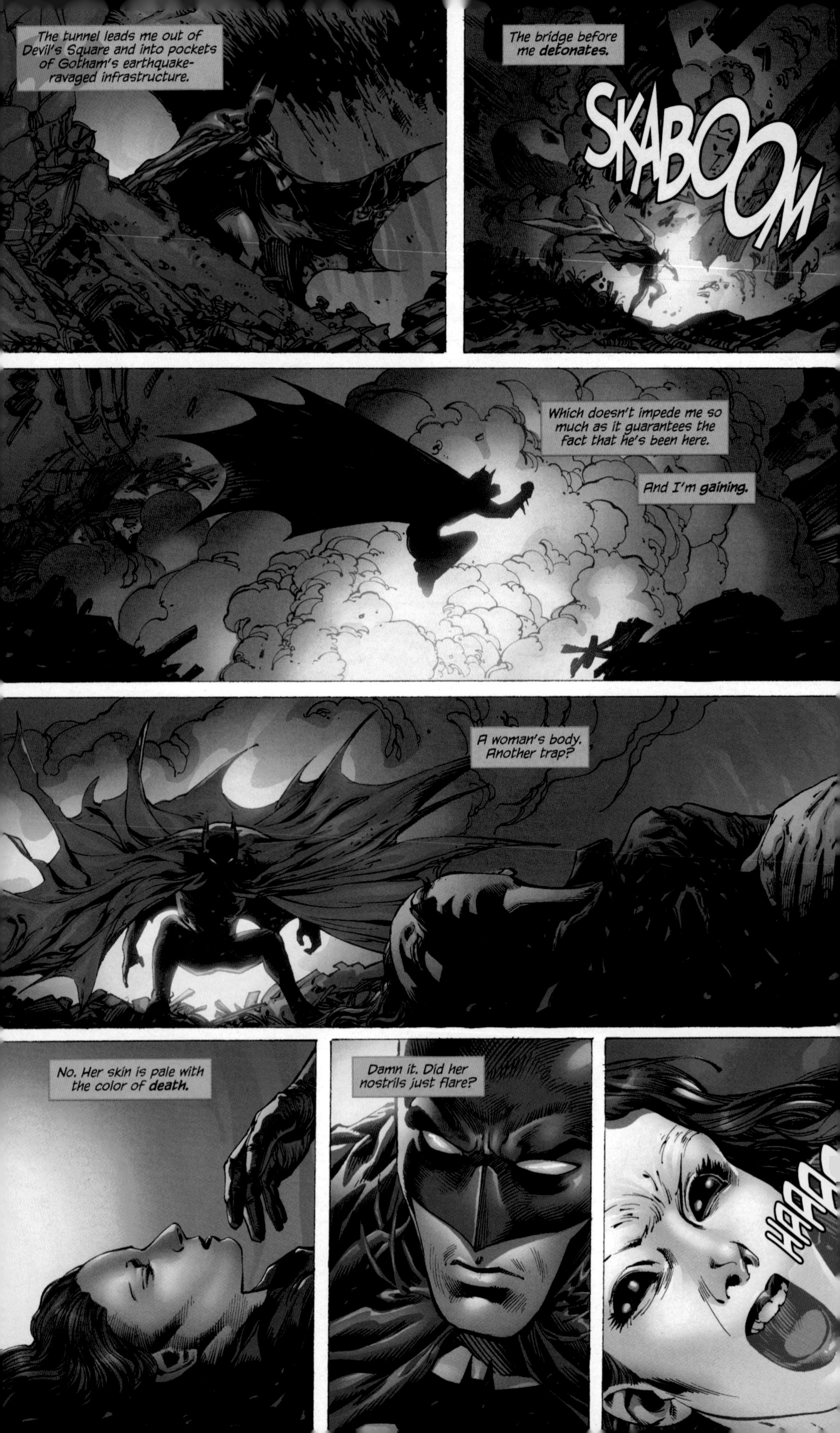

The tunnel leads me out of Devil's Square and into pockets of Gotham's earthquake-ravaged infrastructure.
The bridge before me **detonates.**
SKABOOM
Which doesn't impede me so much as it guarantees the fact that he's been here.
And I'm **gaining.**
A woman's body. Another trap?
No. Her skin is pale with the color of **death.**
Damn it. Did her nostrils just flare?

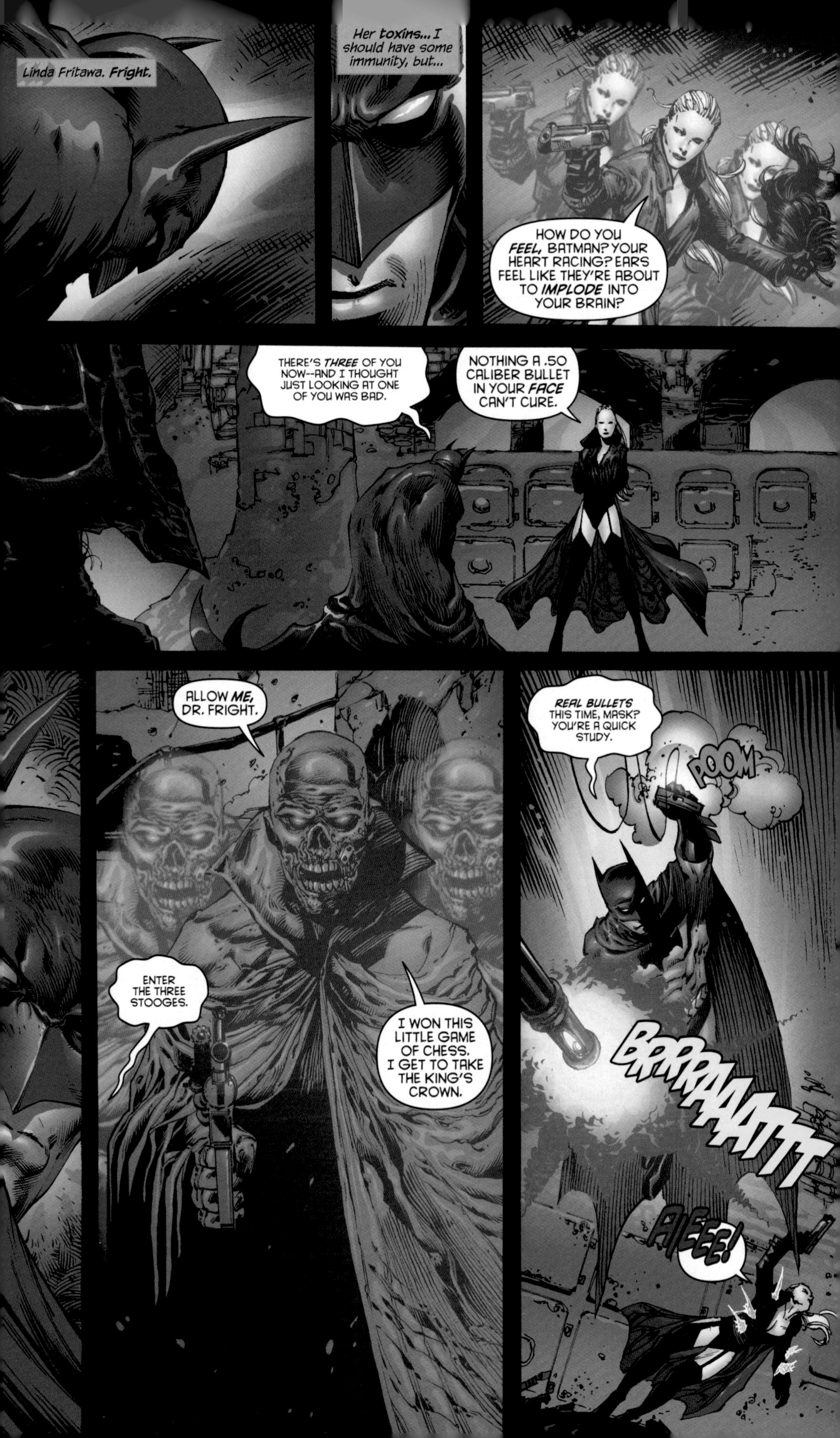
Linda Fritawa. Fright.
Her toxins... I should have some immunity, but...
HOW DO YOU FEEL, BATMAN? YOUR HEART RACING? EARS FEEL LIKE THEY'RE ABOUT TO IMPLODE INTO YOUR BRAIN?
THERE'S THREE OF YOU NOW--AND I THOUGHT JUST LOOKING AT ONE OF YOU WAS BAD.
NOTHING A .50 CALIBER BULLET IN YOUR FACE CAN'T CURE.
ALLOW ME, DR. FRIGHT.
ENTER THE THREE STOOGES.
I WON THIS LITTLE GAME OF CHESS. I GET TO TAKE THE KING'S CROWN.
REAL BULLETS THIS TIME, MASK? YOU'RE A QUICK STUDY.
POOM
BRRRAAATTT
AIEEE!

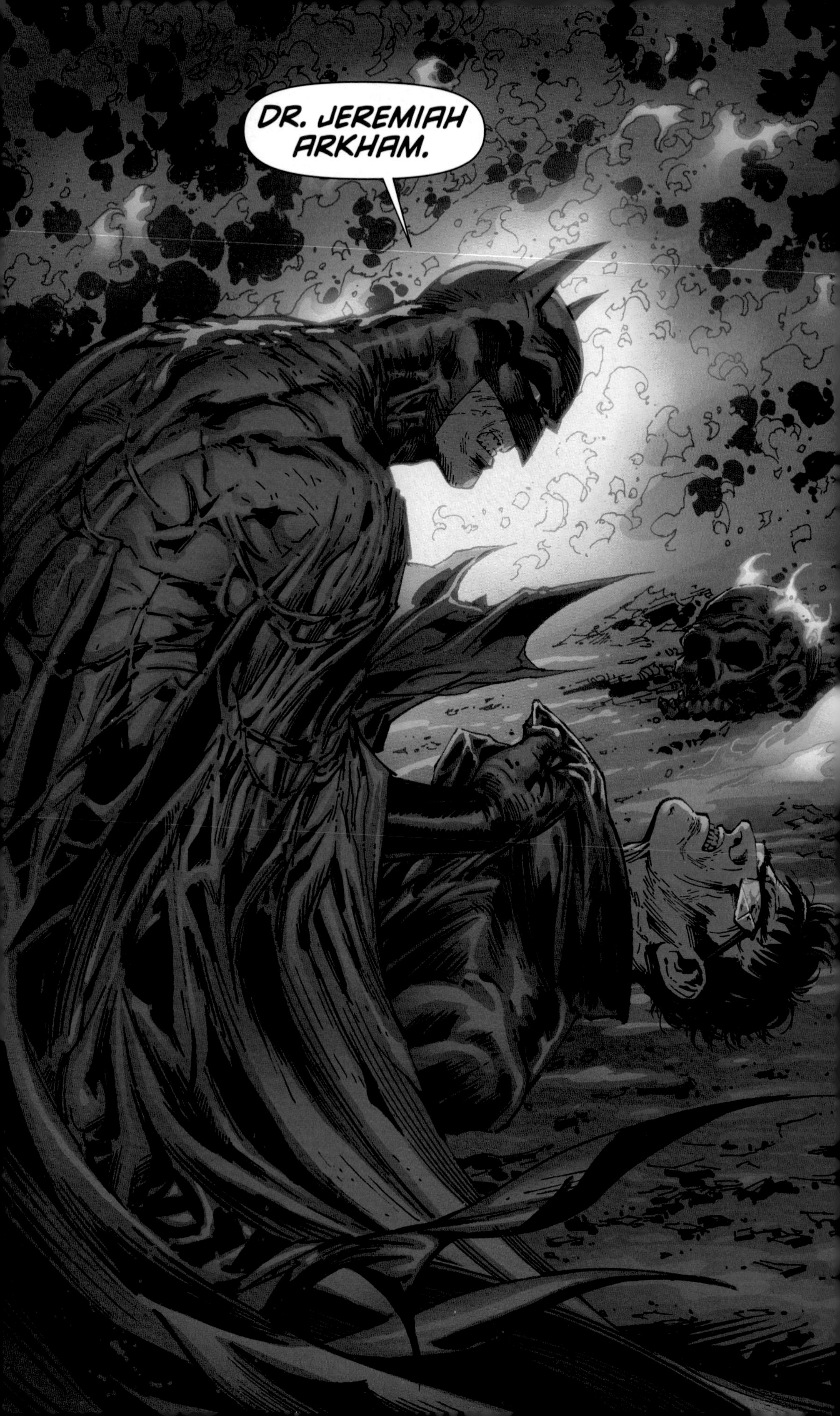
DR. JEREMIAH ARKHAM.

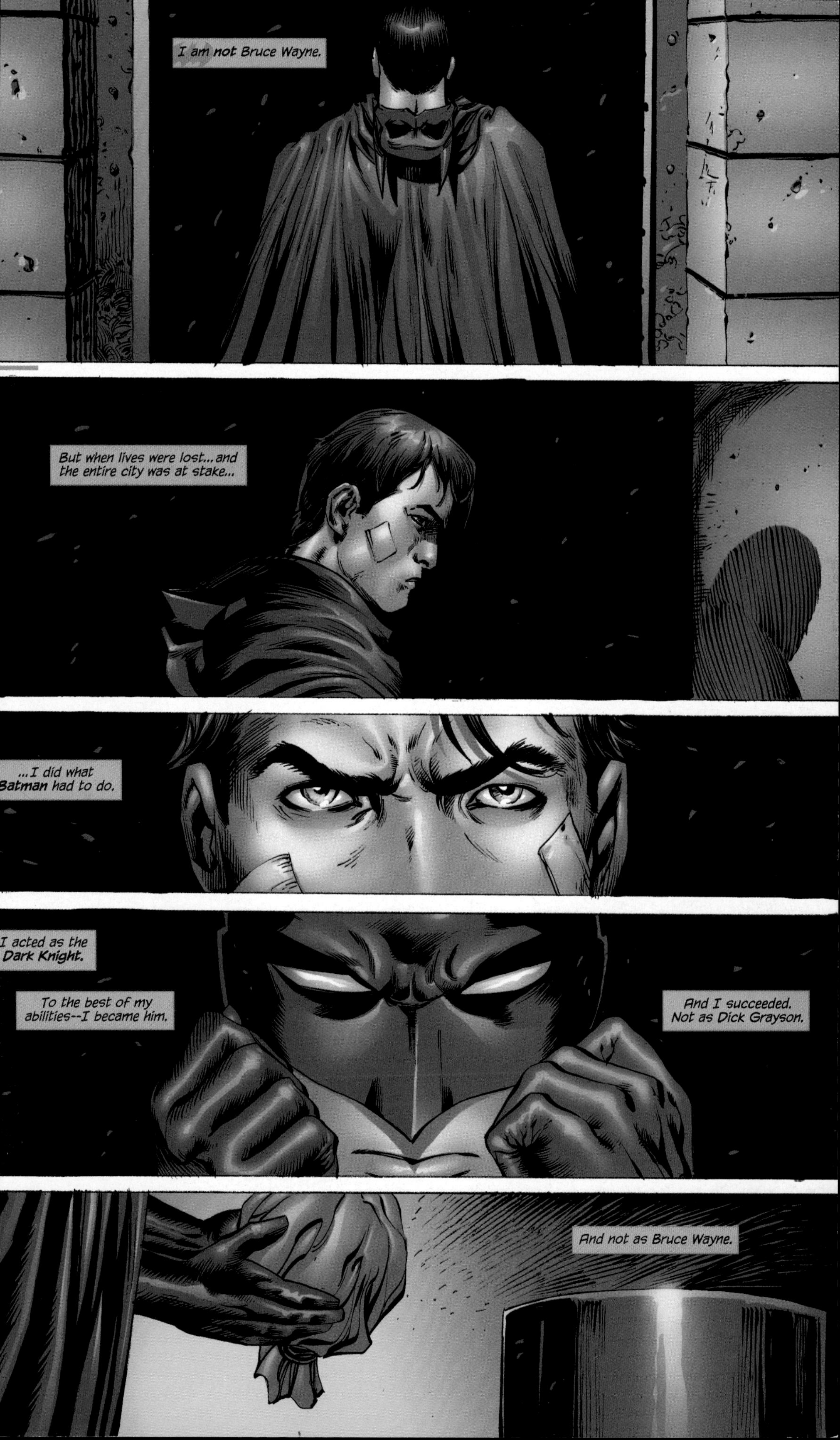
I am not Bruce Wayne.
But when lives were lost...and the entire city was at stake...
...I did what Batman had to do.
I acted as the Dark Knight.
To the best of my abilities--I became him.
And I succeeded. Not as Dick Grayson.
And not as Bruce Wayne.

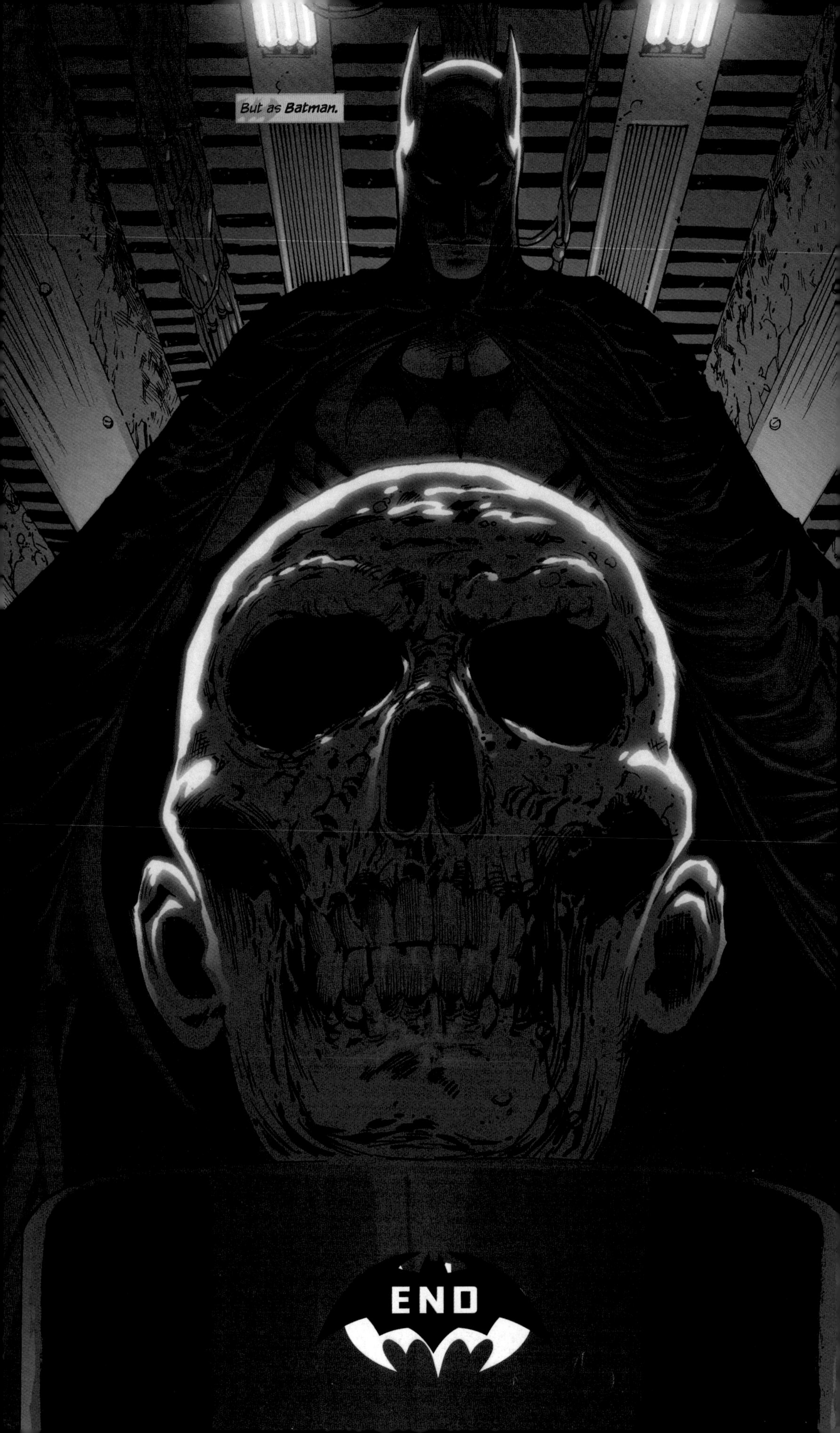
But as Batman.
END

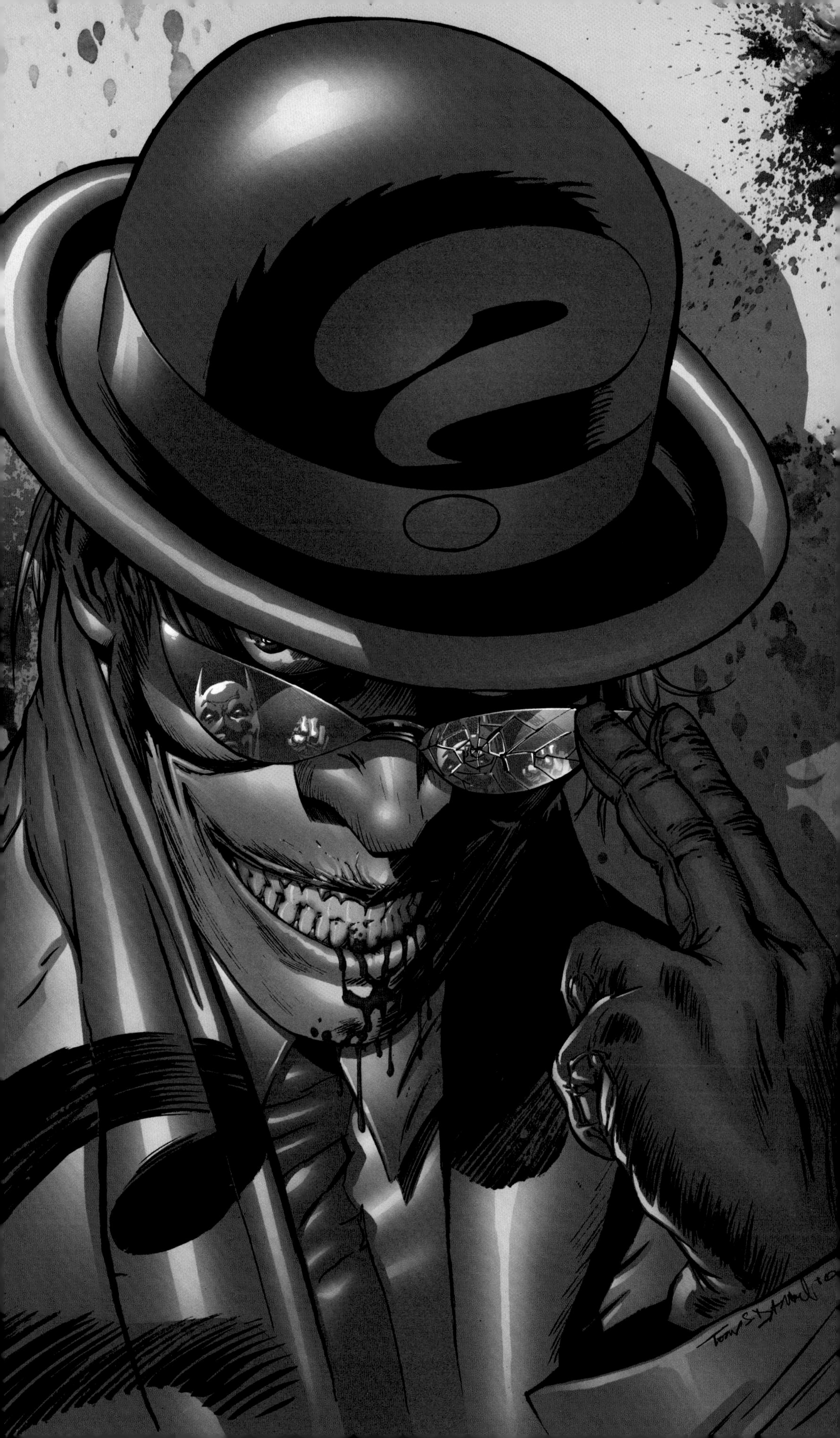

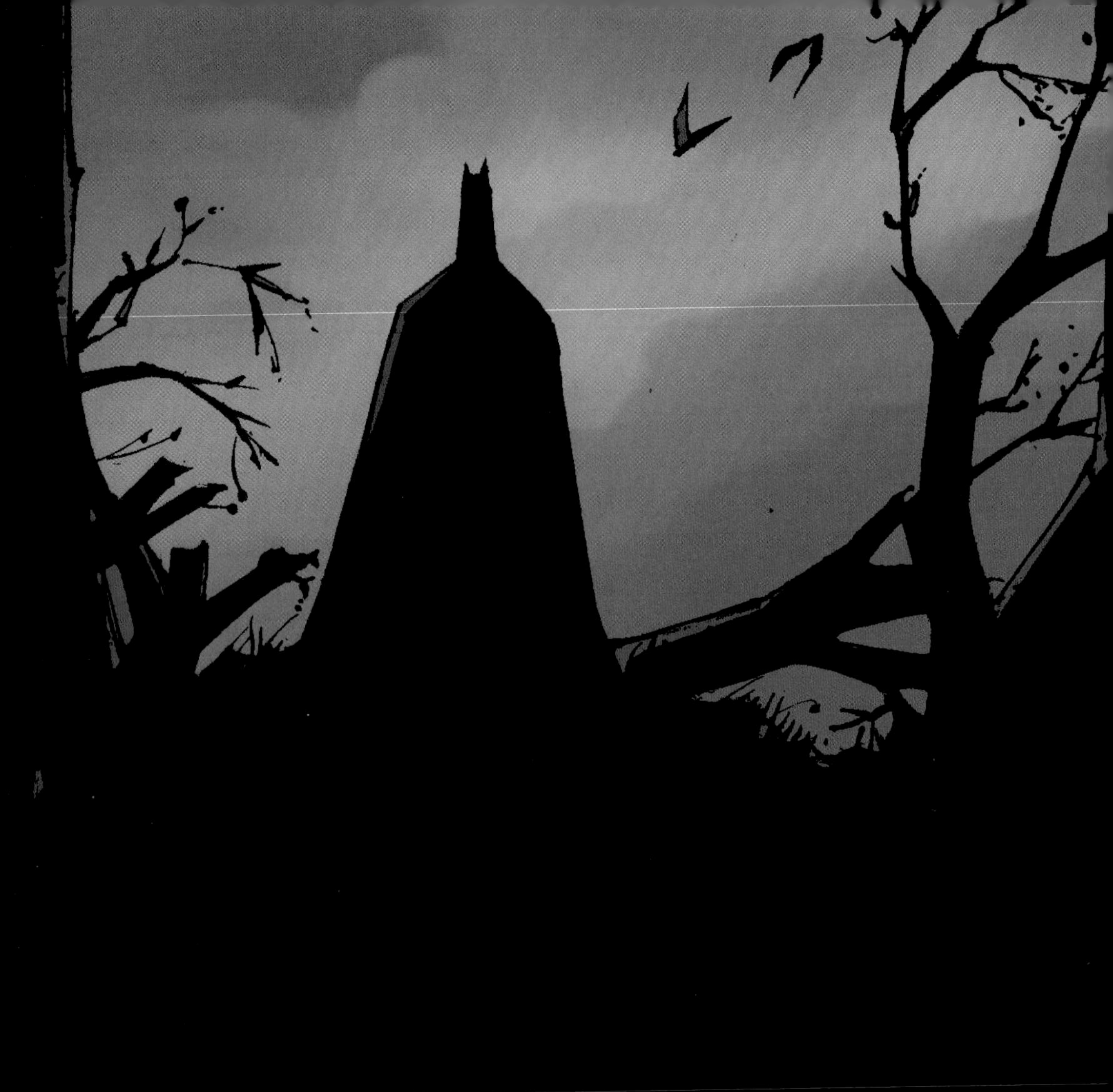

"He's sick in the head. Especially if he thinks he can get away from me."

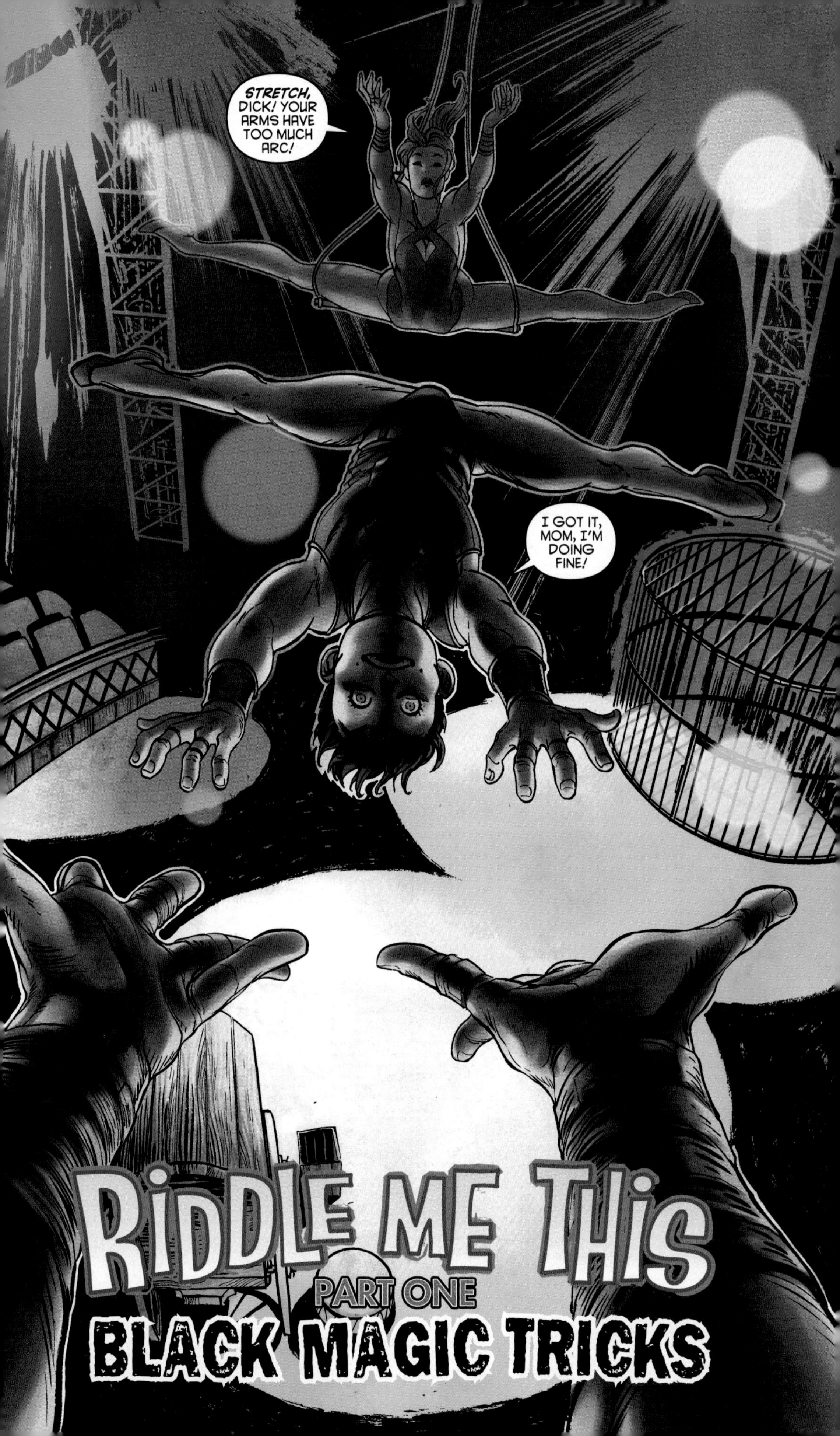
STRETCH, DICK! YOUR ARMS HAVE TOO MUCH ARC!
I GOT IT, MOM, I'M DOING FINE!
RIDDLE ME THIS
PART ONE
BLACK MAGIC TRICKS

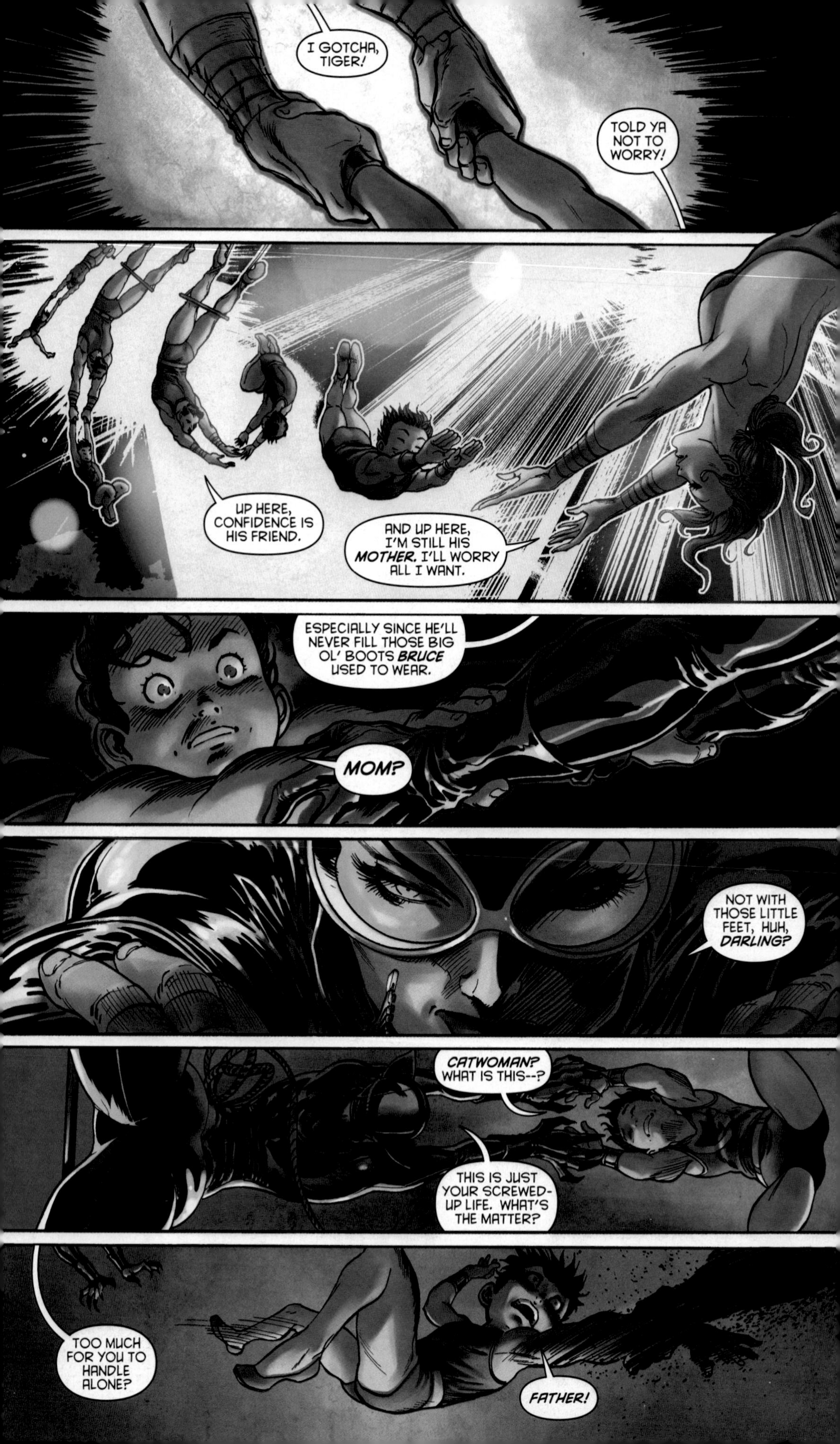
I GOTCHA, TIGER!
TOLD YA NOT TO WORRY!
UP HERE, CONFIDENCE IS HIS FRIEND.
AND UP HERE, I'M STILL HIS MOTHER. I'LL WORRY ALL I WANT.
ESPECIALLY SINCE HE'LL NEVER FILL THOSE BIG OL' BOOTS BRUCE USED TO WEAR.
MOM?
NOT WITH THOSE LITTLE FEET, HUH, DARLING?
CATWOMAN? WHAT IS THIS--?
THIS IS JUST YOUR SCREWED-UP LIFE. WHAT'S THE MATTER?
TOO MUCH FOR YOU TO HANDLE ALONE?
FATHER!

JASON?

YOU'RE TRYING TO *BE HIM*, HUH, KID? TRYING TO BE TOUGHER THAN YOU REALLY ARE. TRYING TO PROVE YOU'RE AS GOOD, OR MAYBE *BETTER?*

LOOK WHAT GOOD IT DID *ME!* HAHAHA!

GET AWAY FROM ME!

DON'T LISTEN TO HIM, DICK. HE'S ALWAYS BEEN JEALOUS OF YOU.

ORACLE... HELP ME GET DOWN!

I THINK YOUR BATMAN IS PRETTY GOOD. IT'S THE DICK GRAYSON PART THAT'S IRKING ME THESE DAYS.

YOU'VE *CHANGED.* AND I DON'T KNOW IF WE CAN BE FRIENDS ANYMORE.

WAIT! I DIDN'T MEAN TO HURT YOU! ORACLE!

BRUCE?! CATCH ME!

BRUUUUUUCE!

NOOOOOO!

HUH-HUH-
HUH-HUH-
HUH--

ANOTHER NIGHT TERROR, MASTER RICHARD?

-GRN- STUPID TOXINS. HOW LONG BEFORE THEY'RE COMPLETELY OUT OF MY SYSTEM?

WITH *HUGO STRANGE'S* CONCOCTIONS, THERE'S NO WAY TO BE CERTAIN.

BUT YOU'VE IMPROVED TENFOLD FROM THURSDAY EVENING, WHICH I THINK IS ENCOURAGING.

AND I'VE BROUGHT YOU A DETOX TEA TO HELP CLEANSE YOUR SYSTEM.

THANKS, ALFRED.

BUT SIR? YOU MAY WISH TO TAKE YOUR TEA DOWNSTAIRS AFTER YOU GET DRESSED.

GREAT. SOME WONDERFUL NEWS WAITING FOR ME DOWN THERE, I BET. WHAT'S UP?

COMMISSIONER GORDON LEFT AN URGENT MESSAGE CONCERNING A HOMICIDE IN CRIME ALLEY. HE MENTIONED A PUZZLING LINK TO *MR. ZSASZ...*

OH

TINK

WONDERFUL.

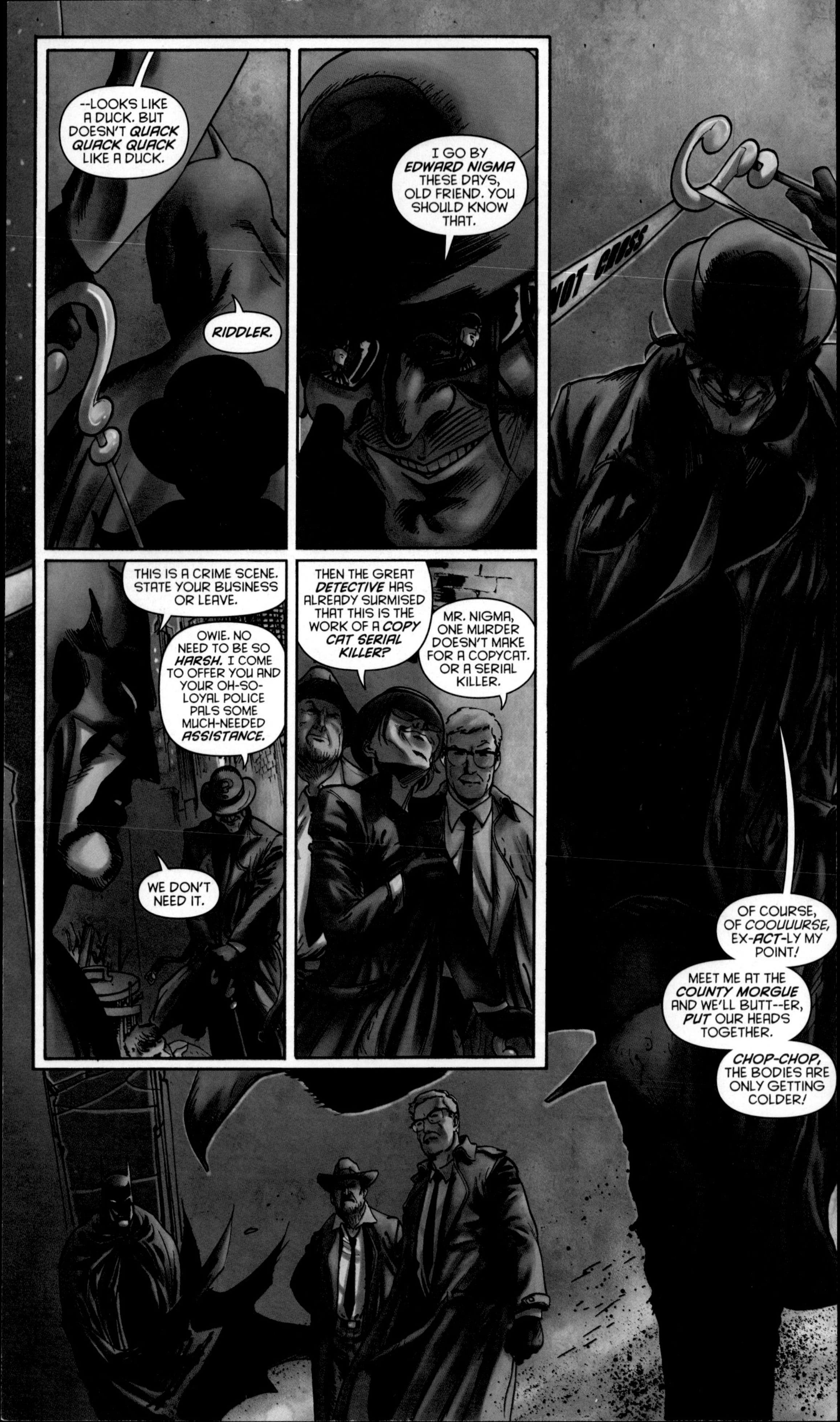
--LOOKS LIKE A DUCK. BUT DOESN'T QUACK QUACK QUACK LIKE A DUCK.
RIDDLER.
I GO BY EDWARD NIGMA THESE DAYS, OLD FRIEND. YOU SHOULD KNOW THAT.
THIS IS A CRIME SCENE. STATE YOUR BUSINESS OR LEAVE.
OWIE. NO NEED TO BE SO HARSH. I COME TO OFFER YOU AND YOUR OH-SO-LOYAL POLICE PALS SOME MUCH-NEEDED ASSISTANCE.
WE DON'T NEED IT.
THEN THE GREAT DETECTIVE HAS ALREADY SURMISED THAT THIS IS THE WORK OF A COPY CAT SERIAL KILLER?
MR. NIGMA, ONE MURDER DOESN'T MAKE FOR A COPYCAT. OR A SERIAL KILLER.
OF COURSE, OF COOUUUURSE, EX-ACT-LY MY POINT!
MEET ME AT THE COUNTY MORGUE AND WE'LL BUTT--ER, PUT OUR HEADS TOGETHER.
CHOP-CHOP, THE BODIES ARE ONLY GETTING COLDER!

THE BATBUNKER.

Numbers. An equation that's adding up to something... but **what?**

Lazlo Rankin worked for the Mayor in the finance department.

And Mr. Barts was the Falcones' legal consultant. Translation: expert money launderer. Both victims were numbers guys.

COULD IT BE JUST A STRANGE COINCIDENCE, MASTER RICHARD?

TWO'S A COINCIDENCE, ALFIE. BUT THREE'S A CONNECTION.

SIR?

I'VE SEARCHED THE CORONER'S DATABANKS GOING BACK FOUR MONTHS-- I FOUND ANOTHER MONEY-MAN.

NAME WAS *DARYL WHITMAN,* USED BY VARIOUS KINGPINS TO TRANSFER STOLEN JEWELRY INTO CASH.

HE DIED IN AN APARTMENT FIRE. THE FIRE ONLY CONSUMED HALF HIS BODY, GIVING HIM A SEMBLANCE TO *TWO-FACE.*

HE ALSO DIED WITHIN DAYS OF BEING RELEASED FROM BLACKGATE.

MONEY AND BLACKGATE. BUT THERE'S ONE MORE CONNECTION THEY ALL SHARE...

FIREFLY

GARFIELD LYNNS. *FIREFLY.*

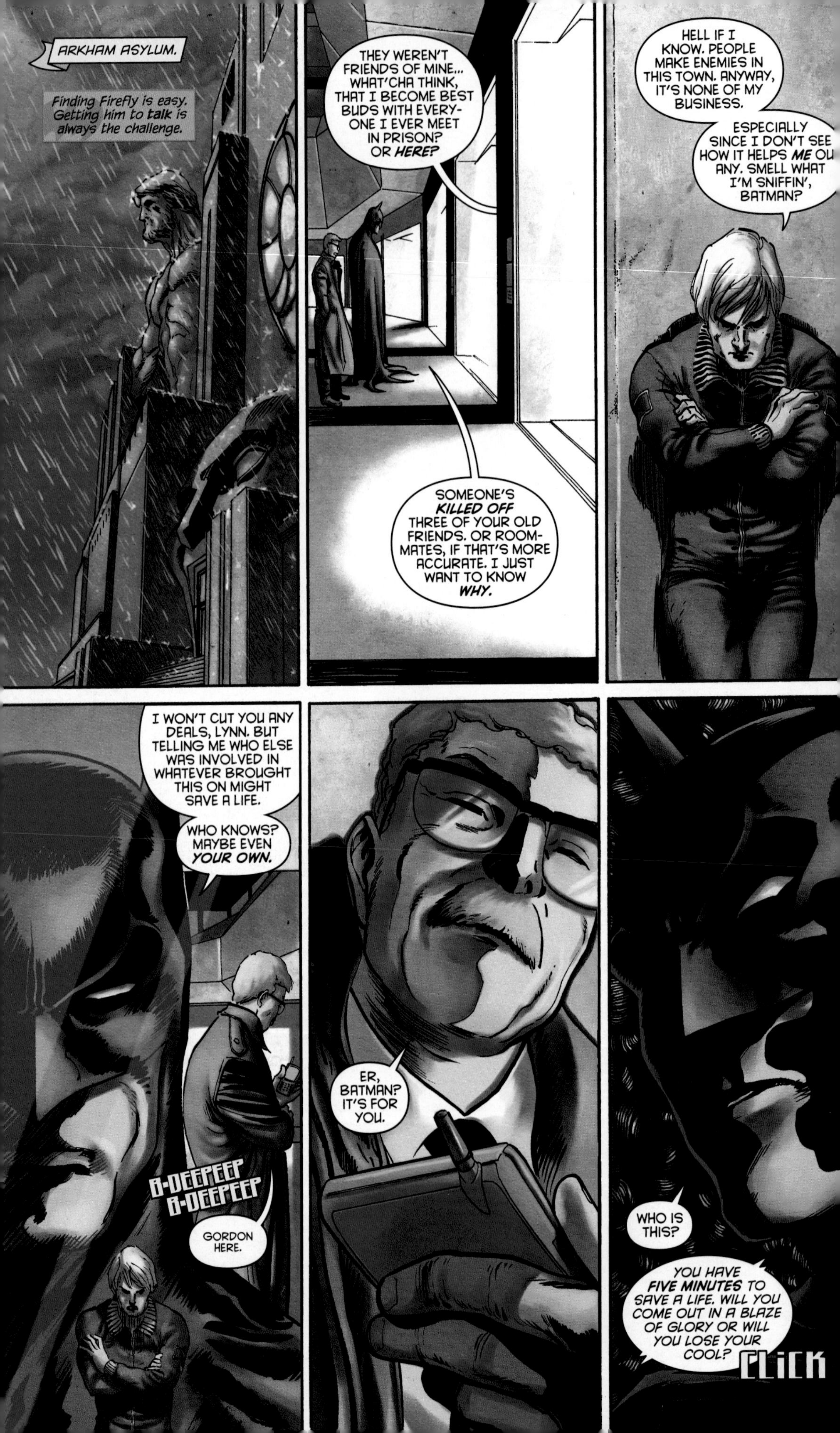
ARKHAM ASYLUM.
Finding Firefly is easy. Getting him to talk is always the challenge.
THEY WEREN'T FRIENDS OF MINE... WHAT'CHA THINK, THAT I BECOME BEST BUDS WITH EVERY-ONE I EVER MEET IN PRISON? OR HERE?
SOMEONE'S KILLED OFF THREE OF YOUR OLD FRIENDS. OR ROOM-MATES, IF THAT'S MORE ACCURATE. I JUST WANT TO KNOW WHY.
HELL IF I KNOW. PEOPLE MAKE ENEMIES IN THIS TOWN. ANYWAY, IT'S NONE OF MY BUSINESS.
ESPECIALLY SINCE I DON'T SEE HOW IT HELPS ME OU ANY. SMELL WHAT I'M SNIFFIN', BATMAN?
I WON'T CUT YOU ANY DEALS, LYNN. BUT TELLING ME WHO ELSE WAS INVOLVED IN WHATEVER BROUGHT THIS ON MIGHT SAVE A LIFE.
WHO KNOWS? MAYBE EVEN YOUR OWN.
B-DEEPEEP B-DEEPEEP
GORDON HERE.
ER, BATMAN? IT'S FOR YOU.
WHO IS THIS?
YOU HAVE FIVE MINUTES TO SAVE A LIFE. WILL YOU COME OUT IN A BLAZE OF GLORY OR WILL YOU LOSE YOUR COOL?
CLICK

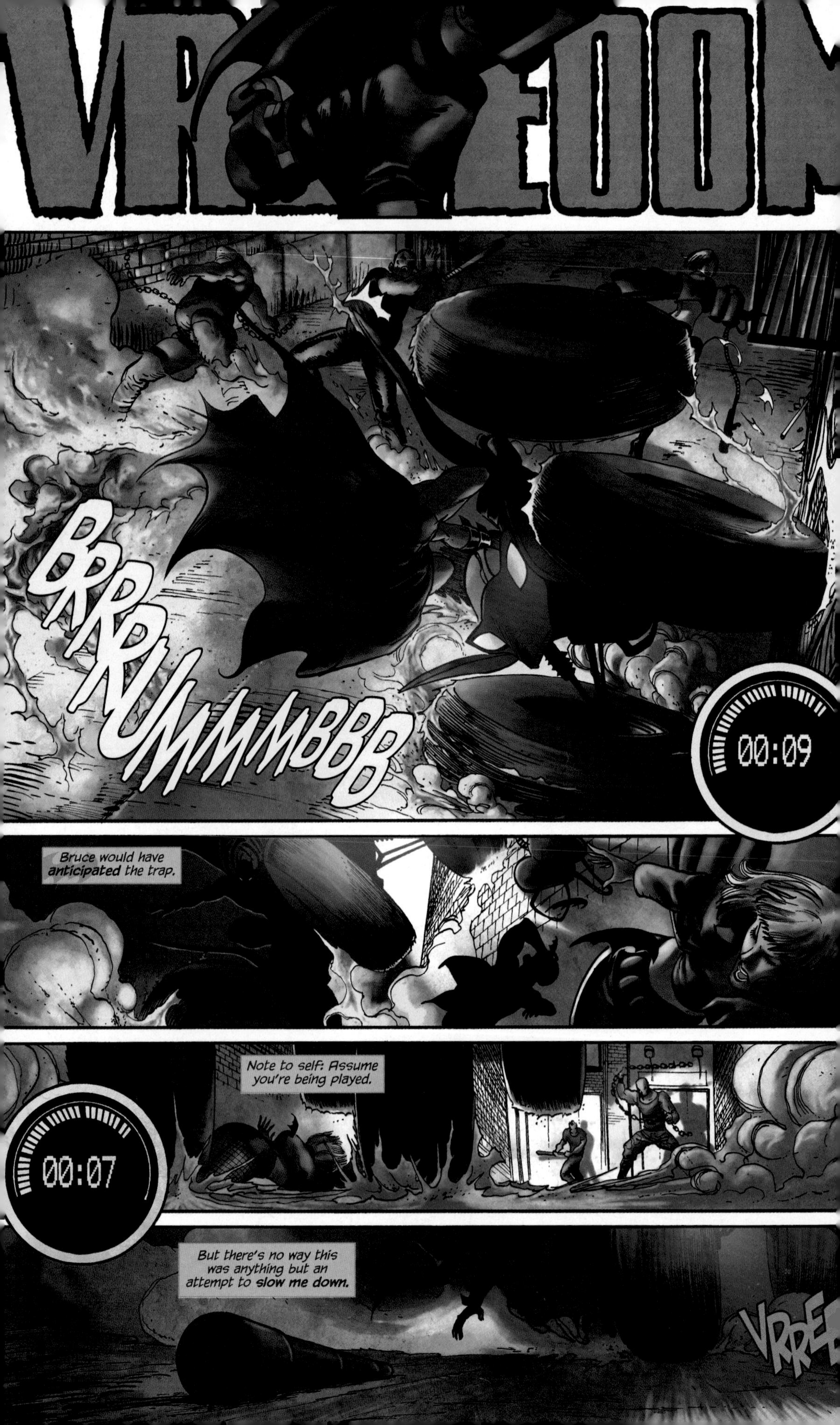
VRRREEOOM
BRRRUMMMBBB
00:09
Bruce would have anticipated the trap.
Note to self: Assume you're being played.
00:07
But there's no way this was anything but an attempt to slow me down.
VRREE

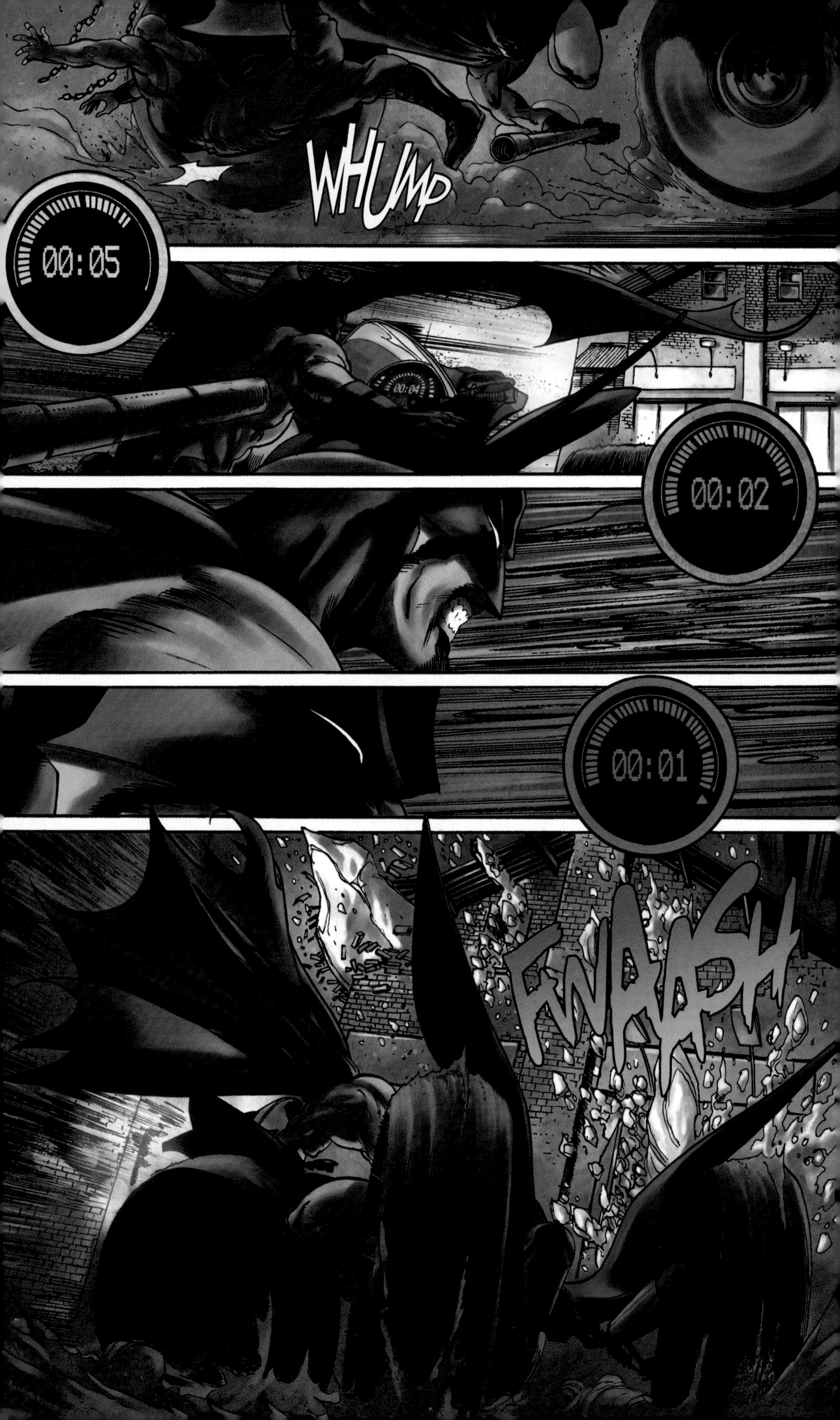
WHUMP
00:05
00:04
00:02
00:01
FWASH

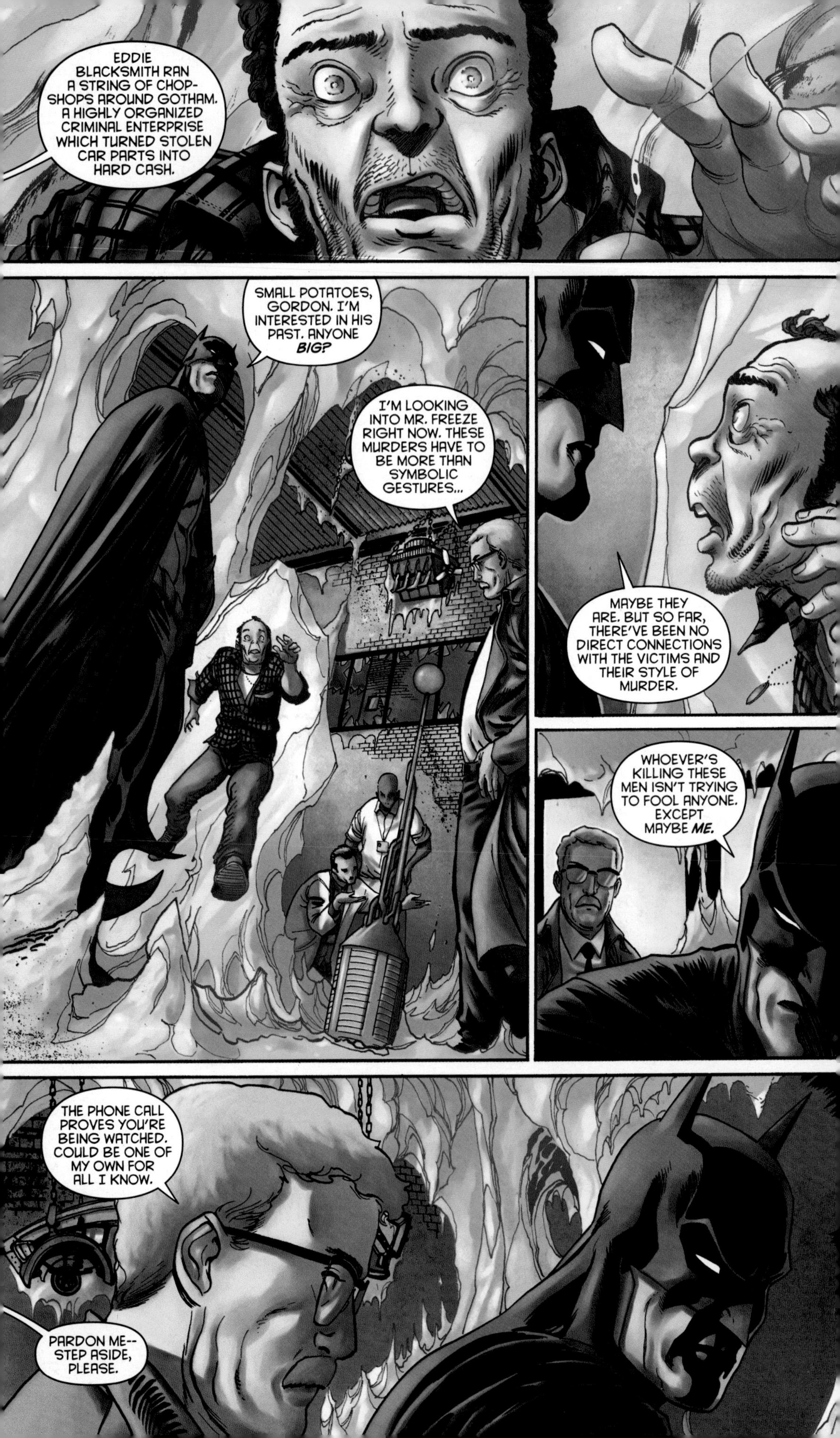
EDDIE BLACKSMITH RAN A STRING OF CHOP-SHOPS AROUND GOTHAM. A HIGHLY ORGANIZED CRIMINAL ENTERPRISE WHICH TURNED STOLEN CAR PARTS INTO HARD CASH.
SMALL POTATOES, GORDON. I'M INTERESTED IN HIS PAST. ANYONE *BIG?*
I'M LOOKING INTO MR. FREEZE RIGHT NOW. THESE MURDERS HAVE TO BE MORE THAN SYMBOLIC GESTURES...
MAYBE THEY ARE. BUT SO FAR, THERE'VE BEEN NO DIRECT CONNECTIONS WITH THE VICTIMS AND THEIR STYLE OF MURDER.
WHOEVER'S KILLING THESE MEN ISN'T TRYING TO FOOL ANYONE. EXCEPT MAYBE *ME.*
THE PHONE CALL PROVES YOU'RE BEING WATCHED. COULD BE ONE OF MY OWN FOR ALL I KNOW.
PARDON ME-- STEP ASIDE, PLEASE.

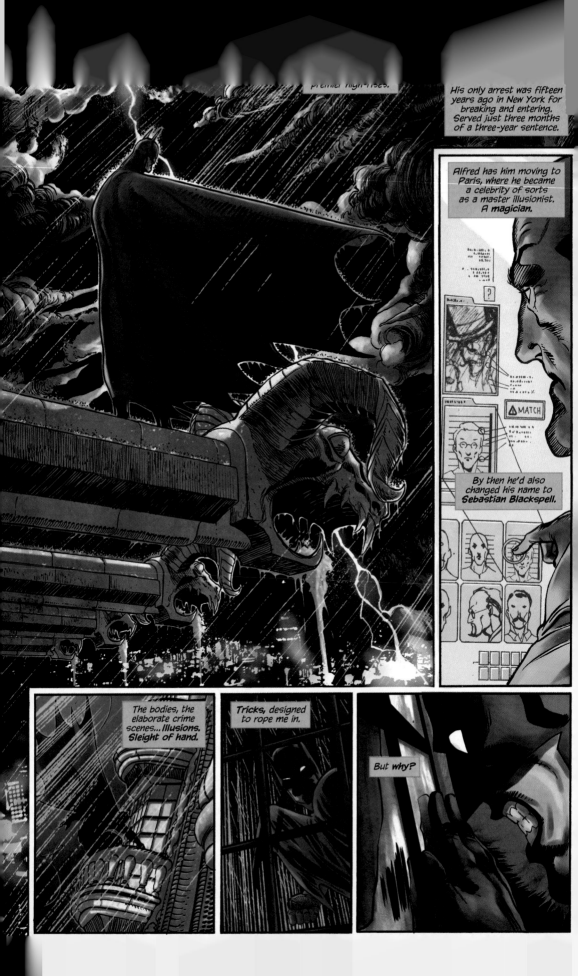

premier high-rises.

His only arrest was fifteen years ago in New York for breaking and entering. Served just three months of a three-year sentence.

Alfred has him moving to Paris, where he became a celebrity of sorts as a master illusionist. **A magician.**

MATCH

By then he'd also changed his name to Sebastian Blackspell.

The bodies, the elaborate crime scenes... Illusions. Sleight of hand.

Tricks, designed to rope me in.

But why?

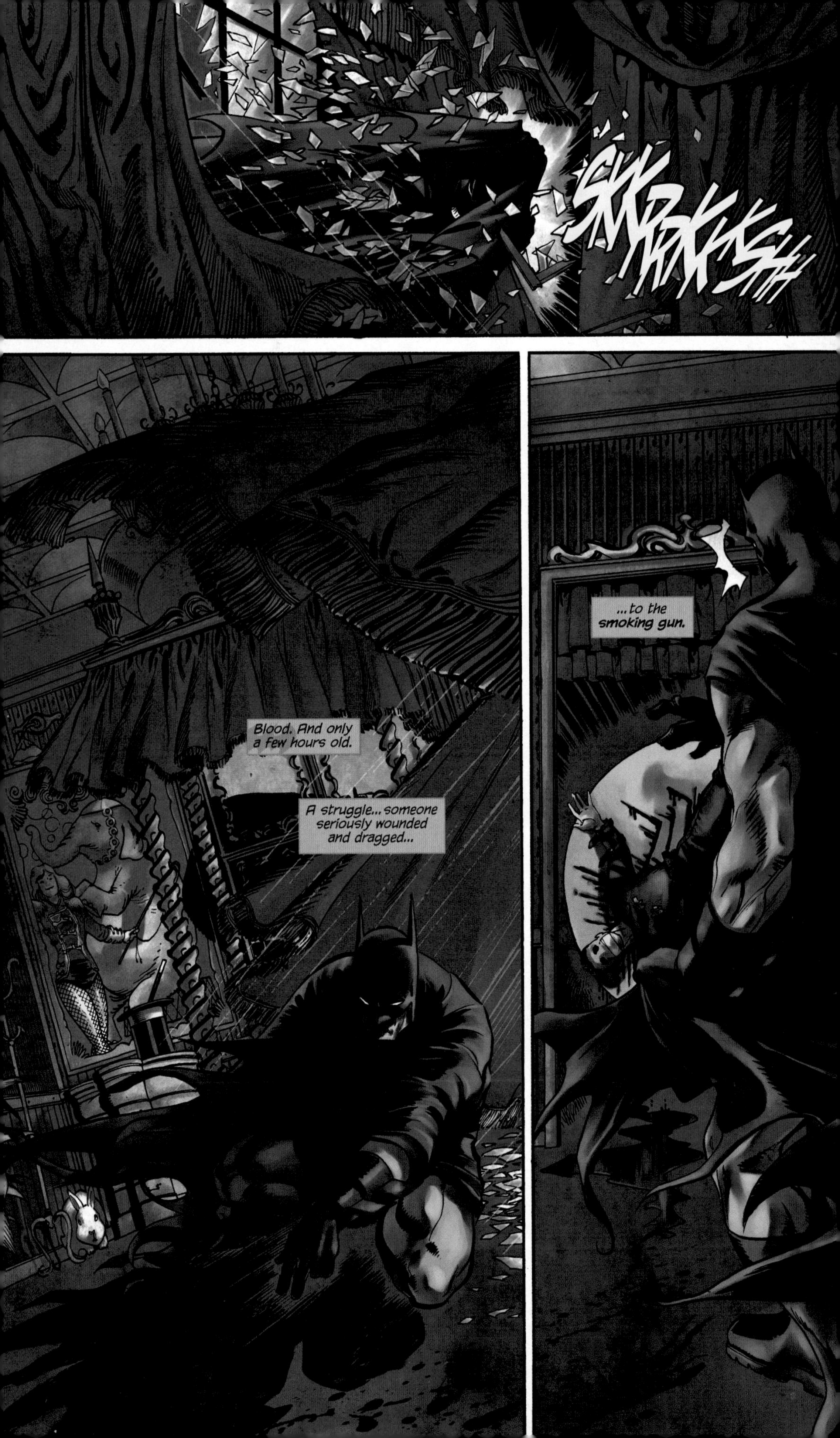
SKKRKKKSH
Blood. And only a few hours old.
A struggle... someone seriously wounded and dragged...
...to the smoking gun.

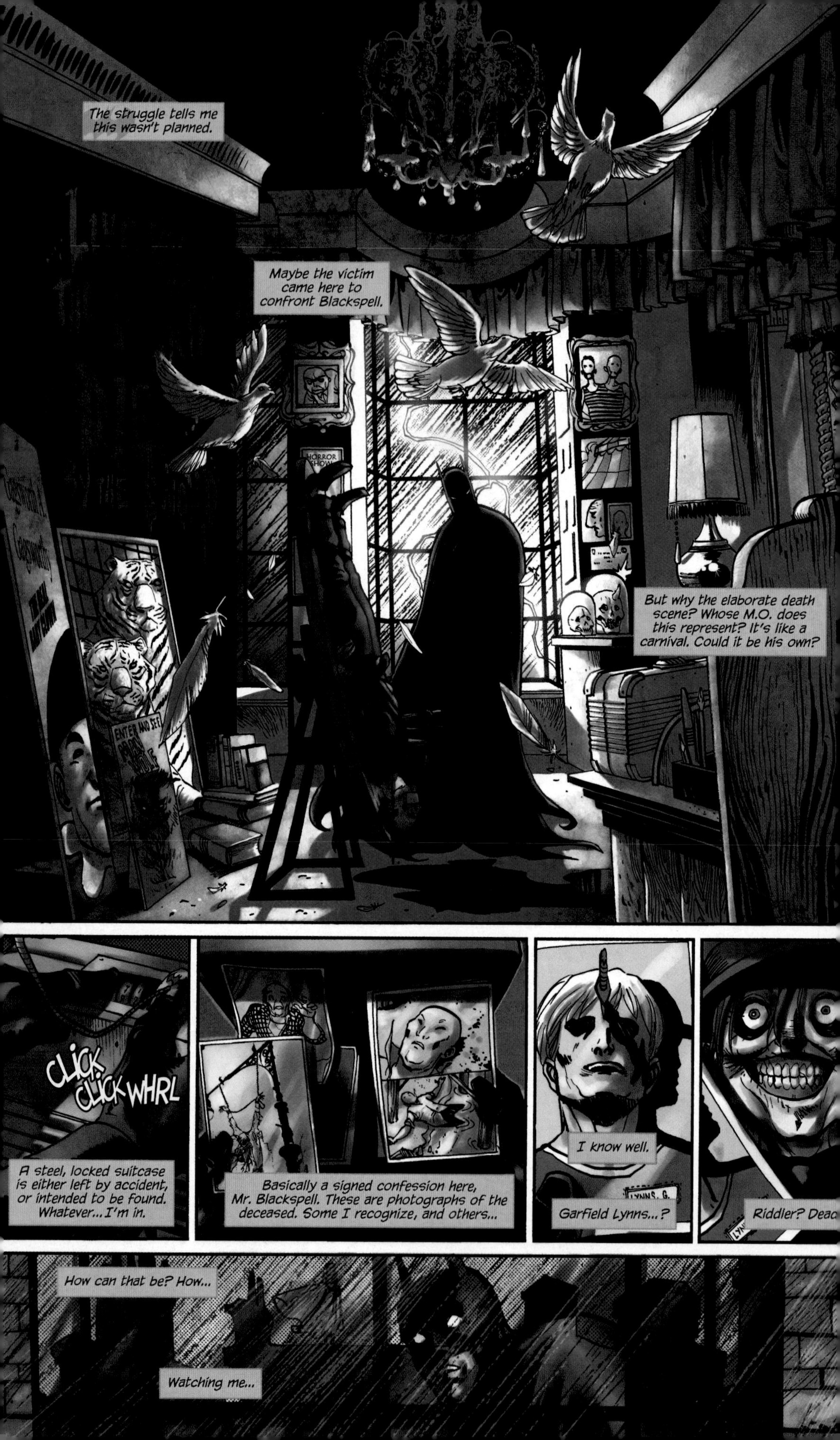
The struggle tells me this wasn't planned.
Maybe the victim came here to confront Blackspell.
HORROR SHOW
ENTER AND SEE!
But why the elaborate death scene? Whose M.O. does this represent? It's like a carnival. Could it be his own?
CLICK CLICK WHRL
A steel, locked suitcase is either left by accident, or intended to be found. Whatever... I'm in.
Basically a signed confession here, Mr. Blackspell. These are photographs of the deceased. Some I recognize, and others...
I know well.
LYNNS, G.
Garfield Lynns...?
Riddler? Deac
How can that be? How...
Watching me...

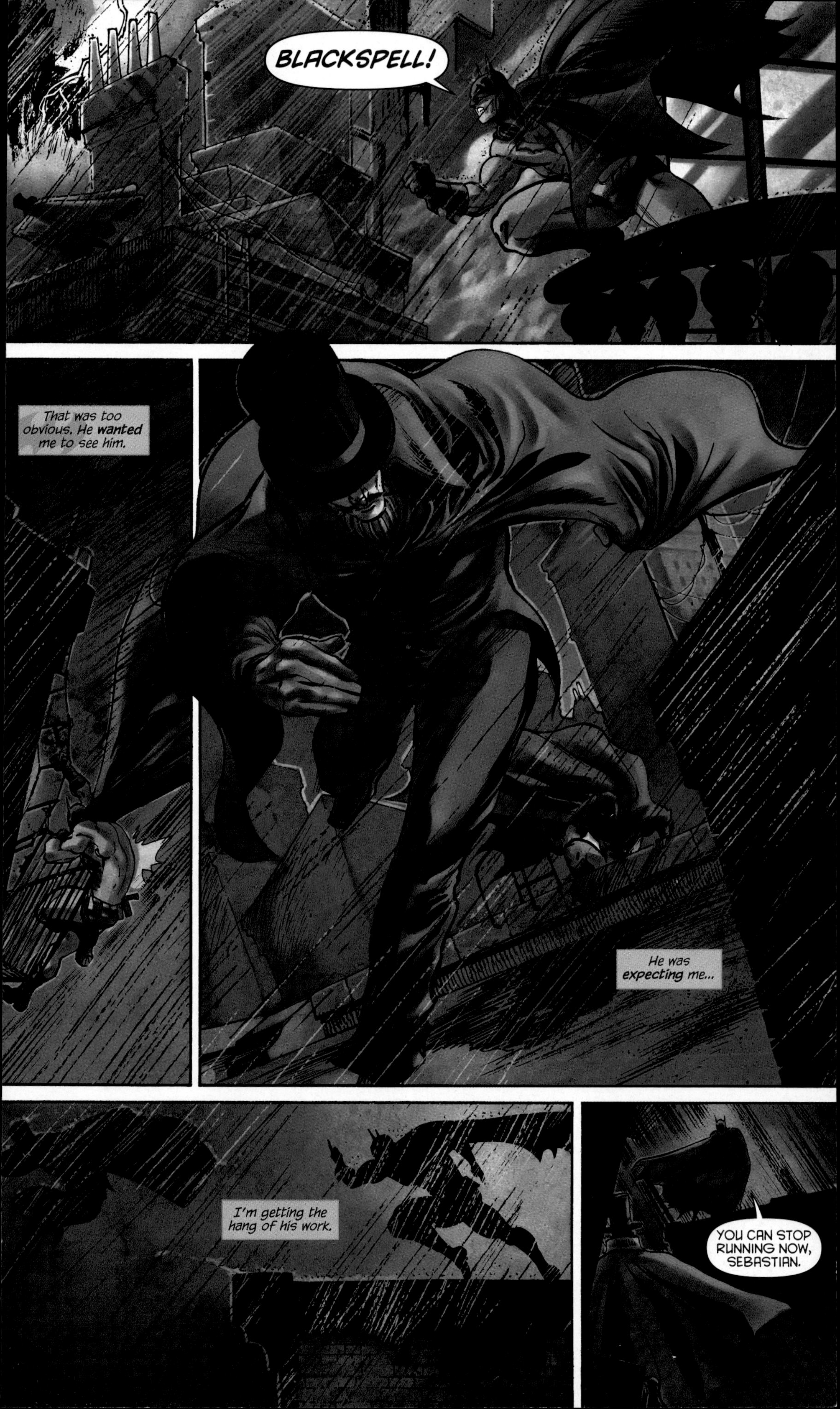

BLACKSPELL!
That was too obvious. He wanted me to see him.
He was expecting me...
I'm getting the hang of his work.
YOU CAN STOP RUNNING NOW, SEBASTIAN.

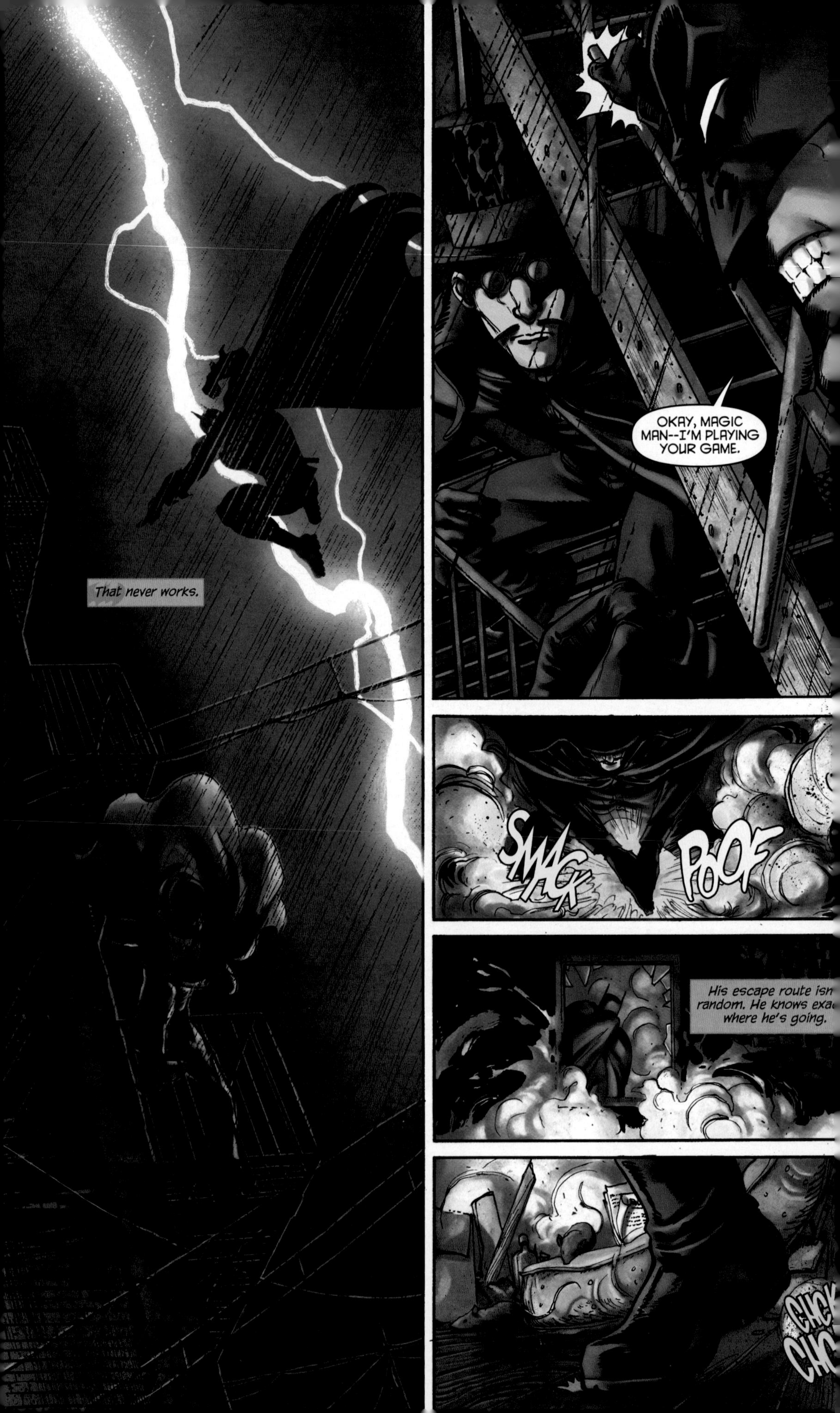
That never works.
OKAY, MAGIC MAN--I'M PLAYING YOUR GAME.
SMACK
POOF
His escape route isn
random. He knows exa
where he's going.

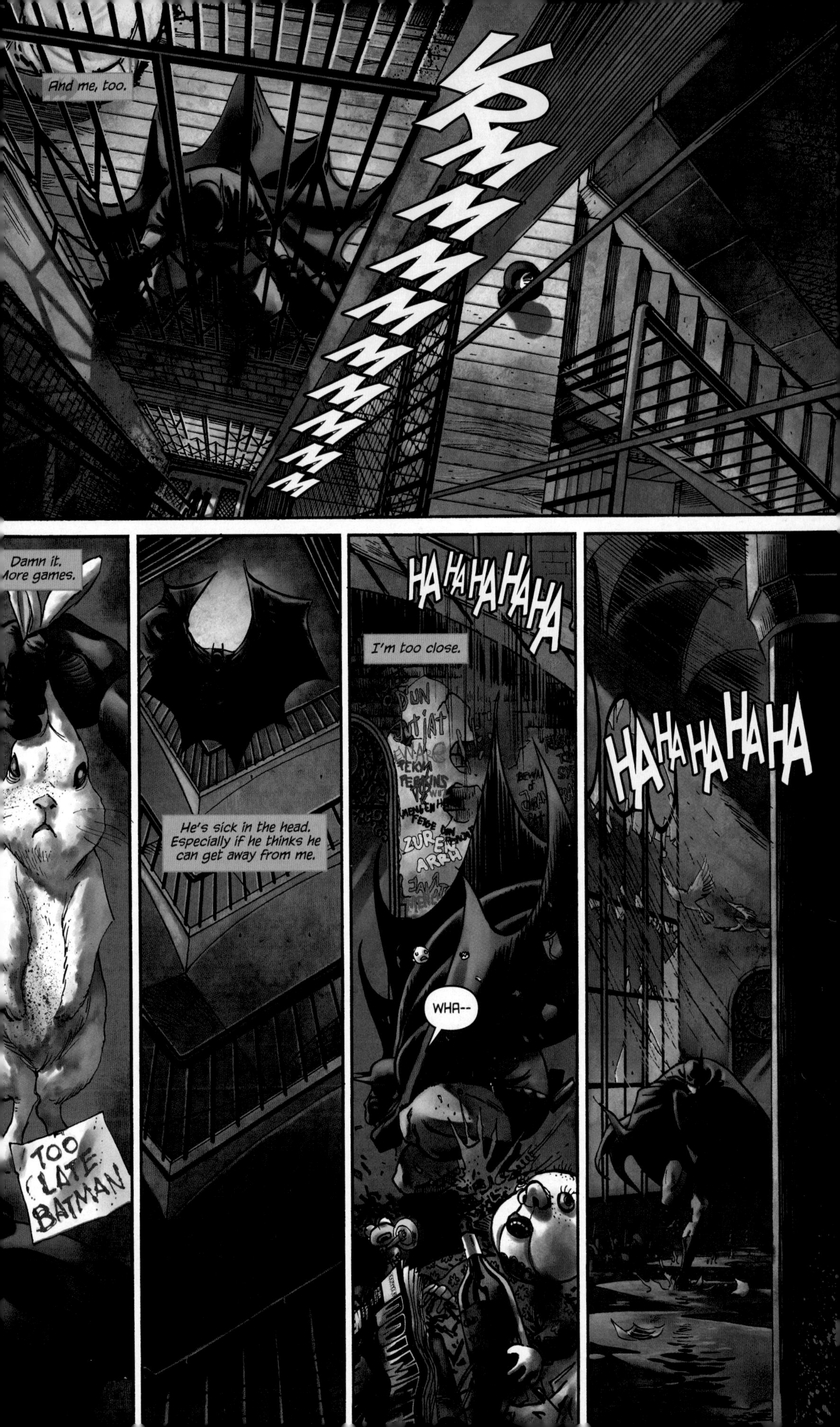

And me, too.
KRMMMMMMMMMMM
Damn it. More games.
TOO LATE BATMAN
He's sick in the head. Especially if he thinks he can get away from me.
HA HA HA HA HA HA
I'm too close.
WHA--
HA HA HA HA HA HA

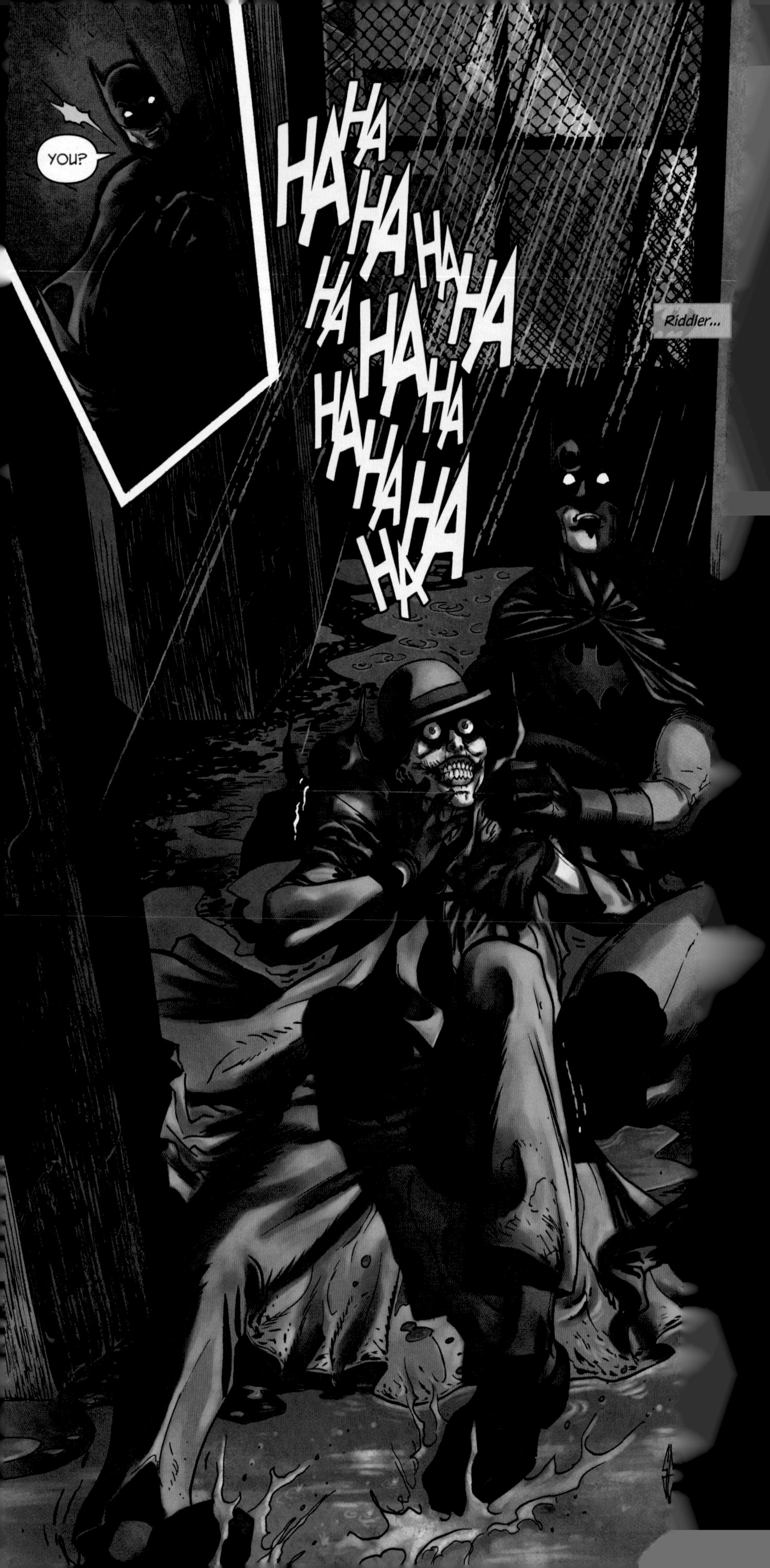
YOU?
HA HA HA HA HA HA HA HA HA HA HA HA HA HA HA HA HA
Riddler...

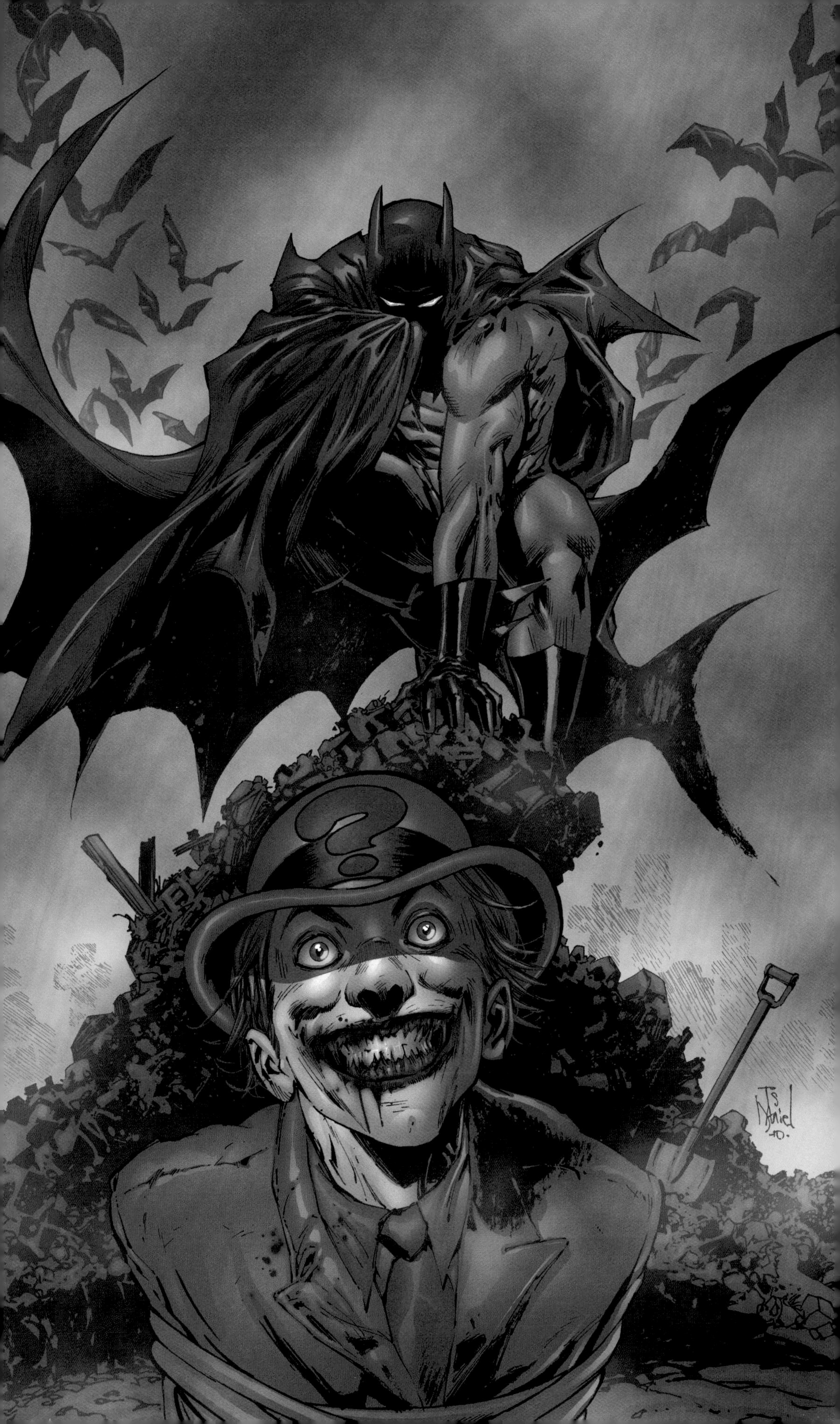

"Be thankful I will need you one day."

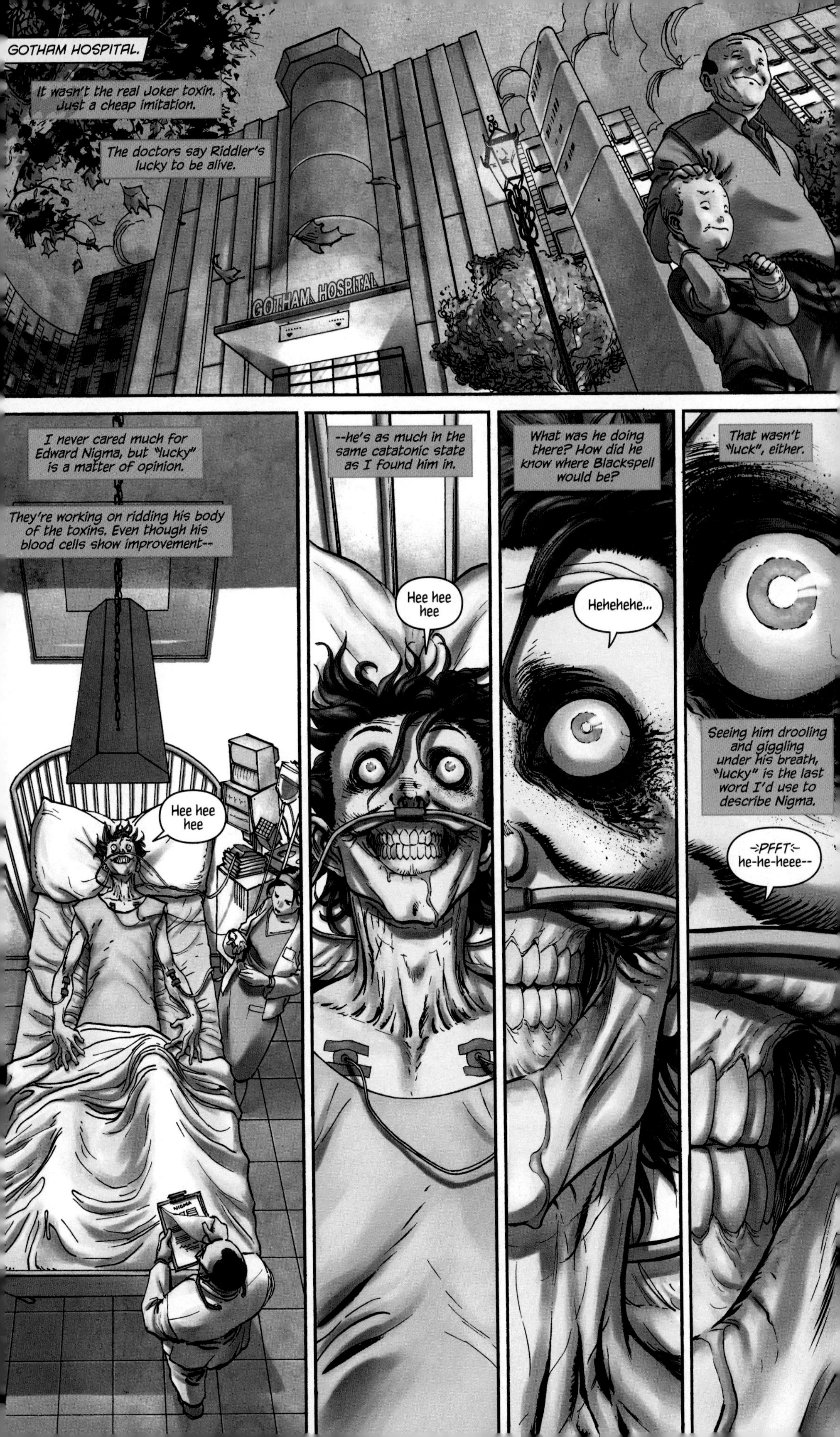
GOTHAM HOSPITAL.
It wasn't the real Joker toxin. Just a cheap imitation.
The doctors say Riddler's lucky to be alive.
GOTHAM HOSPITAL
I never cared much for Edward Nigma, but "lucky" is a matter of opinion.
They're working on ridding his body of the toxins. Even though his blood cells show improvement--
Hee hee hee
NIGMA
--he's as much in the same catatonic state as I found him in.
Hee hee hee
What was he doing there? How did he know where Blackspell would be?
Hehehehe...
That wasn't "luck", either.
Seeing him drooling and giggling under his breath, "lucky" is the last word I'd use to describe Nigma.
PFFT he-he-heee--

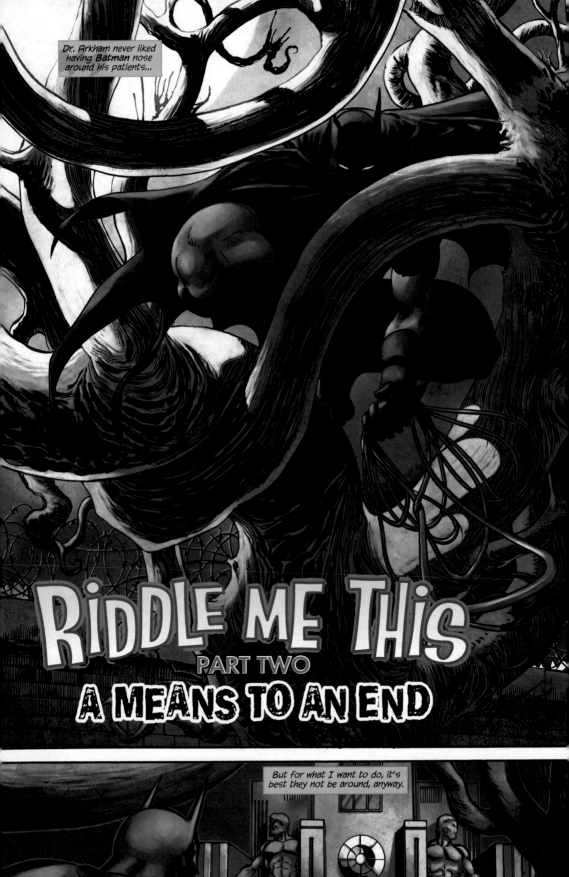

Dr. Arkham never liked having *Batman* nose around his patients...

RIDDLE ME THIS
PART TWO
A MEANS TO AN END

But for what I want to do, it's best they not be around, anyway.

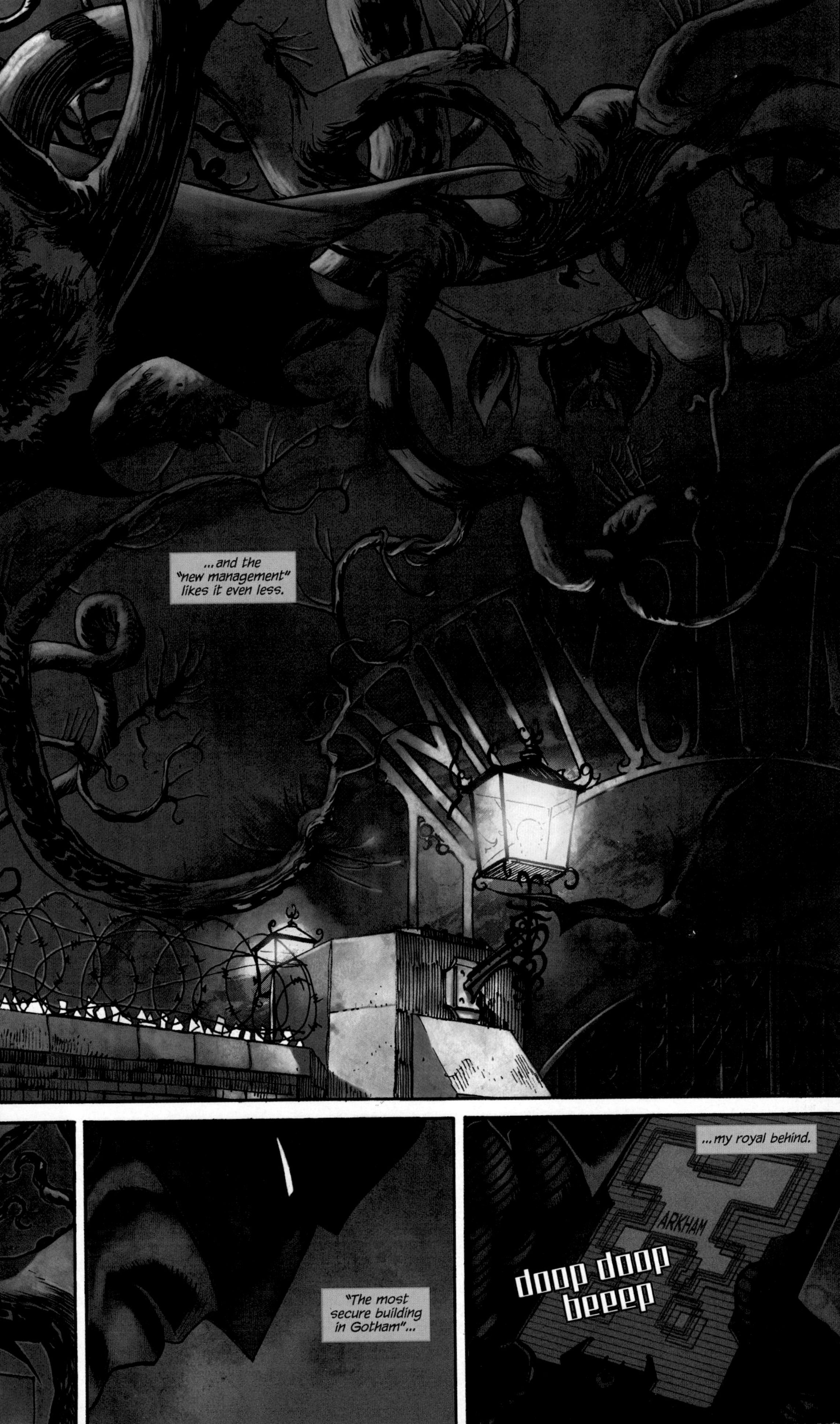
...and the "new management" likes it even less.
"The most secure building in Gotham"...
...my royal behind.
ARKHAM
doop doop beeep

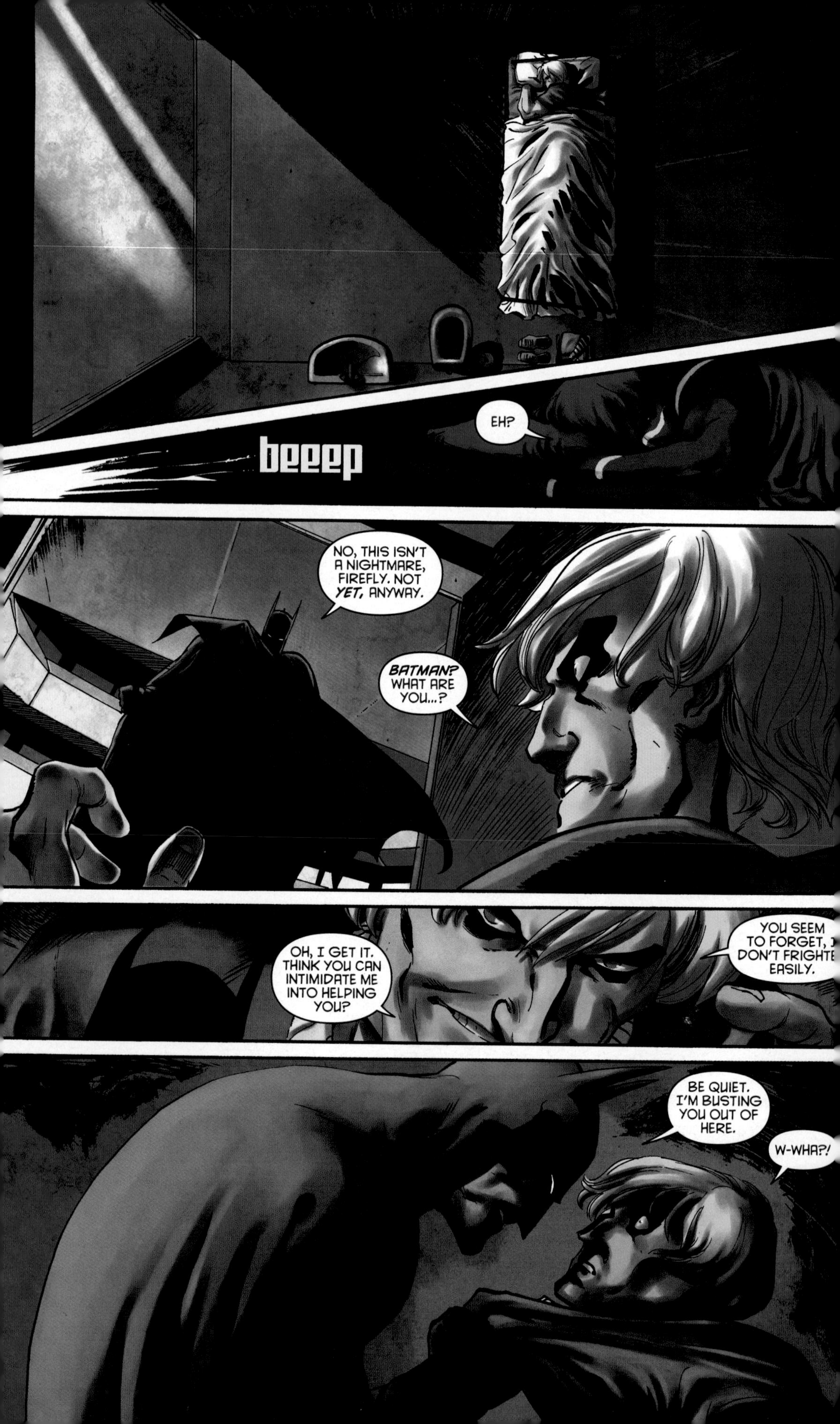
EH?
beeep
NO, THIS ISN'T A NIGHTMARE, FIREFLY. NOT *YET,* ANYWAY.
BATMAN? WHAT ARE YOU...?
OH, I GET IT. THINK YOU CAN INTIMIDATE ME INTO HELPING YOU?
YOU SEEM TO FORGET, I DON'T FRIGHTE EASILY.
BE QUIET. I'M BUSTING YOU OUT OF HERE.
W-WHA?!

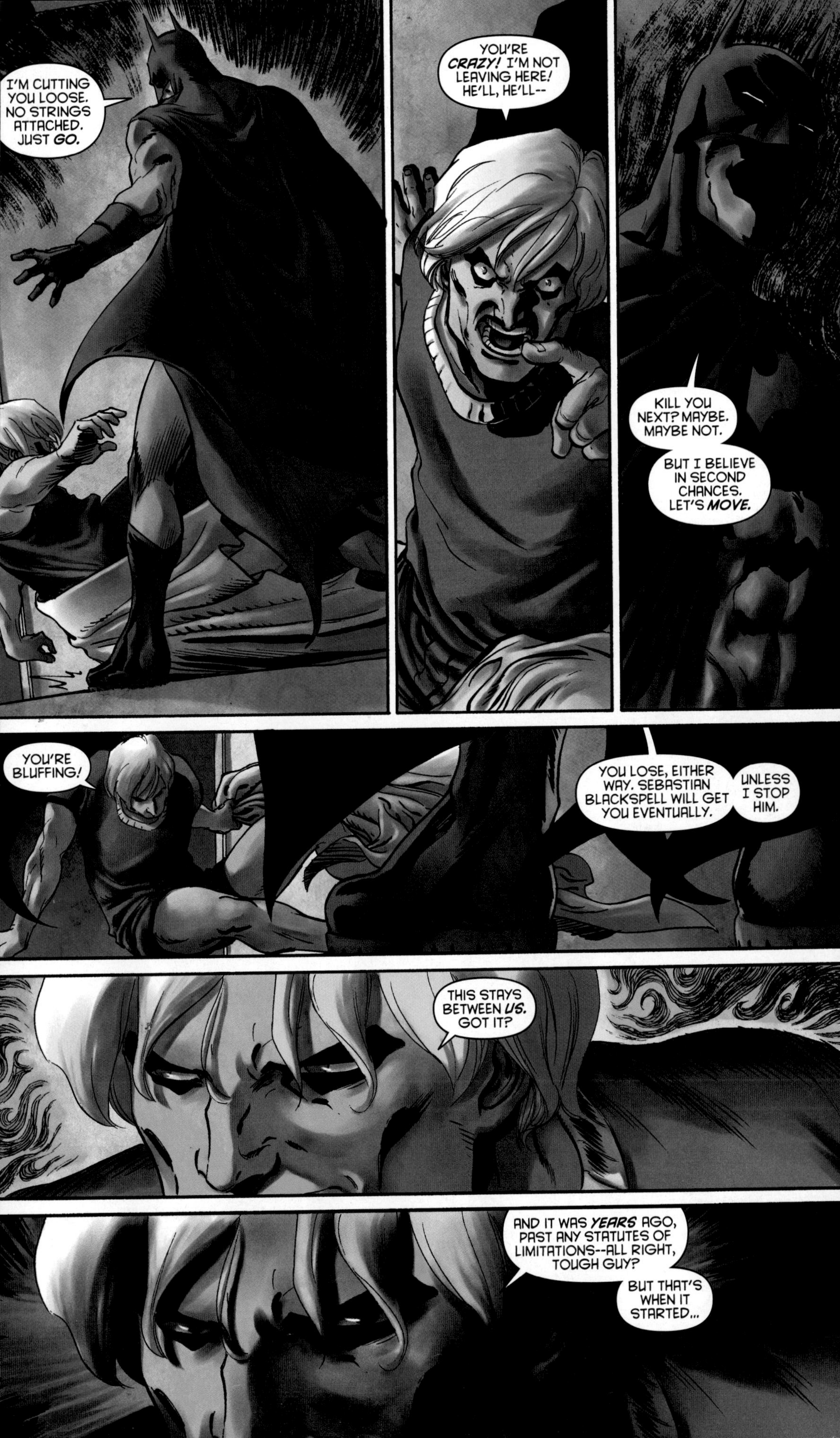
I'M CUTTING YOU LOOSE. NO STRINGS ATTACHED. JUST GO.
YOU'RE CRAZY! I'M NOT LEAVING HERE! HE'LL, HE'LL--
KILL YOU NEXT? MAYBE. MAYBE NOT.
BUT I BELIEVE IN SECOND CHANCES. LET'S MOVE.
YOU'RE BLUFFING!
YOU LOSE, EITHER WAY. SEBASTIAN BLACKSPELL WILL GET YOU EVENTUALLY.
UNLESS I STOP HIM.
THIS STAYS BETWEEN US. GOT IT?
AND IT WAS YEARS AGO, PAST ANY STATUTES OF LIMITATIONS--ALL RIGHT, TOUGH GUY?
BUT THAT'S WHEN IT STARTED...

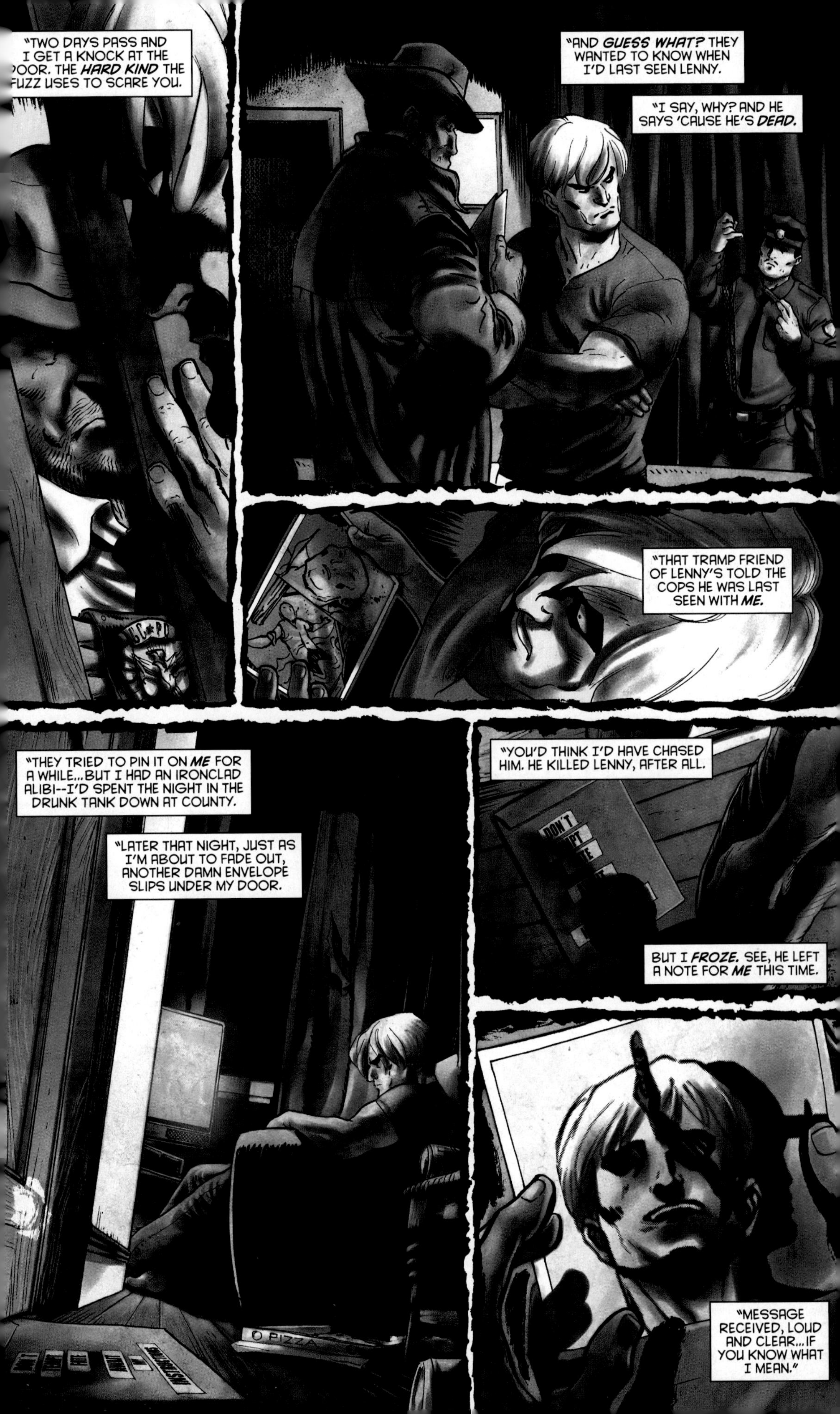
"TWO DAYS PASS AND I GET A KNOCK AT THE DOOR. THE HARD KIND THE FUZZ USES TO SCARE YOU.
"AND GUESS WHAT? THEY WANTED TO KNOW WHEN I'D LAST SEEN LENNY.
"I SAY, WHY? AND HE SAYS 'CAUSE HE'S DEAD.
"THAT TRAMP FRIEND OF LENNY'S TOLD THE COPS HE WAS LAST SEEN WITH ME.
"THEY TRIED TO PIN IT ON ME FOR A WHILE... BUT I HAD AN IRONCLAD ALIBI--I'D SPENT THE NIGHT IN THE DRUNK TANK DOWN AT COUNTY.
"LATER THAT NIGHT, JUST AS I'M ABOUT TO FADE OUT, ANOTHER DAMN ENVELOPE SLIPS UNDER MY DOOR.
PIZZA
"YOU'D THINK I'D HAVE CHASED HIM. HE KILLED LENNY, AFTER ALL.
BUT I FROZE. SEE, HE LEFT A NOTE FOR ME THIS TIME.
"MESSAGE RECEIVED, LOUD AND CLEAR... IF YOU KNOW WHAT I MEAN."

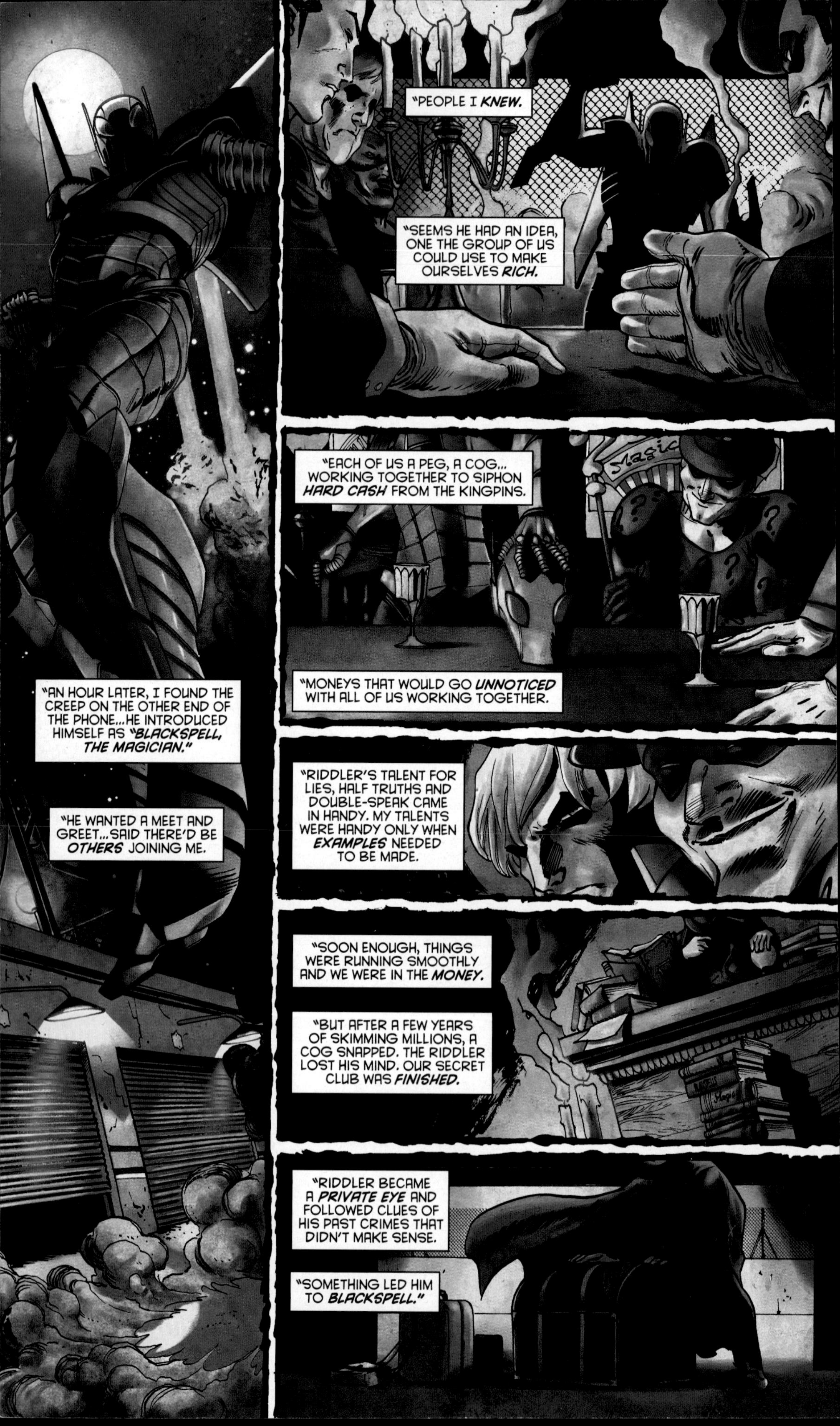
"AN HOUR LATER, I FOUND THE CREEP ON THE OTHER END OF THE PHONE...HE INTRODUCED HIMSELF AS "BLACKSPELL, THE MAGICIAN."
"HE WANTED A MEET AND GREET...SAID THERE'D BE OTHERS JOINING ME.
"PEOPLE I KNEW.
"SEEMS HE HAD AN IDEA, ONE THE GROUP OF US COULD USE TO MAKE OURSELVES RICH.
"EACH OF US A PEG, A COG... WORKING TOGETHER TO SIPHON HARD CASH FROM THE KINGPINS.
"MONEYS THAT WOULD GO UNNOTICED WITH ALL OF US WORKING TOGETHER.
"RIDDLER'S TALENT FOR LIES, HALF TRUTHS AND DOUBLE-SPEAK CAME IN HANDY. MY TALENTS WERE HANDY ONLY WHEN EXAMPLES NEEDED TO BE MADE.
"SOON ENOUGH, THINGS WERE RUNNING SMOOTHLY AND WE WERE IN THE MONEY.
"BUT AFTER A FEW YEARS OF SKIMMING MILLIONS, A COG SNAPPED. THE RIDDLER LOST HIS MIND. OUR SECRET CLUB WAS FINISHED.
"RIDDLER BECAME A PRIVATE EYE AND FOLLOWED CLUES OF HIS PAST CRIMES THAT DIDN'T MAKE SENSE.
"SOMETHING LED HIM TO BLACKSPELL."

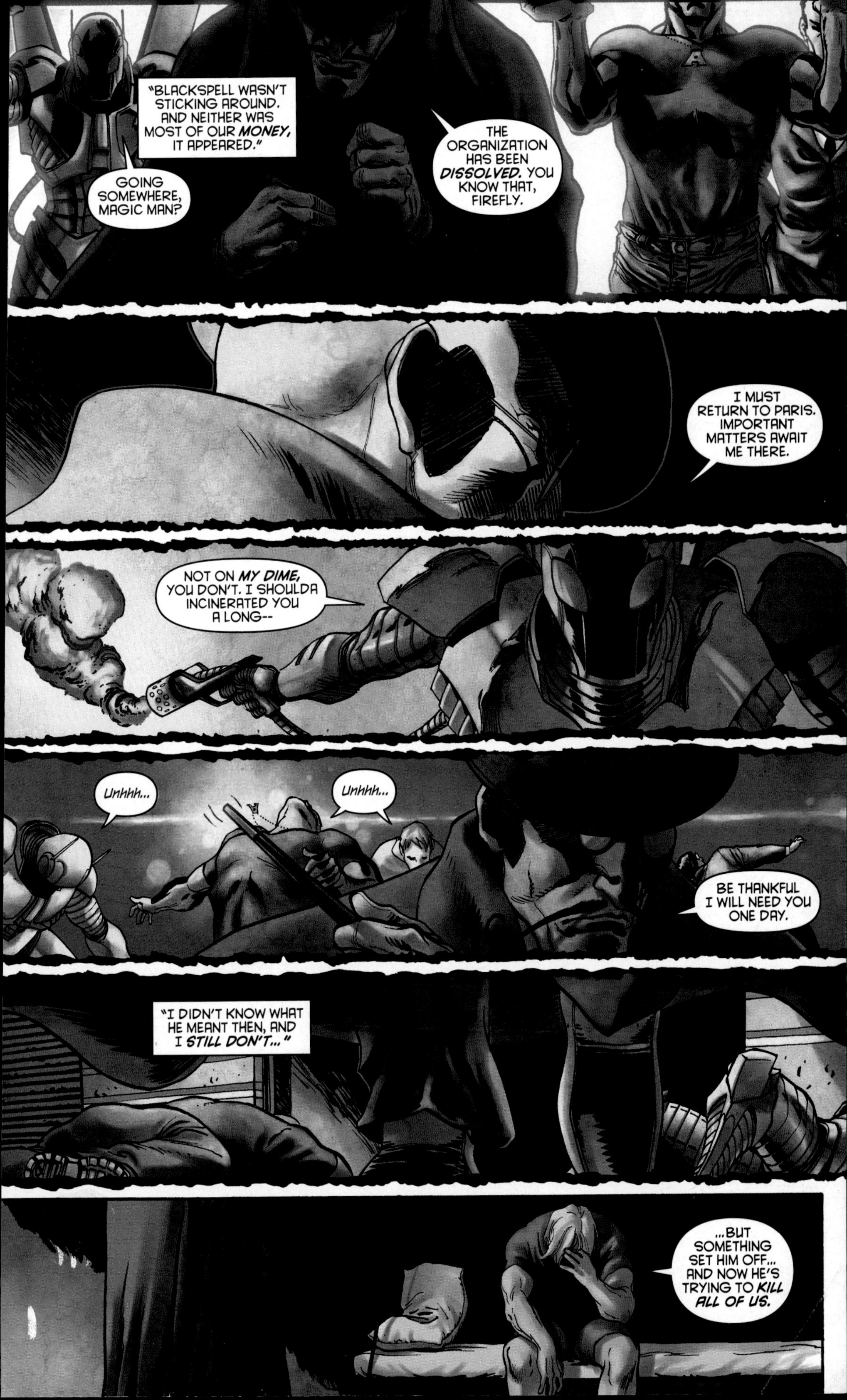
"BLACKSPELL WASN'T STICKING AROUND. AND NEITHER WAS MOST OF OUR MONEY, IT APPEARED."
GOING SOMEWHERE, MAGIC MAN?
THE ORGANIZATION HAS BEEN DISSOLVED. YOU KNOW THAT, FIREFLY.
I MUST RETURN TO PARIS. IMPORTANT MATTERS AWAIT ME THERE.
NOT ON MY DIME, YOU DON'T. I SHOULDA INCINERATED YOU A LONG--
Unhhh...
Unhhh...
BE THANKFUL I WILL NEED YOU ONE DAY.
"I DIDN'T KNOW WHAT HE MEANT THEN, AND I STILL DON'T..."
...BUT SOMETHING SET HIM OFF... AND NOW HE'S TRYING TO KILL ALL OF US.

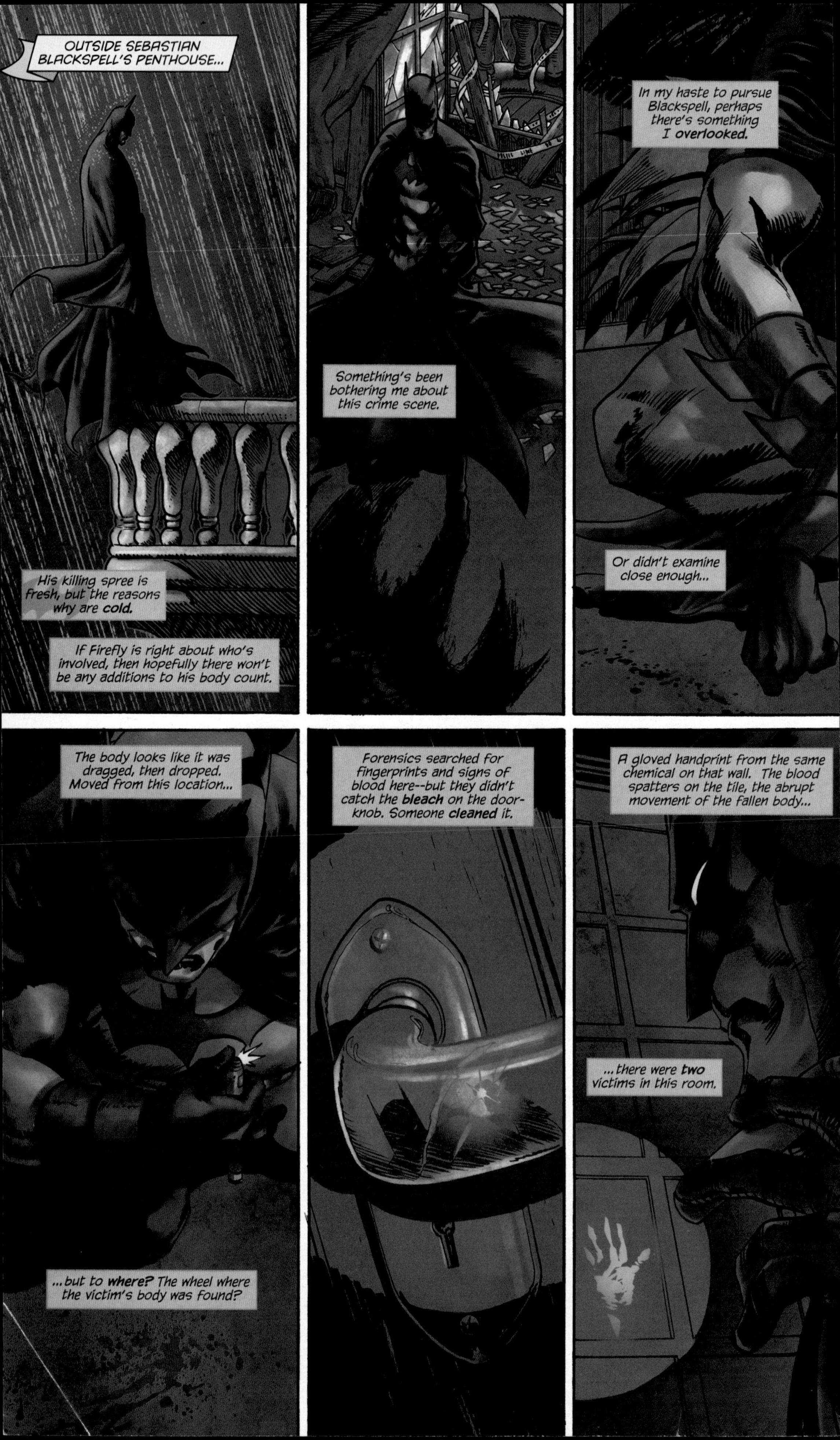
OUTSIDE SEBASTIAN BLACKSPELL'S PENTHOUSE...
His killing spree is fresh, but the reasons why are **cold.**
If Firefly is right about who's involved, then hopefully there won't be any additions to his body count.
Something's been bothering me about this crime scene.
In my haste to pursue Blackspell, perhaps there's something I **overlooked.**
Or didn't examine close enough...
The body looks like it was dragged, then dropped. Moved from this location...
...but to **where?** The wheel where the victim's body was found?
Forensics searched for fingerprints and signs of blood here--but they didn't catch the **bleach** on the door-knob. Someone **cleaned** it.
A gloved handprint from the same chemical on that wall. The blood spatters on the tile, the abrupt movement of the fallen body...
...there were **two** victims in this room.

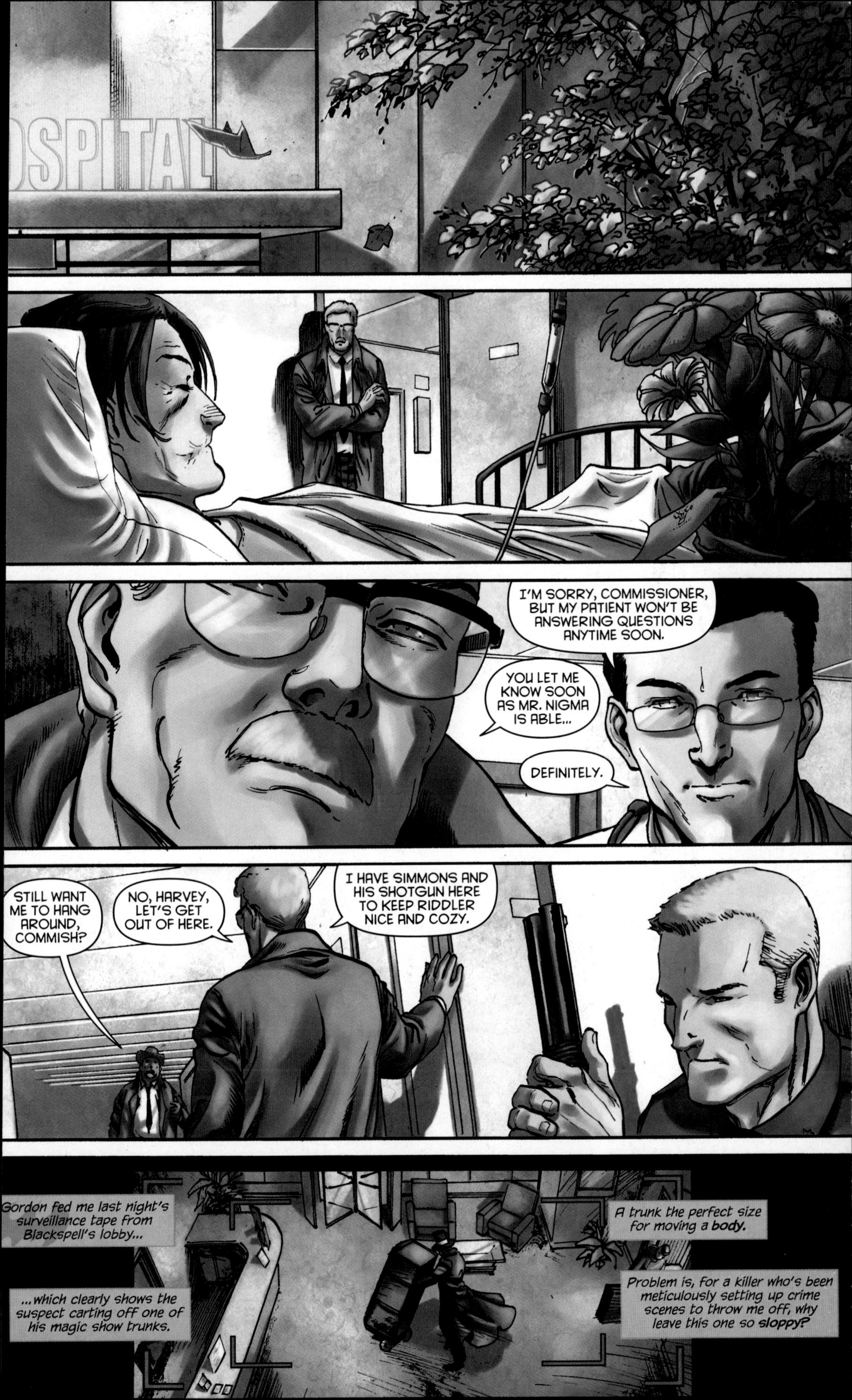
OSPITAL
I'M SORRY, COMMISSIONER, BUT MY PATIENT WON'T BE ANSWERING QUESTIONS ANYTIME SOON.
YOU LET ME KNOW SOON AS MR. NIGMA IS ABLE...
DEFINITELY.
STILL WANT ME TO HANG AROUND, COMMISH?
NO, HARVEY, LET'S GET OUT OF HERE.
I HAVE SIMMONS AND HIS SHOTGUN HERE TO KEEP RIDDLER NICE AND COZY.
Gordon fed me last night's surveillance tape from Blackspell's lobby...
...which clearly shows the suspect carting off one of his magic show trunks.
A trunk the perfect size for moving a **body.**
Problem is, for a killer who's been meticulously setting up crime scenes to throw me off, why leave this one so **sloppy?**

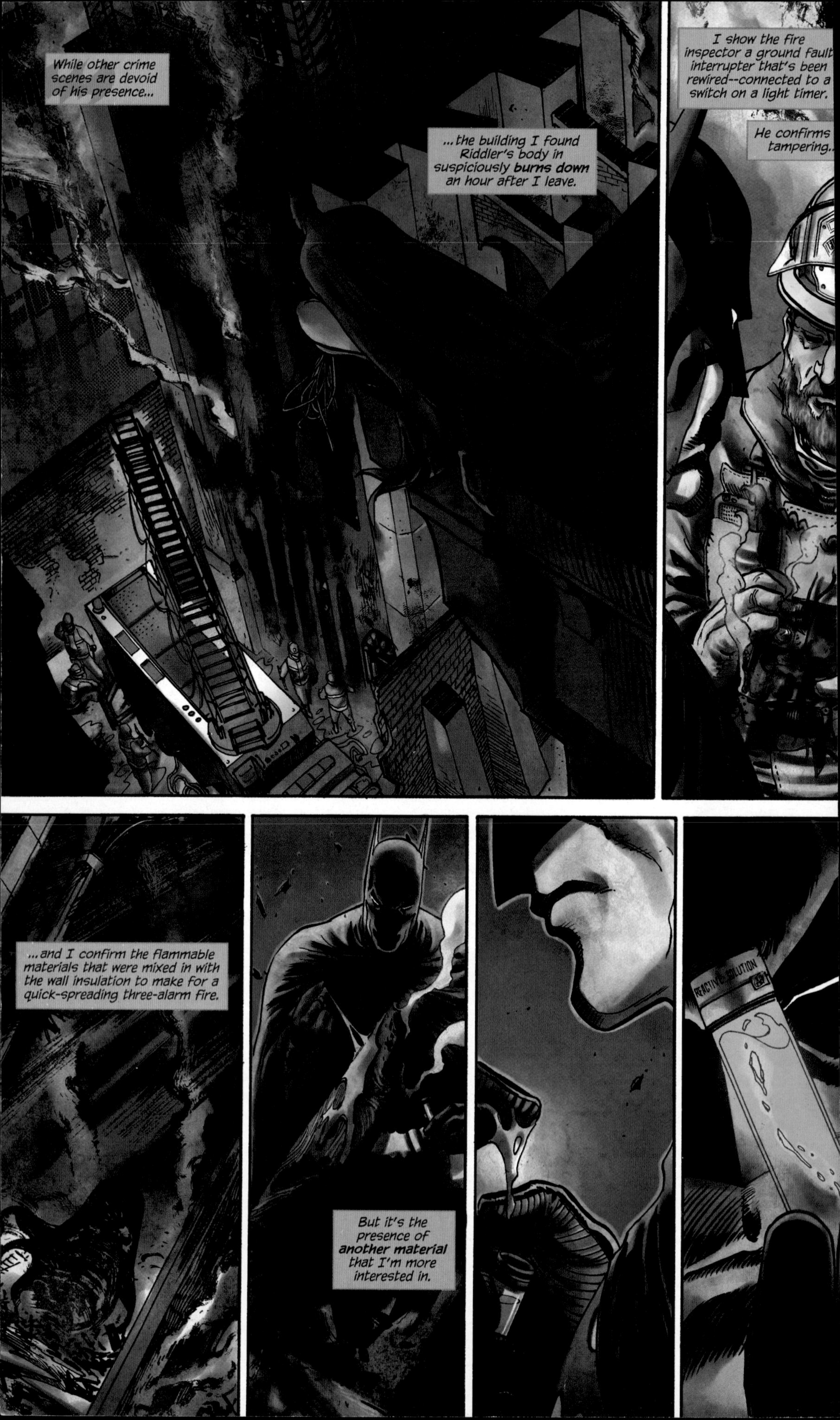
While other crime scenes are devoid of his presence...
...the building I found Riddler's body in suspiciously **burns down** an hour after I leave.
I show the fire inspector a ground fault interrupter that's been rewired--connected to a switch on a light timer.
He confirms tampering...
...and I confirm the flammable materials that were mixed in with the wall insulation to make for a quick-spreading three-alarm fire.
But it's the presence of **another material** that I'm more interested in.
REACTIVE SOLUTION

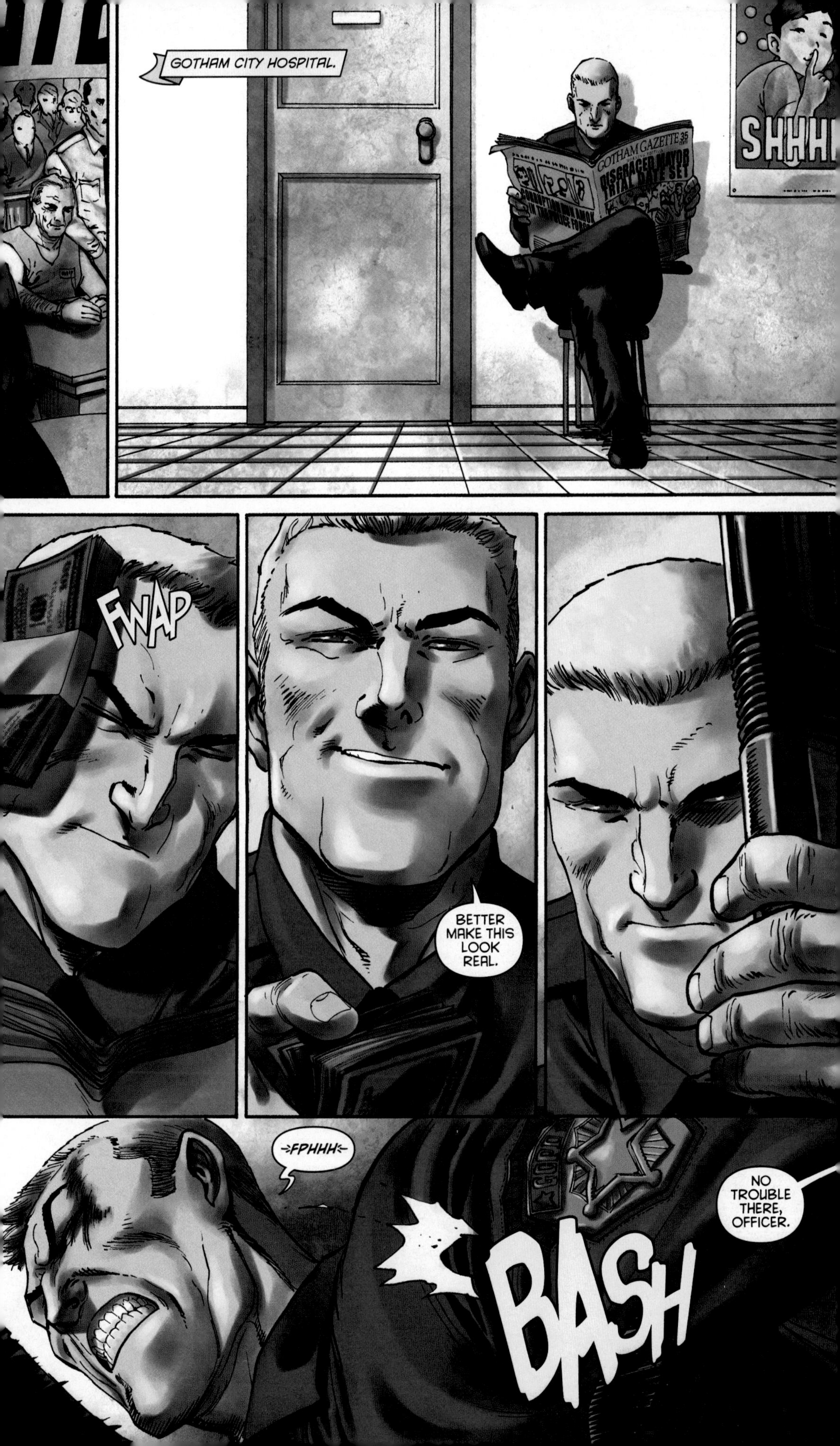
GOTHAM CITY HOSPITAL.
GOTHAM GAZETTE
DISGRACED MAYOR TRIAL DATE SET
SHHH
FWAP
BETTER MAKE THIS LOOK REAL.
FPHHH
NO TROUBLE THERE, OFFICER.
BASH

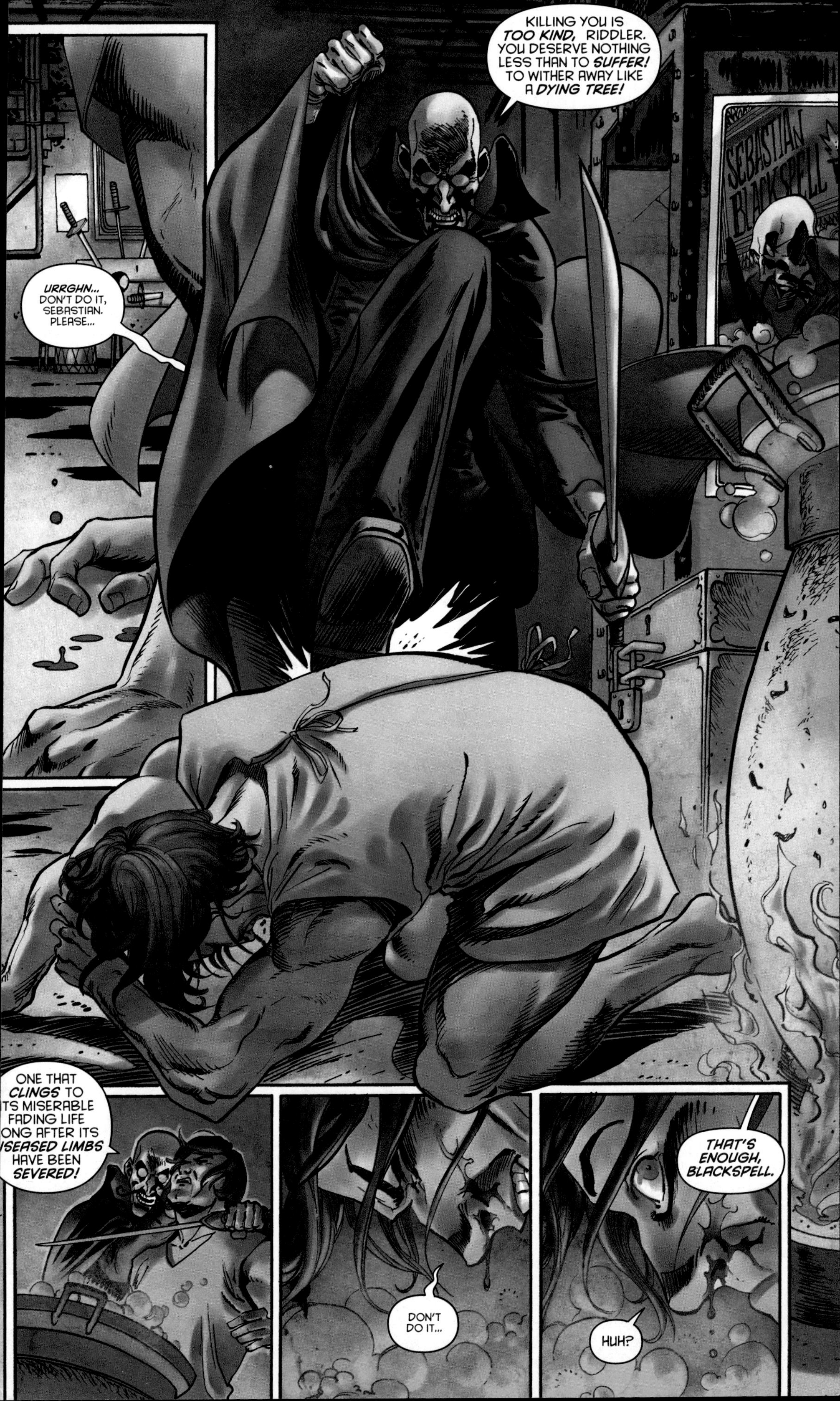
KILLING YOU IS *TOO KIND,* RIDDLER. YOU DESERVE NOTHING LESS THAN TO *SUFFER!* TO WITHER AWAY LIKE A *DYING TREE!*
SEBASTIAN BLACKSPELL
URRGHN... DON'T DO IT, SEBASTIAN. PLEASE...
ONE THAT *CLINGS* TO TS MISERABLE FADING LIFE ONG AFTER ITS *ISEASED LIMBS* HAVE BEEN *SEVERED!*
DON'T DO IT...
THAT'S ENOUGH, BLACKSPELL.
HUH?

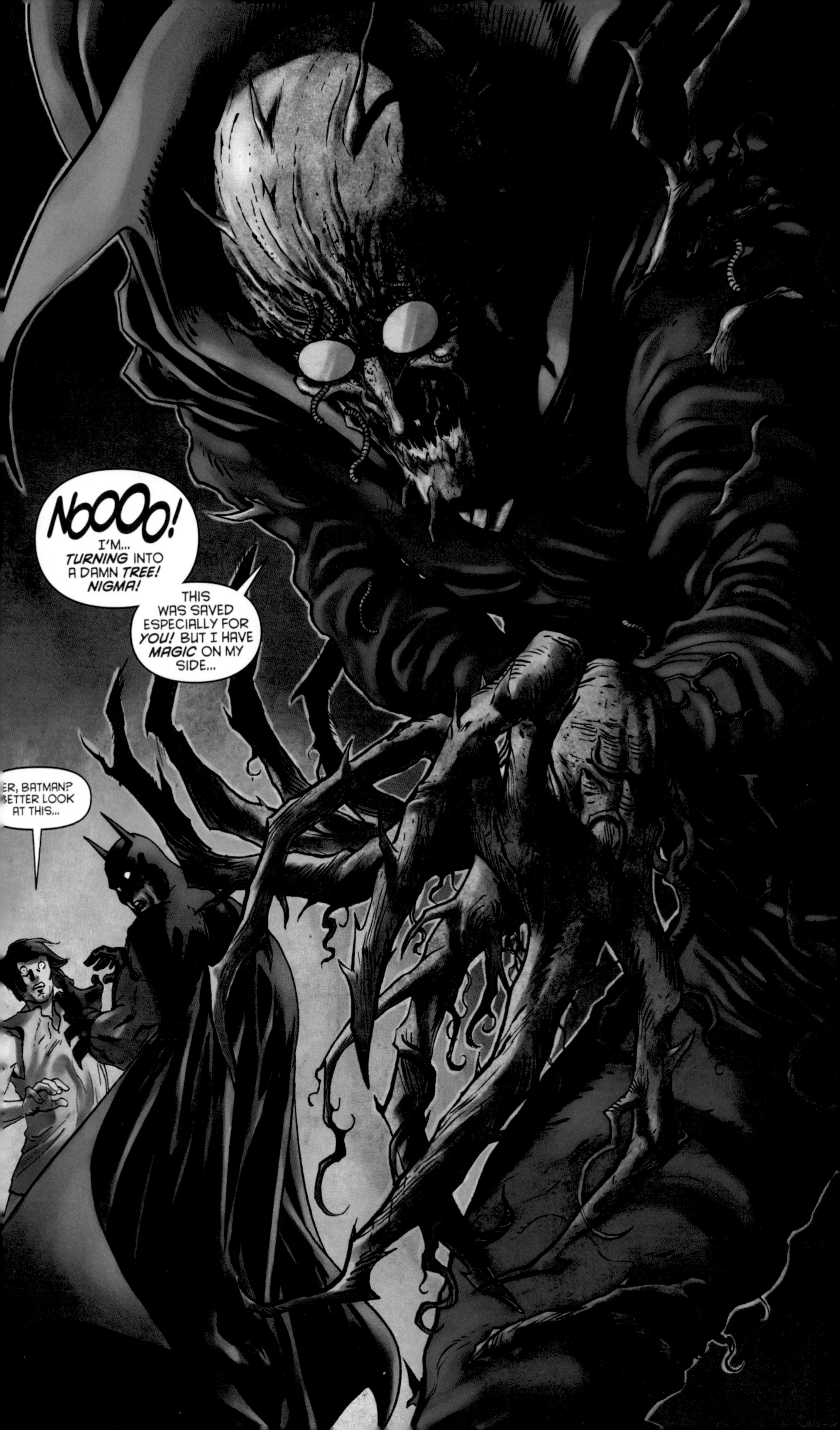
NOOOO! I'M... TURNING INTO A DAMN TREE! NIGMA!
THIS WAS SAVED ESPECIALLY FOR YOU! BUT I HAVE MAGIC ON MY SIDE...
ER, BATMAN? BETTER LOOK AT THIS...

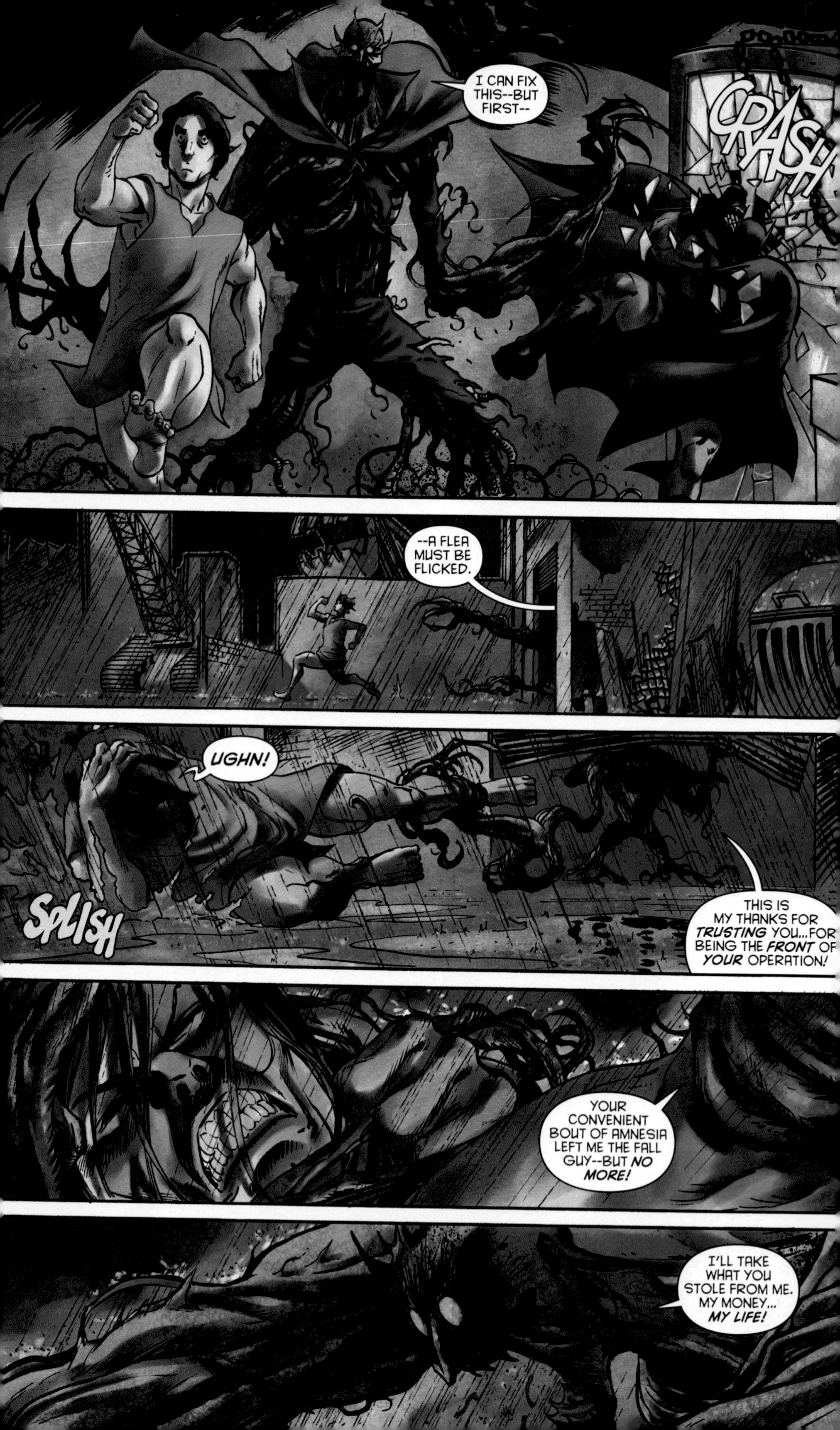
I CAN FIX THIS--BUT FIRST--
CRASH
--A FLEA MUST BE FLICKED.
UGHN!
SPLISH
THIS IS MY THANKS FOR *TRUSTING* YOU...FOR BEING THE *FRONT* OF *YOUR* OPERATION!
YOUR CONVENIENT BOUT OF AMNESIA LEFT ME THE FALL GUY--BUT *NO MORE!*
I'LL TAKE WHAT YOU STOLE FROM ME. MY MONEY... *MY LIFE!*

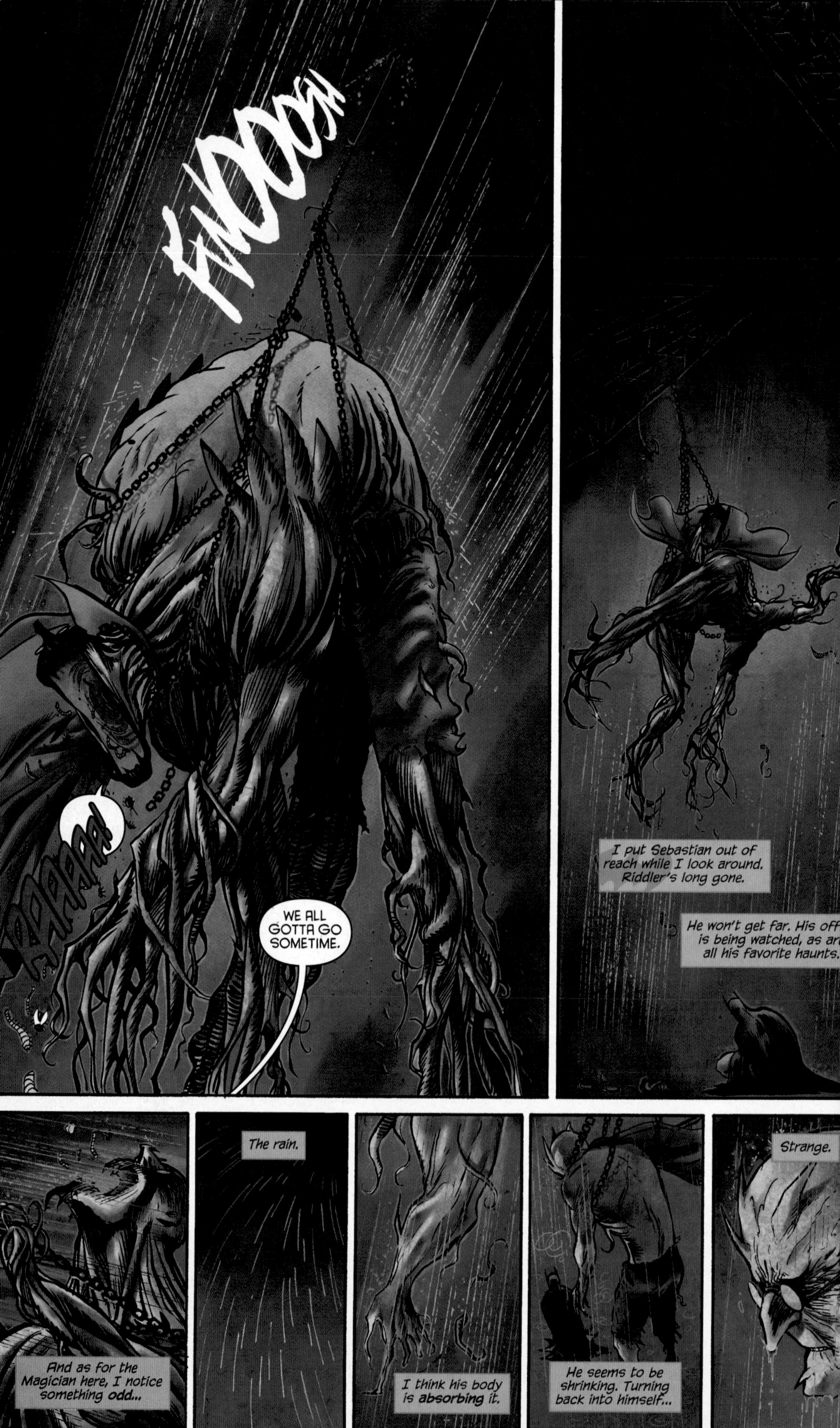
FWOOOSH
RRAAAAAA!
WE ALL GOTTA GO SOMETIME.
I put Sebastian out of reach while I look around. Riddler's long gone.
He won't get far. His off is being watched, as ar all his favorite haunts.
And as for the Magician here, I notice something odd...
The rain.
I think his body is absorbing it.
He seems to be shrinking. Turning back into himself...
Strange.

I HAVEN'T HAD MUCH TIME TO CONDUCT A THOROUGH EVALUATION ON SEBASTIAN BLACKSPELL YET, COMMISSIONER...

...BUT IN MY PROFESSIONAL OPINION, HE'S A DEEPLY TROUBLED MAN.

TROUBLED ENOUGH TO BE A *SERIAL KILLER*, MS. SINNER?

WELL, HE DOES SHARE TRAITS WITH YOUR COMMON GARDEN VARIETY SERIAL KILLER... LONER, SINGLE WHITE MALE, HIGH IQ...

...BUT I DON'T SEE A PSYCHOLOGICAL *THRILL* FOR THE KILLINGS.

HE'LL STAND TRIAL FOR THE MURDERS OF HIS ASSOCIATES AND THE ATTEMPTED MURDERS OF EDWARD NIGMA AND BATMAN.

AS SOON AS YOU DEEM HIM CAPABLE.

MAYBE WHEN HE FEELS LIKE TALKING HE'LL TELL ME WHERE HE SUSTAINED HIS INJURIES.

WHAT DO YOU MEAN?

FIREFLY, YOU FEEL LIKE OFFERING UP ANY INFORMATION THAT MIGHT HELP US BETTER UNDERSTAND MR. BLACKSPELL?

WHAT DO YOU PEOPLE THINK Y-YOU'RE *DOING?*

YOU CAN'T PUT HIM NEXT TO ME! THIS IS A *DEATH SENTENCE!*

THE DOCTOR WHO EXAMINED HIM NOTED SIGNS OF SEVERE *TORTURE.* IT *COULD* HAVE BEEN SELF-INFLICTED...BUT I NEED TO HEAR IT FROM HIM.

I WANT TO SPEAK TO AN ATTORNEY. YOU *HEAR ME?!*

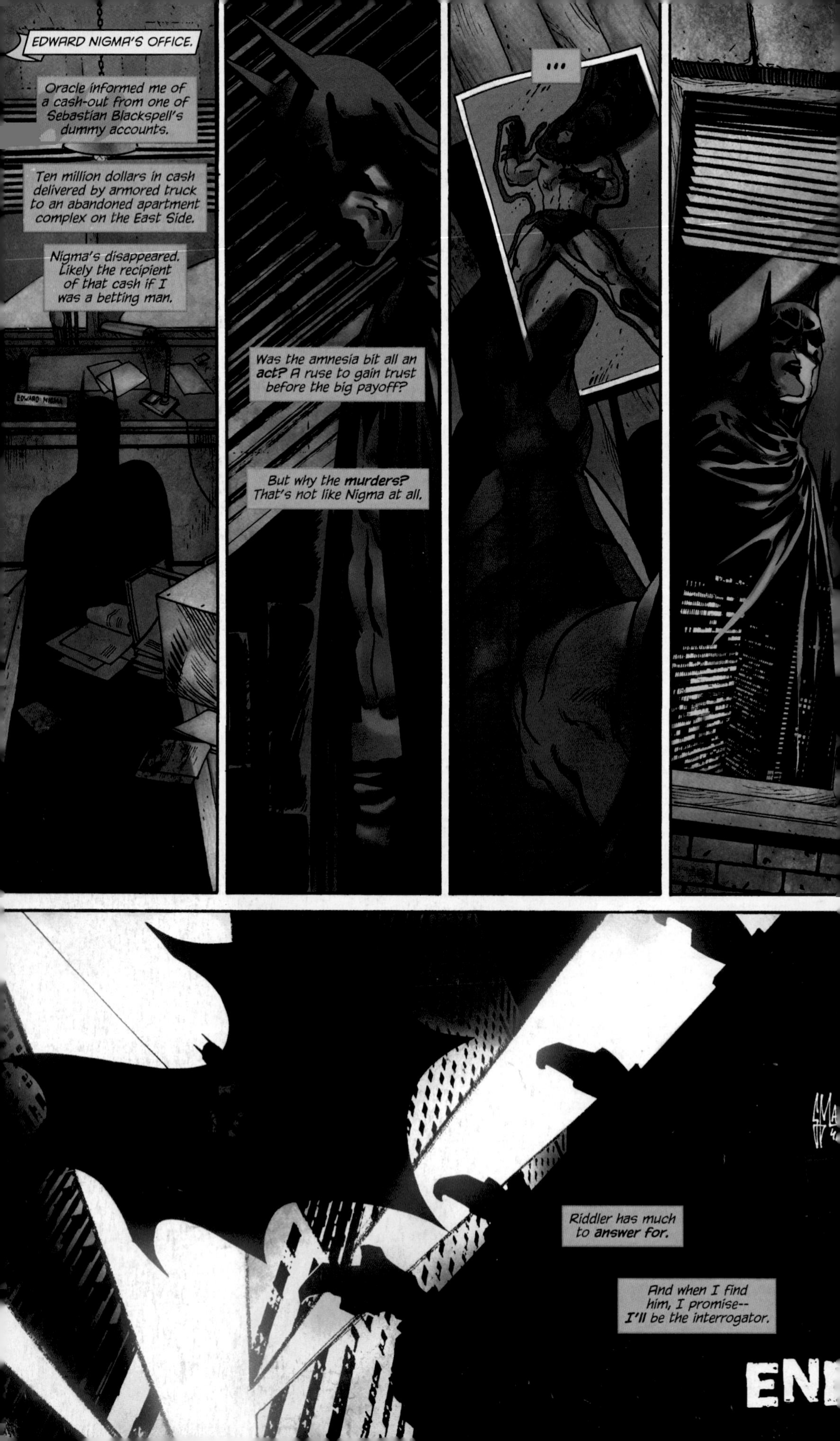
EDWARD NIGMA'S OFFICE.
Oracle informed me of a cash-out from one of Sebastian Blackspell's dummy accounts.
Ten million dollars in cash delivered by armored truck to an abandoned apartment complex on the East Side.
Nigma's disappeared. Likely the recipient of that cash if I was a betting man.
EDWARD NIGMA
Was the amnesia bit all an act? A ruse to gain trust before the big payoff?
But why the murders? That's not like Nigma at all.
...
Riddler has much to answer for.
And when I find him, I promise-- I'll be the interrogator.
END

FROM THE WRITER OF
300 & SIN CITY

FRANK MILLER

Frank Miller's classic graphic novel features a Gotham City that has sunk into decadence and lawlessness ten years after an aging Batman retired. The Dark Knight returns in blaze of glory when his city needs him most to end the threat of a brutal new generation of criminals while encountering the Joker, Two-Face and the Man of Steel for the final time.

"Groundbreaking."
– USA TODAY

"It's film noir in cartoon panels."
–VANITY FAIR

BATMAN: THE DARK KNIGHT RETURNS

FRANK MILLER
with KLAUS JANSON and LYNN VARLEY

BATMAN:
THE DARK KNIGHT
STRIKES AGAIN

BATMAN: YEAR ONE

ALL STAR BATMAN & ROBIN,
THE BOY WONDER VOL. I

with
DAVID MAZZUCCHELLI

with
JIM LEE

SEARCH THE GRAPHIC NOVELS SECTION OF
DCCOMICS.COM
FOR ART AND INFORMATION ON ALL OF OUR BOOKS!

MORE CLASSIC TALES OF THE DARK KNIGHT

BATMAN: HUSH

BATMAN: UNDER THE HOOD
VOLS. 1 & 2

BATMAN:
THE LONG HALLOWEEN

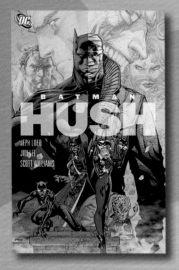

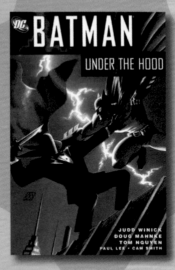

**JEPH LOEB
JIM LEE**

**JUDD WINICK
DOUG MAHNKE**

**JEPH LOEB
TIM SALE**

BATMAN:
DARK VICTORY

BATMAN:
HAUNTED KNIGHT

BATMAN:
YEAR 100

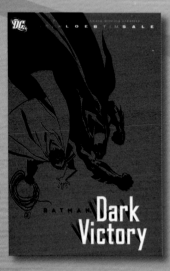

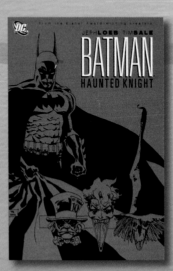

**JEPH LOEB
TIM SALE**

**JEPH LOEB
TIM SALE**

PAUL POPE

SEARCH THE GRAPHIC NOVELS SECTION OF
DCCOMICS.COM
FOR ART AND INFORMATION ON ALL OF OUR BOOKS!